Table of contents

Foreword

This book's primary goal is to give you a nice introduction, tackle advanced features and to teach you as many best practices as possible. If you have not only understood how something works, but also grasped the 'why', then I have reached my goal. Every developer has different opinions on which methods are best and how to write code in a simple, beautiful and efficient fashion. However, I have tried to stay as close as possible to: the advice of the core engineers at Facebook; suggestions from the greatly appreciated folks at AirBnB; and some great minds of the React scene — all sprinkled with a little seasoning of my own years of expertise.

There are always a number of ways to publish your application, creating a bundle with tools such as **Browserify, Rollup** or **Webpack**. You can write your components as ES2015 classes or decide to use `createClass` from the old "ES5-times". Whenever I think it necessary, I will not only show you the various well-established ways, but also some alternatives.

Foremost, I want to delve deeper into the most modern, current and in most cases, the easiest, methods to use React, which is why I have chosen to use **Webpack, Babel** and **ES2015** (and newer) for most of the code examples. Worry not though, I will explain this in more detail later in the book. People who have never come into contact with ES2015+ might take a little longer to understand some of the examples, however I will try my utmost to keep the examples concise and explain things further if necessary. You should possess basic JavaScript knowledge to get the most out of this book though.

Furthermore, this book is intended as an **introduction to React**. It is not an introduction to JavaScript. I assume you have a basic understanding of JavaScript and sometimes deeper understanding of its inner workings but I will aim to explain everything in this book to the best of my ability. This means that even if you have only used JavaScript in a superficial or broad sense, you should be able to understand most of the material covered in this book. I do not assume that you can recite the internals of a JavaScript interpreter from memory, but I assume that you know about the basics of scope in JavaScript, what a callback is and how `Promise.then()` and `Promise.catch()` work and how to make use of asynchronous programming with JavaScript.

But do not worry: it all sounds more complicated than it actually is. Every reader that has worked with something like jQuery in the past, should not have any problems working through the examples in this book and understanding the explanations.

A few words on this book

I self-published this book to retain full control on all channels of distribution, the pricing model and all rights and freedom. I am not "in it for the money" or to get rich, but I primarily want to have as many of you benefit from the book as possible. This is why you can still find a free German version of this book online at the following URL: https://lernen.react-js.dev.

Self-publishing indicates that while I retained full control, I was on ultimately on my own. There was no publisher that helped me to distribute the book or granted me access to an editor. Keeping this in mind, you might find this book a little rough around the edges and not as clean as you might be used to from a normal textbook. I apologize for this and urge you to contact me if you find any mistake — be it a spelling mistake, a grammatical error or an error in the content. Just open a ticket on GitHub[1].

The book has been written entirely in Markdown format. I have used Gitbook.com[2] for my writing, loving the writing process on some days and hating it on others. The service is great for writing technical documentation, less so for writing entire books. Even if the name suggests otherwise.

If you loved the book or if you simply have a question, you can reach out to me via Twitter. I always like to receive feedback. It does not matter if it is words of encouragement or constructive criticism.

And now, I hope you enjoy the book!

About the Author

Manuel Bieh has worked as a Freelancer in Frontend-/JavaScript Development since 2012.

Before deciding to enter the life of a freelancer, I had roughly 10 years of experience under my belt — helping companies of different scales with Frontend Development. For a long time, I have identified as more of a generalist rather than a specialist. It will be hard to find a technology I have not at least tried or touched upon in my career. With the exception of JavaScript itself, I have never really thought of myself as a specialist in any field or technology. This changed drastically and suddenly when a friend of mine, who is also a developer, told me about React in 2014. Driven by my curiosity and an opportunity to use it professionally for Zalando, I delved deeper into React.

I have to admit, at the start I found React a little strange — this is not uncommon by the way, especially for people new to React — but the more I explored and researched, the more I tried to expose myself to React, the more my initial skepticism turned into enthusiasm. Ever since, React has been the tool of choice in all of my projects where I deemed it a good fit. During this time, I have learned a ton and I'm still learning every day. I've worked in teams with fewer than 5 people but also in bigger teams of over 30 people and shared my React knowledge with them while, of course, soaking up more knowledge myself.

The complexity of React should not be underestimated, however. It's possible to start out with React and build applications fairly quickly. If you value quality though, there is much to learn to increase code quality, performance and maintenance. Some of this wisdom is not even known to people who have worked with React professionally for quite a while. Hence, I would not describe myself as an expert, despite years of daily and intense exposure to React. Nevertheless, I hope I have amassed a substantial amount of knowledge that I can share with you all in the form of this book, to ease the transition and to provide you with a few tips.

About the Translator

Sibylle Sehl is a Berlin-based Software Engineer.

Sibylle discovered Technology and Programming as more of a means to an end during her undergraduate degree. During a competition that centered on entrepreneurship, she discovered the fundamentals of Frontend Development, HTML and CSS, and how they allowed her to create things from scratch. Whilst still completing her business degree, she started studying in her own time and enrolled in a Programming Fundamentals Course. She was lucky enough to have the chance to intern in a few organizations that were either shaped by digital resources and a means of managing those or selling a digital product, allowing her to see work in Technology from the inside.

In 2016, she decided that Programming professionally was no longer a dream but something she wanted to pursue full-time and enrolled at The University of Edinburgh's MSc in Computer Science. This year was tough and very intense, especially since her peers had studied Computer Science beforehand. Fast forward to 2017 with a degree in the bag, she started working at Skyscanner as a Product Manager, where she first heard about React. While being a PM was insightful and incredibly rewarding, the lack of programming led her to reevaluate her career choice.

Studying in her free time and basically teaching herself JavaScript in the evenings, she started applying for Frontend Development jobs in Berlin, moving there in 2018. For her first job, she chose to work for a vibrant and young agency to get exposed to a variety of technologies and different projects. It was during this time, that she saw how incredibly useful and simple React made Frontend Development. Whilst still having to support vanilla JavaScript projects as well, she could see in many instances in which situations React was a great choice for a client and when it was possibly not. This love for React and its declarative approach to programming user interfaces also influenced her next career move, where she made working with React a hard requirement. She now works at ResearchGate as a Software Engineer continuing to use React and also learning PHP and GraphQL.

I – Introduction

General

What React is and what it is not

Let's cite the React documentation at this point that has summarized it nicely:

> [React is] a library for building user interfaces.

Even if this explanation might seem a little short, we can deduce a few key points from it in order to understand React better. In the first instance, React is just a *library,* not a framework. It does not boast with an abundance of in-built functions with which we can create complex web applications with ease. The second part of the sentence is equally important: *for building user interfaces.*

Strictly speaking, React is just a **library** that makes it easy to develop **user interfaces**. There are no services or methods to make API calls or built-in models or ORM. React is only concerned with user interfaces. One could say, it is the view layer in our application. And that's it! In this context, we occasionally read that React can be thought of the "V" in **MVC** (Model-View-Controller) or **MVVM** (Model-View-ViewModel). This is a pretty good explanation in my eyes.

React offers a declarative way to model state, state here referring to the state of the user interface itself. Put simply, this means that we declare in our code how our user interface should look given each state of the component. Let's look at a simple example to illustrate this: If a user is logged in, show the dashboard. If they are not, show the login form.

The logic itself is found in the JavaScript part of the application (where it should live anyway) and not in templates, as opposed to many other web frameworks who mix the two. This sounds complicated at first, but it will become clearer soon what this means.

React is **component-based**. We write **encapsulated, Functional components** that can be composed together at will and reused at our leisure. Extending or inheriting components is possible in theory, but rather uncommon in the world of React. Rather than working with *inheritance,* React encourages *composition,* the act of combining multiple components into a "whole".

Does this mean that we cannot build complex web applications with React? No. Absolutely not. React boasts a large, high quality and very active ecosystem of libraries that, in turn is based on, extends, or complements React in such a way that it does not need to hide behind large scale frameworks like Ember or Angular. Quite the opposite actually. Once we have entered the React ecosystem and gained a first impression, we quickly find a number of really good tools and libraries with which we can build professional, super individual and highly complex applications.

When should I use React and when is it best to avoid it?

The more React gained in popularity, the more the question arose whether jQuery's days were numbered. Should we develop everything in React now? Is it useful to use React or maybe not so much?

As mentioned previously, React is primarily a *library for building user interfaces.* User Interfaces always contain interaction which mandates the usage of state management. For example, I am pressing a button and a dropdown opens. The state of the dropdown changes from *closed* to *open*. Or, I could enter information into a form input and receive feedback whether the data I entered is correct. If it is not valid, the state of the form input will change from *valid* to *invalid*. React is great at modelling these changes. If I do not have a large amount of changing data or user interactions on my page (for example if am developing a static website for a client), I *probably* do not need React.

In the wrong context, React can cause more harm than good. If we put more focus on the content of our page and have not pre-rendered our components on the server, search engines could have difficulty processing our page. Thankfully, React is making it easy for us to do server-side rendering with our components, so we can often neglect this concern.

If we have a large amount of interaction and changing data on our site, React will save us time and energy. The more interaction we have on our site and the more complex it is, the more we will benefit from using React. The best example here is a **Single Page Application** *(SPA)* that is only visited and initialized once by the browser and where each subsequent interaction and communication with the server is processed over fetch requests or XHR (more commonly known as "AJAX-Requests").

Only a little while ago, I had to build a signup form which initially seemed simple enough. I started out without using React but quickly regretted my decision as the complexity grew and more interaction was needed to increase usability. Implementing live-validation of form data and separating the signup process into two steps is no easy feat, which quickly drove me back to using React. Managing these different states and **imperative** changes of the interface manually would have been too much to handle without it.

Imperative refers to instructing the browser precisely what it should do. *Declarative* code on the other hand (which we write with React) defines the end-goal based on our current state which is one of the fundamental principles of React. Instead of saying: "I am now logged in, dear browser, please proceed to hide the login form and show me the dashboard", we can define two views: "This is what the interface looks like when I am logged in" (dashboard view) and "this is what it looks like if I am not (login view)". React decides which of these views to show based on the current state of our component.

How did React come into existence?

React was originally created at **Facebook** and open sourced under a BSD-Licence in 2013. Following some public protest though, the license was changed to MIT. Given Facebook's involvement in React's creation, it is no surprise that a large chunk of Facebook's code is also based on React. An estimated amount of around **50.000** components is currently in use in Facebook's products, a number so great that it is easy to understand that Facebook has a high interest to maintain the technology it's based upon and come up with ideas to ensure its continuous development. So for anyone worried about using React in their own projects, you need not worry about React becoming unmaintained anytime soon.

The core engineers on the React Team do a great job to get the community involved with React's development early on. A call for React RFC[3] (*"Request for Comments"*) means that developers and interested parties can discuss changes early on in a designated GitHub repository and also enables users to bounce around ideas with the React team themselves.

While maintaining and developing React, the core engineers are ensuring that **breaking changes** follow a clear **deprecation schema**. Breaking changes in this instance refer to changes in the codebase that are **not backwards compatible**. Any methods, properties or functions that are due to be deprecated will be flagged with a visible and easy-to-notice **deprecation warning**. They furthermore provide a tool to safely amend old code with the new changes, called React-Codemod[4], which follows strict Semver conventions.

For a release, this can have a number of implications. Only *major releases* will involve breaking changes, i.e (`16.x.x` to `17.x.x`) , whereas a *minor release* will only contain new features or deprecation warnings (for example `16.6.x` to `16.7.x`). A minor release can safely prepare and inform developers to upgrade their existing code. Bug fixes will be dealt with in a so-called *patch release*, denoted by only bumping the version from `16.8.0` to `16.8.1`.

For the curious among us, there's the possibility to inspect soon-to-be released features for major and minor releases by checking out Alpha, Beta and RC- (*"Release Candidate"*) versions. However, these features are subject to changes and we should be careful when implementing them.

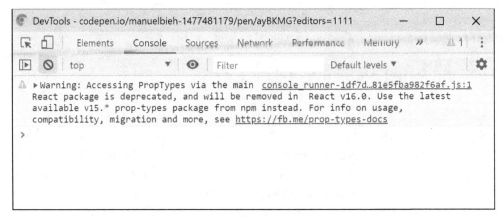

An example of a deprecation warning

While this is useful for React's user base, one can assume that it is in Facebook's own interest to not cause problems by unplanned changes — given that they have a large number of React components in their own codebase. However, transparency is always a given and you can follow along on GitHub's issue tracker where all important changes are neatly summarized in so-called Umbrella-Tickets[5].

Into the deep end

We have just talked about the "what", "when" and "where" but we have not yet talked about the "how". Let's write our first **React component**. In order to display our component in the browser, we need to not only install **React** but also **ReactDOM**, a package that enables us to mount our application in the browser — put simply: to use it in the browser.

Let's have a look at a very minimalist setup to get started with React:

```
<!DOCTYPE html>
<html>
<head>
<meta charset ="UTF-8" />
<title>Hello React! </title>
</head>
<body>
<div id="root"></div>
<script crossorigin src="https://unpkg.com/react@16.8.4/umd/react.development.js"  >
</script>
<script crossorigin src="https://unpkg.com/react-dom@16.8.4/umd/react-
dom.development.js"></script>
<script>
// Placeholder for our first component
</script>
</body>
</html>
```

We build up the bare bones set up for a regular HTML document and load in **React** and **ReactDOM** in their latest *stable* version from unpkg-CDN. We can now use React and ReactDOM as a global variable in the window object as window.React and window.ReactDOM. Apart from that we only see an empty page here with an empty <div id="root"></div> . This div is going to be used as our **mount node** to show our first React component.

> (i) If we deal with a number of React components, we normally refer to this as an **app**, **web app** or **single page app**. The boundaries of when we call a component an app are fluid though. A few developers talk of an **app** if we only have a single component in our code. A clear definition of this does not exist though.

Let's start with a classic "Hello-World" example and include the script where we put the placeholder earlier.

```
class HelloWorld extends React.Component {
  render() {
    return React.createElement( 'div', { id: 'hello-world' },  'Hello World');
  }
}

ReactDOM.render(
  React.createElement(HelloWorld),
  document.getElementById('root' )
);
```

And just like that we have implemented our first React component. If we include this snippet where we have put the placeholder earlier, we can see the following in the browser:

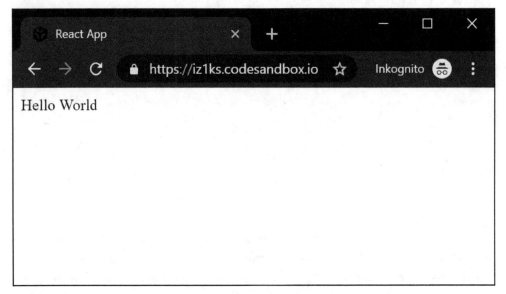

Our first React component in the browser

That does not look that complicated, does it? Let's go through the code one step at a time. I have highlighted all the relevant parts in the code in bold.

```
class HelloWorld
```

Here, we are giving a name to a child component. We have named our first component **HelloWorld.** We can name our components anything we like, but there is one rule to keep in mind: React components start with a capital letter. Using helloWorld as a component name would not be valid, HELLOWORLD, however, would be — albeit very rarely seen in the wild.

Naming components follows the **UpperCamelCase** convention. It is not unusual to have long, self-explanatory names for our components — **UserNotificationView** is an entirely normal name, for example.

```
extends React.Component
```

With this snippet, we are extending the internal React class `React.Component`. This transforms our own class into a component that we can use in React. Apart from `React.Component` there is also a `React.PureComponent` and a so-called *Functional component*. This is simply a JavaScript function that follows a particular pattern. We are going to look at both of these at a later stage, for now we can neglect them.

```
render();
```

So far, our component only contains the obligatory `render()` method. This method is necessary to inform React how the component is displayed — we say "rendered" in the React world. A component has to have a `return` value. This value can either be an explicit `null` value to show nothing (but not `undefined`), another **React element**, or from Version 16 onward, a **string** or **array**.

In terms of an array, the array can include strings, numbers, React elements or `null` as values. The `render()` method **declaratively** describes the current state of our user interface. Everything that is included in our render method right after `return` is what the browser will display after rendering.

Even if it is entirely up to us how to structure our JavaScript classes, a common pattern has evolved to put our `render()` method at the end of all our methods. This is not mandatory of course but it aids readability. Many renowned engineers in the React scene advocate for this guideline too. The code guidelines by AirBnB also include this rule. Speaking from my own experience here, I can say that it does help to follow this guideline to make your day-to-day React work easier.

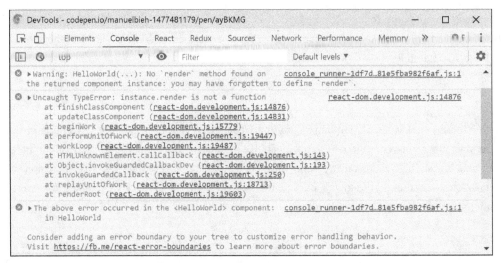

Error message for missing render() method

Error message for missing render() method

```
React.createElement();
```

As mentioned previously, the `render()` method of a React component returns a **React element** in most cases. React **elements** are the smallest but also most significant building blocks in a React application and describe what a user will see on their screen. Apart from `React.cloneElement()` and `React.isValidElement()` , `React.createElement()` has been one of of the only 3 top level API methods for a long time. Since then though, a few other methods have been added but they are mainly for performance optimizations.

The `createElement()` method expects 1-n parameters:

1. "Type" - this can be a HTML element as a string, i.e. `'div'` , `'span'` or `'p'` but also other React components.
2. So-called "Props" - these are read-only "property objects" of a component. The name is derived from - you guessed it - properties.
3. As many child elements as you wish to put in. These can be React elements themselves, or arrays, functions or simply plain text. However, a component does not necessarily need to contain other child elements.

At the end of the day, **React elements** are nothing more than a never changing (immutable) JavaScript objects that contain properties to tell React how and what exactly needs displayed. This description of properties is used by React to construct a virtual blueprint of the component hierarchy. It resembles the representation of the HTML tree in the form of a JavaScript object. You often hear it being referred to as the VirtualDOM, however the term is losing popularity with the React team and they have distanced themselves from using it. This tree is used by React to only refresh the parts of the tree that have actually changed, e.g. when a user interacts with an app and changes data or fires an event. To do this, the previous tree is compared to the current tree.

As React does not refresh the entire application at once, or writes it to the DOM in its entirety once any state changes, it is a lot more performant than other frameworks or libraries. Other libraries or frameworks can often lead to unnecessarily many DOM mutations at the cost of performance. Using a special **reconciliation** algorithm that compares previous state with current state, React processes what exactly has changed, and can reduce the number of writes to a minimum.

However, in our day-to-day development we will hardly ever call `React.createElement()` in this form. Facebook has developed its own syntax extension for JavaScript called **JSX**. JSX reduces a great amount of work and simplifies a lot of work with React. Nevertheless, I am of the opinion that it is good to know of `React.createElement()` 's existence to understand how JSX works behind the scenes and to reduce the number of errors when debugging.

JSX resembles HTML or XML/XHTML in parts, however it is a lot more powerful as we can include JavaScript expressions within it. JSX is an abstraction that makes it a lot **easier** for the developer to create React elements. Our previous example

```
React.createElement( 'div', { id: 'hello-world' }, 'Hello World' );
```

would look like this in JSX:

```
<div id= "hello-world" >Hello World< /div>
```

For many beginners, this can look a little strange. I have heard this referred to as **JSX shock** but after playing around with JSX for a little while, it practicality becomes obvious. In my opinion, JSX is one of the reasons why React's usage has gained so much traction in such a short time.

Let's have a look at our example again. The `return` value of the `render()` method indicates that it will display an element of type `div` which shall contain the id `hello-world` and the child element (a text node in this case) containing `Hello World`.

```
ReactDOM.render(Element, Container);
```

We have talked about most of the parts in our example but we have not yet looked at **ReactDOM**. This library enables React to interact with the DOM (*Document Object Model*) — put simply, it allows us to interact with the browser. Just like React itself, **ReactDOM** only contains a few top level API methods. We are going to concentrate on the `render()` method — the core of **ReactDOM** in the browser.

Although the naming might suggest otherwise, **ReactDOM**'s internal `render()` method does not directly relate to its counterpart used in React components. Using it in this case, enables us to render a **React element** onto a **"root node"**, meaning to display it on the screen. In our example, we render our `HelloWorld` component onto the `<div id="root"></div>` . It is important to understand that the root node is **not replaced**, but that the content is inserted **into the container**.

ReactDOM enables us to actually see our component in the browser. The content that we can see is described in the `render()` method, which contains a React element after the `return`. Calling `ReactDOM.render()` with the two parameters as shown above, will insert the **React** element into the given **container**.

> (i) Calling the `ReactDOM.render()` function for the first time, any possibly existing content in the destination container is being replaced. With every subsequent call, React uses an internal comparison algorithm for best performance and to avoid re-rendering the entire application.
>
> While this is good to know in theory, we normally do not call `ReactDOM.render()` more than once and only use it to initialize our Single Page App to load the page. React never changes the root node itself, only its contents. This means that if our container element has classes, ids or a data-attribute, these will remain intact after calling `ReactDOM.render()` .

And just like that, we have discussed the basics of how React works under the hood, implemented our first component and finally displayed it in the browser. Congrats!

Tools and Setup

Tools

In order to work with React comfortably and without interruptions, a few conditions should be met. Installing these tools is not entirely necessary but it does make our development workflow much easier. My suggestion would be to install all the tools and I will assume in the following chapters that you have done so.

Node.js and npm

Most of you will know **Node.js** as server-side JavaScript, however this is only partly true. First of all, **Node.js** is a **JavaScript Runtime Environment** that is very well suited to write network applications, such as a server. **Node.js** also comes with a package management tool, commonly known as **npm**. It enables us to easily install new JavaScript libraries on our own machines and also lets us write and run our own command line scripts.

Instead of installing **Node** directly, I suggest to use <u>nvm</u>[6] (*"Node Version Manager"*) for Mac or Linux, and <u>nvm-windows</u>[7] for Windows. One of **nvm**'s advantages is that it does not require root privileges to install packages globally. Moreover, we can update your installed node version with a simple command line expression (`nvm install [version]`). If we want to see the list of all available versions, we can run `nvm ls-remote` (Max/Linux) or `nvm list available` (Windows). For the rest of this book, I would suggest you use the LTS (Long Term Support) version as its stable and will receive updates over a longer time frame.

Yarn

While **Node** and **npm** already offer a very solid package manager, **yarn** takes it a little bit further and offers simpler commands, and better caching — and thus better performance. Similar to React, **yarn** was created at Facebook to make working with React a little bit nicer. Everything that I am going to describe in the rest of the book will also work seamlessly with **npm** but I would still suggest installing **yarn** instead. Especially in the React ecosystem, it is gaining popularity due to its ease of use and its better performance compared to **npm**. Once **Node** and **npm** have been installed, **yarn** can be added as a global package via **npm**:

```
npm install --global yarn
```

Or in short:

```
npm i -g yarn
```

Just like that we have installed our first package. Easy! The so-called command line flags `--global` and `-g` make sure that the `yarn` executable is installed globally and can be called from the command line anywhere on our machine by typing `yarn` .

Babel

Babel is usually only used as a dependency in React based projects, namely as an npm package. It does not need to be installed explicitly at this stage. Babel allows us to interpret and then *transpile* JavaScript that is not standardized, or not yet conforming to standards that are supported by all modern browsers, into code that can be executed without issues.

 Transpiling is the process of transforming the source code of one language into a functionally identical piece of code in another language. In our case, that's transforming JSX or ES2015+ into valid and executable JavaScript that is understood by all browsers.

Babel consists of a core module (`@babel/core`) that offers a few APIs that can then be used by **plugins** for each respective transpilation. These plugins are often grouped together by so-called **presets**. Presets can in turn install many **plugins** at once. In React, the most common presets are `@babel/preset-react` and `@babel/present-env` . The former is used to read and translate **JSX** and the latter transforms modern JavaScript based on its destination environment and translates it into something that even older browsers can understand.

The @ sign in the name indicates that the package originates from an organization within the npm registry (the npm package registry) and can been understood as some sort of a namespace. In the case of Babel, you can find all of its official packages in the organization that have been published there by the Babel maintainers. Before Babel version 7 was released, this organization did not exist and the packages were simply separated by hyphens. `@babel/preset-react` was called `babel-preset-react` and `@babel/core` was named `babel-core` and so on.

So do not be confused if you encounter `babel-core` instead of `@babel/core` in a project. In this case we are simply dealing with an older version of Babel (6 or below). However, sometimes we might come across plugins or presets that are not officially part of Babel, but the developer has still prefixed the package with `babel-` although it works with Babel 7. In this case, we can only really check the readme of the package to understand what is going on.

The **presets** that I have used in my work with React (and which I also suggest you should use are):

- @babel/preset-env
- @babel/preset-react
- @babel/plugin-proposal-object-rest-spread
- @babel/plugin-proposal-class-properties
- @babel/plugin-syntax-dynamic-import

If you want to work with static type checking like Flow or TypeScript, you also need to install `@babel/preset-flow` or `@babel/preset-typescript` respectively.

You can install these via:

```
npm install --save-dev [package]
```

or:

```
yarn add --dev [package]
```

The `--dev` or `--save-dev` flag indicates that we are only dealing with a `devDependency`, meaning that it is only relevant for our development and that it should not be included in production code.

Webpack

Webpack is one of the most central tools in the React ecosystem. Without it, an efficient workflow with React is almost impossible or at least a lot harder to achieve. **Webpack** is a module-bundler that has brought module based development (that you might know from Node.js) to the browser. It enables us to structure our application code neatly in their own files and allows us to use their dependencies via `import` or `require()` . This way, the dependencies are loaded into their own **module scope** and made available within the module. In the end, only a single JavaScript file is produced (if we wanted to, we could tell Webpack to produce more). Thus avoiding having to single-handedly import each and every JavaScript file in a `<script src="...">`</script> in the HTML. Without bundling, we would need to import hundreds of scripts manually.

Wow. That sounds complicated, but after a few examples it almost happens intuitively and on its own. Once you get used to it, you ask yourself how you could ever work without a module-bundler.

But **Webpack** can be used for much more than module-bundling. It can also be taught to transpile files with JSX into JavaScript with Babel, it can copy images, stylesheets and other assets into a `build` folder that can then be deployed on the server. There are a lot of other things Webpack can do, but we are going to investigate this deeper at a later point and show

19

what such a configuration could look like. Thus, we will not look at the Webpack command line tools at this stage.

ESLint

ESLint is a very practical tool for static code analysis. It helps us to spot errors in our code, but it can also be used to enforce consistent rules for code style or to give helpful tips on how to optimize code during development. ESLint titles itself as a "pluggable linting utility", which promises to place the most value on extensibility. You can find a number of useful plugins for different tools, runtime environments and frameworks.

In most professional contexts, as well as many open source projects, an ESLint config has become the de-facto standard. In React projects, you will likely see `eslint-plugin-react` , `eslint-plugin-babel` and `eslint-plugin-react-hooks` which have proven themselves to be a solid choice for development workflows.

Your editor of choice will reveal easy to spot error messages to you in those places where the code apparently does not work as intended:

```
  ❌  23          const NotUsed = 'Should not be here'
      24

  PROBLEMS   2     OUTPUT    DEBUG CONSOLE    TERMINAL

  ⌄  Js  App.js  src\shared   2
        ❌  'NotUsed' is assigned a value but never used.  eslint(no-unused-vars) [23, 11]
        ❌  Insert ';'  eslint(prettier/prettier) [23, 41]
```

Warning for an unused variable and a missing semicolon in VSCode

Prettier

Some love it, some hate it. The latter often only hate it for a short amount of time. Once you have seen the value this tool can bring, you ask yourself how you could ever work without it — I felt the same back in the day, as did my colleagues.

Prettier is a tool that can automatically format our code according to a predefined set of rules — neatly and consistently. We can either run it on the command line or we can install the **Prettier** plugin that is available for most editors and IDEs. **Prettier** does not offer many formatting options on purpose. This keeps the number of fruitless discussions on how best to format our code to a minimum and also avoids the additional discussion "which **Prettier** option would be best".

In the beginning, it might feel alienating to some and you might not always agree with **Prettier** 100%. However, not having to worry about where to place a line break and which line of code should be indented reduces the cognitive overload immensely. In my eyes, this justifies the use of **Prettier**.

IDE-/Editor Plugins

All the common editors (and many smaller ones too) such as Webstorm, Atom, Visual Studio Code or Sublime offer plugins or have natively integrated functionality to support working with **React** and **JSX**. I strongly suggest that you install these plugins as they normally lead to better syntax highlighting, code completion and usually add more nice features on top.

Atom offers language-babel[8], **VS Code** has Babel ES6/ES7[9] and for **Sublime** users it is worth checking out babel-sublime[10]. If you are using **Webstorm**, you get automatic support for React syntax highlighting from version 10 onward. The previously mentioned plugins for **ESLint** and **Prettier** are also very useful. Search the plugin manager of your editor of choice for ESLint or Prettier and select the plugin with the most installations. This plugin is usually the official ESLint or Prettier plugin.

Browser Plugins

Concerning your browser, I urge you to install the **React Dev Tools** for Chrome[11] and Firefox[12] as well as the **Redux Dev Tools** for later use (Chrome[13], Firefox[14]). These dev tools neatly integrate with your already existing dev tools and will appear as a separate tab in the browser. They offer great advantages during development.

Chrome and newly installed dev tools plugins for React and Redux

Using these tools, we can manipulate state and watch it change directly in the browser. I would almost argue that efficient debugging is close to impossible without these dev tool plugins.

Zero Config Setup

Some people have joked in the past that you can easily spend days plugging away at your setup and perfecting it before you actually write any lines of code. A solid setup is important and somewhat decides whether the quality and maintenance of your application will continue in the future.

However, the React community has done a lot of work for us already. The site JavaScriptStuff contains a grand total of **198 projects** for <u>React Starter Projects</u>[15]. Facebook itself also offers a starter, or more concretely **Dan Abramov** who is part of the React core team and creator of Redux, named **Create React App** (or *"CRA"* for short). The project has surpassed 75.000 stars on GitHub and has become the standard for React projects. **Create React App** is described on GitHub as:

> Create React apps with no build configuration

And this is true. **Create React App** makes it easy to create a robust and good setup with only a single command on the command line, especially for beginners:

```
yarn create react-app projectname
```

If you prefer using npm, you still need to enter two commands:

```
npm install -g create-react-app
```

... which will install the **Create React App** executable globally and then:

```
create-react-app projectname
```

And just like that we have created a complete React setup with a few little example components in our *"projectname"* folder. I would advise you to go ahead and execute the last few steps right now because the following code examples will all assume that you have set up **Create React App**.

 The project name has to fit the <u>criteria for the name property</u>[16] for the package.json format of **npm**. This means that it is **not allowed to contain capital letters**, it can have **no spaces,** and can only have **up to 214 characters max**. The other criteria can be found in the **npm** documentation.

This setup is quite extensive and has dealt with many aspects beforehand, so we do not need to spend as much time with the setup and can dive into the code straight away.

Once CRA has created the basic setup and has installed all the relevant dependencies, it will give us a prompt on the command line as to how we can work with CRA in our first React project.

```
$ create-react-app foobar

Creating a new React app  in /home/manuel/my-react-app.

Installing packages. This might take a couple of minutes.
Installing react, react-dom, and react-scripts...

Success! Created foobar at /home/manuel/my-react-app
Inside that directory, you can run several commands:

  yarn start
    Starts the development server.

  yarn build
    Bundles the app into static files  for production.

  yarn test
    Starts the test runner.

  yarn eject
    Removes this tool and copies build dependencies, configuration files
    and scripts into the app directory. If you  do this, you can't go back!

We suggest that you begin by typing:

  cd my-react-app
  yarn start

Happy hacking!
```

yarn start

This command starts the development server, which lets us see our newly created application in the browser. The dev server is also taking care of files which are changing in the different directories and "compiles" our app and its dependencies again if we have made changes.

yarn build

Creates a build folder of our app which we can then deploy to a public server. Compared to the development build (yarn start), this build is optimized for performance. Due to this, running yarn build takes much longer than running yarn start.

yarn test

Runs tests. CRA comes pre-installed with **Jest**, another tool developed at Facebook. In comparison to other testing frameworks, it also allows for **snapshot testing**, that is creating some form of a copy of the current state of your component and compares it with future test states. This way, changes — wanted or unwanted — are detected easily right from the get go.

yarn eject

Using yarn eject, we can bid our app goodbye. All the build scripts, dependencies and config files are copied to our current project directory. From this point onwards, it is *our* responsibility to ensure that everything is working as intended. While we have more responsibility, we also gain more freedom as we can now make changes to the standard configuration of CRA. If or when this step ever needs taken depends on the project. I have been working on projects where I have used the CRA standard setups for months but also worked on others where I needed to eject much earlier (days or weeks) as I needed to make changes to setup.

> (i) In order to understand all the code examples in the book, I strongly suggest to install **Create React App** at this stage. Most of the examples can then be copied and pasted into the App.js file and then run. To maximize your learning experience though, I would advise you to type out the examples instead of simply copying them.
>
> If you do not want to install CRA locally or if you are in a hurry, you can try working with CodeSandbox[17]. It allows you to create a new setup with **Create React App**[18] in seconds and then allows you interact with it in a browser environment.

II – Basics

Introduction to ES2015+

The "new" JavaScript

ES2015 is a modern, up-to-date version of JavaScript with lots of new functionality and syntax. **ES2015** is the successor to **ECMAScript** version 5 (or **ES5**) and is thus often referred to as **ES6** in many articles and blogs. So if you come across **ES6** anywhere in an article or elsewhere, you know now that it applies to **ES2015**. In most of the book, I will refer to **ES2015+** which means any changes in the JavaScript language since 2015 will be marked accordingly. This includes ES2016 (ES7), ES2017 (ES8), ES2018 (ES9).

> (i) The **ES** in **ES2015** and **ES6** stands for **ECMAScript**. The organization ECMA International is responsible for the standardization of the **ECMA-262** specification. Since 2015, a new specification has been published every year. Historically, they attributed each version with an increasing number, however to increase clarity and understanding the versions now include the year in which they were published. This way, **ES6** becomes **ES2015**, **ES7** is **ES2016** and so on.

People that work with React most definitely also use **Babel** as their **transpiler** to change **JSX** into its respective `createElement()`, but this is not the only thing **Babel** can do. Previously named **6to5**, it did exactly what its name suggests: transpile **ES6** syntax JavaScript into **ES5**. This unlocks the ability to use newer, or soon-to-be-supported, features and syntax extensions today whilst still supporting older browsers that do not natively support these features.

In this chapter I want to show and explain the most important and useful functionality and opportunities that **ES2015** and the following versions have brought about. I will focus on those features that you would commonly come across when developing with React and those that make life easiest for you.

If you already have experience working with ES2015 and its subsequent versions, feel free to skip this chapter!

Variable declarations with `let` and `const`

For a long time, we could only use `var` to declare a variable in JavaScript. Since 2015 however, JavaScript has gained two new keywords which we can use to declare variables: `let` and `const`. Using `var` for variable declarations has become somewhat superfluous and in almost all cases `let` and `const` are the better choices. But what is the difference?

As opposed to `var`, the new variable declarations, `let` and `const`, only exist **inside of the scope in which they were defined**. These scopes can be a function, as was the case with `var`, but it can also be a loop or an `if` statement.

Tip: Whenever you find an open curly bracket in your code, you are opening a new scope. Similarly, a closing curly bracket closes the scope again. Using these new variable declarations, we have encapsulated our variables to a greater degree and limited their usage — which is usually considered a good thing.

On the one hand, if you want to override the value of a variable (e.g. in a loop), you have to use `let` to achieve this. On the other hand, if the reference of the variable should stay the same, i.e. constant, one should use `const`.

But be careful: As opposed to other languages, `const` does not disable every mutation on the variable. If you have declared an object or an array with `const`, the actual content of the variable can still be changed. The reference of the variable however is fixed and cannot be changed anymore.

The difference between `let`/`const` and `var`

Let's look at an example to further demonstrate the differences between `let` and `const` versus `var`, and see how the former are only visible in the scope which they are defined in:

```
for (var i = 0; i < 10; i++) { }
console.log (i);
```

Result:

ⓘ 10

An now let's look at the same example with `let`

```
for (let j = 0; j < 10; j++) { }
console.log (j);
```

Result:

ⓧ Uncaught ReferenceError: j is not defined

While the variable var i is accessible outside of the `for` loop, the variable defined with `let` is limited to the scope in which it is defined, the `for` loop in this case. Remember, a loop creates a new scope.

This information forms part of one of the building blocks which will help us to write encapsulated components without any side effects.

The differences between `let` and `const`

The following code is valid and works for as long as the variable is declared with `let` (or var):

```
let myNumber = 1234;
myNumber = 5678;
console.log(myNumber) ;
```

Result:

 5678

If we try and run the same code with const :

```
const myNumber = 1234;
myNumber = 5678;
console.log(myNumber) ;
```

Result:

 Uncaught TypeError: Assignment to constant variable.

If we try to directly override a previously declared variable with const, the JavaScript interpreter will give us a warning. But what about just changing a property *inside* of an object declared with const?

```
const myObject = {
    a: 1
};
myObject.b = 2;
console.log(myObject) ;
```

Result:

`{a: 1, b: 2}`

In this instance, we do not encounter any problems as we are changing the object itself but not the reference to `myObject`. Arrays, similarly, follow the same rules. The elements in the array can be changed, but the value of the variable cannot.

Allowed:

```
const myArray = [] ;
myArray.push(1 );
myArray.push(2 );
console.log(myArray) ;
```

Result:

 `[1, 2]`

Conversely, the following code would not be allowed as the variable would be directly overridden:

```
const myArray = [];
myArray = myArray.concat(1, 2);
```

⊗ Uncaught TypeError: Assignment to constant variable.

If we want to ensure that `myArray` can easily be overridden, we have to use `let` instead or we accept that we can only change the elements in the array but not the actual value itself while declaring it with `const`.

Arrow functions

Arrow functions are yet another great addition in terms of simplicity since the introduction of ES2015. Previously, function declarations were written in the following fashion: the keyword `function`, followed by an optional function name, parentheses in which the function arguments were given as well as the **function body**. The function body comprises the actual content of the function:

```
function(arg1, arg2) {}
```

Arrow functions simplify this greatly by making the `function` keyword redundant:

```
(arg1, arg2) => {}
```

If we only pass one parameter into the function, even the parentheses for the arguments is optional. Our pre-ES2015 function:

```
function(arg) {}
```

would be transformed into this **arrow function**:

```
arg => {}
```

Yep, this is a valid function in ES2015!

And it is getting wilder. If our function should only return an expression in the `return` value, the parentheses become optional as well. Let's compare a function that takes a number as its single argument, doubles it and `returns` it. This is ES5:

```
function double(number) {
  return number * 2;
}
```

... and this is the same code as a ES2015 **arrow function**:

```
const double = number => number * 2;
```

In both cases, the declared functions yield the same result. For example, if we called the functions with `double(5)`, the results would be `10` in both cases.

But there is another even greater advantage when it comes to arrow functions. This will be especially useful once we fully start to work with React. Arrow functions do not have their own constructor meaning they cannot be instantiated using the `new MyArrowFunction()` form. On top of this, they do not bind their own `this` but inherit `this` from their **parent scope**. The latter will become useful in the future.

This sounds more complicated than it actually is and can be explained quickly using an example. Let's assume we define a button which should write the current time into a `div` once it is being pressed. A typical function in ES5:

```
function TimeButton() {
  var button = document.getElementById('btn');
  var self = this;
  this.showTime = function() {
```

```
      document.getElementById('time' ).innerHTML = new Date();
  }
  button.addEventListener( 'click', function() {
    self.showTime();
  });
}
```

As the function supplied an **event listener**, and does not have access to its **parent scope** — the **TimeButton** in this case — we have to make amends with saving this in the variable self. This is not an uncommon pattern for ES5 JavaScript. Alternatively, the scope of the function could be **explicitly** bound to this and thus teach the **event listener** which scope to execute the code in:

```
function TimeButton() {
  var button = document.getElementById('btn');
  this.showTime = function() {
    document.getElementById('time' ).innerHTML = new Date();
  }
  button.addEventListener( 'click', function() {
    this.showTime();
  }.bind( this));
}
```

self becomes superfluous in this example. This example is entirely valid as well, however also not very elegant.

Let us look at an example using **arrow functions** which inherit this from their **parent scope**, in this case from the TimeButton.

```
function TimeButton() {
  var button = document.getElementById('btn');
  this.showTime = function() {
    document.getElementById('time' ).innerHTML = new Date();
  }
  button.addEventListener( 'click', () => {
    this.showTime();
  });
}
```

And just like that we gained access to the outer this in the **event listener**.

Gone are the days of var self = this and .bind(this). We can pretend we are still using the scope of the TimeButton scope even though the code is being written inside the **event listener**. This is especially useful for working with complex React components that contain many class properties and methods themselves. It avoids confusion as new scopes are not being opened every time.

New String, Array and Object methods

With the introduction of ES2015, a lot of static and prototype methods were added to JavaScript. Even if many of these are not directly relevant to React, they are still very powerful, which is why I will explain these in bit more detail.

String methods

In the past, we had to use `indexOf()` or regular expressions for operations such as checking if a value is present in a string or whether the string starts or ends with a specific value. With ES2015, the string data type gets its own methods to achieve these:

```
string.includes(value);
string.startsWith(value);
string.endsWith(value);
```

In each of these, a boolean value is returned by the function — meaning either `true` or `false`. If I want to test whether the string `Example` contains the word egg, I can check for it like this:

```
'Example'.includes ('egg')
```

Similarly, we can test for `startsWith`:

```
'Example'.startsWith ('Ex')
```

… and for `endsWith`:

```
'Example'.endsWith ('ample')
```

All of these are case-sensitive, meaning that differences in capitalization are taken into account.

Another two useful methods added in ES2015 are `String.prototype.padStart()` and `String.prototype.padEnd()`. Both of these can be used to extend a string to a specific length by inserting a number of characters at the beginning or end. The first parameter denotes the desired length of the string whereas the optional second parameter describes the character with which you want to fill up the string to the given length. If no second parameter is provided, spaces are used instead.

A common use case is to prepend numbers with leading zeros to give them all the same length:

```
'7'.padStart( 3, '0'); // 007
'72'.padStart( 3, '0'); // 072
'132'.padStart( 3, '0'); // 132
```

The same applies to `String.prototype.padEnd()` although the string is filled up at the end (not at the start).

Arrays

The Array has also gained new static and prototype methods. What do I even mean when I talk about prototype methods? Prototype methods work "with the actual array" — an already existing **array instance**. Static methods on the other hand can be thought of as helper methods which "do things" that are related to arrays.

Static array methods

```
Array.of(3); // [3]
Array.of(1, 2, 3); // [1, 2 ,3]
Array.from('Example'); // ['E', 'x', 'a', 'm', 'p', 'l', 'e']
```

`Array.of()` creates a new array instance from any given number of parameters. It does not matter if their types are different. `Array.from()` also creates an array instance but from an "array-like" iterable object. The most common examples are probably an `HTMLCollection` or a `NodeList`. These are created by DOM methods such as `getElementsByClassName()` or the more modern `querySelectorAll()`. `HTMLCollection` and `NodeList` do not own methods such as `.map()` or `.filter()`. If you want to iterate over any of the two, you need to convert them to an array first. It's easily done by using `Array.from()` though.

```
const links = Array.from(document.querySelectorAll('a'));
Array.isArray(links); // true
```

Methods on the array prototype

The methods on the array prototype can be **directly executed on the array instance**. The most applicable methods for React and Redux are:

```
Array.find(func);
Array.findIndex(func);
Array.includes(value);
```

`Array.find()` finds the **first** element in an array that fulfills the given criteria (as can be inferred from its name). It uses a function which is supplied as the first parameter to check for this value.

```
const numbers = [ 1, 2, 5, 9, 13, 24, 27, 39, 50];
const biggerThan10 = numbers.find((number) => number >  10); // 13

const users = [
  {id: 1, name: 'Manuel'},
  {id: 2, name: 'Bianca'},
  {id: 3, name: 'Brian' }
];

const userWithId2 = users.find((user) => user.id ===  2);
// { id: 2, name: 'Bianca'}
```

The `Array.findIndex()` method follows a similar pattern but returns only the index of element which has been found as opposed of the `Array.find()` method which returned the value. In the above example, the first function would yield 4, the second 1.

`Array.includes()`, added in ES2016, checks whether a value exists within the array it is called upon and returns a boolean. **Finally!** If you tried to reproduce the same functionality in the past, you had to make do with `Array.indexOf()`. `Array.includes()` simplifies this greatly:

```
[1,2,3,4,5].includes(4); // true
[1,2,3,4,5].includes(6); // false
```

But be careful: `.includes()` is case sensitive. If you try to check for `['a', 'b'].includes('A')`, it will return `false`.

Objects

Static object methods

Arrays and strings are not the only data structures which have gained new functionality. Objects have received a lot of new methods and improvements. Let's look at the most important ones briefly:

```
Object.assign(target, source [, source[,...] ]);
Object.entries(Object)
Object.keys(Object)
Object.values(Object)
Object.freeze(Object)
```

In my opinion the most useful addition has been `Object.assign()`. This method enables the merge of one or more objects into an existing object and returns the result as an object. But beware: the existing object is **mutated**. Hence, you should use this method sparingly. Another example to illustrate the point:

```
const user = { id: 1, name: 'Manuel' };
const modifiedUser = Object.assign( user, { role: 'Admin' });
console.log( user);
// -> { id: 1, name: 'Manuel', role: 'Admin' }
console.log(modifiedUser);
// -> { id: 1, name: 'Manuel', role: 'Admin' }
console.log( user === modifiedUser);
// -> true
```

The property `role` of the object in the second parameter of the `Object.assign()` function is added to the **existing destination object**.

React embraces the principle of **pure functions** which denote functions which are encapsulated in themselves and do not modify their entry parameters. Taking this into account, it becomes apparent that such mutations should be avoided if at all possible. We can circumvent this problem by providing an empty object literal as the first argument:

```
const user = { id: 1, name: 'Manuel' };
const modifiedUser = Object.assign({}, user, { role: 'Admin' });
console.log( user);
// -> { id: 1, name: 'Manuel' }
console.log(modifiedUser);
// -> { id: 1, name: 'Manuel', role: 'Admin' }
console.log( user === modifiedUser);
// -> false
```

By providing a newly created object as the destination object, the result is also a different object. In few cases, it can be advantageous to mutate the **destination object**, in React however this practice is best avoided.

The method can process any given objects as parameters. If a property name appears more than once in an object, the properties added later take precedence.

```
const user = { id: 1, name: 'Manuel' };
const modifiedUser = Object.assign(
  {},
  user,
  { role: 'Admin' },
  { name: 'Not Manuel' , job: 'Developer' }
```

```
);
console.log(modifiedUser);
// -> { id: 1, name: 'Not Manuel' , role: 'Admin' , job: 'Developer' }
```

`Object.entries()`, `Object.keys()` and `Object.values()` offer similar functionality. They return the properties (keys), the values (values) or the entries (`entries()`) as an **array**. **Entries** however returns a nested array of the following form:

```
[[key, value], [key2, values2], …]
```

Applying these methods to our example above, we receive the following results:

```
Object.keys({ id: 1, name: 'Manuel'});
// -> ['id', 'name']
Object.values({ id: 1, name: 'Manuel'});
// -> [1, 'Manuel']
Object.entries({id: 1, name: 'Manuel'});
// -> [['id' , 1], ['name', 'Manuel']]
```

Lastly, let us look at `Object.freeze()` which does just what you would expect. It freezes an object and prohibits any further mutations, be it the adding of new properties, deleting old properties or even just changing values. Following React's principle of immutable objects, this is very useful.

```
const user = Object.freeze({ id: 1, name: 'Manuel' });
user.id = 2;
delete user.name;
user.role = 'Admin';
console.log( user);
// -> { id: 1, name: 'Manuel' }
```

If an object created with `Object.freeze()` is attempted to be changed, for example using `Object.assign()`, it will throw a `TypeError`, thus preventing unwanted and accidental mutations on the object.

Syntax extensions and simplifications

The rest of the changes that were added to objects are not methods but syntax extensions.

First, **computed properties** were introduced to have the possibility of using expressions as object properties. In the past, one had to manually create the object (for example using an **object literal** `{}` or using `Object.create()`), assign it to a variable and then add it as a new property to the object:

```
const nationality = 'german';
const user = {
  name: 'Manuel',
};
user[nationality] = true;
console.log( user );
// -> { name: 'Manuel', german: true };
```

With the addition of **ES2015**, expressions can now be directly used as object properties by surrounding them with brackets [] avoiding the clunky detour of adding properties to the already existing object:

```
const nationality = 'german';
const user = {
  name: 'Manuel',
  [nationality]: true,
};
console.log( user );
// -> { name: 'Manuel', german: true };
```

So far so good. I have tried to keep the examples very simple at this point but its implications are evident. In more complex situations, this technique will allow us to write clean and easily readable code especially with regard to **JSX**.

Another noteworthy addition for objects has been the introduction of **shorthand property names**. Previously, code had to be written in the following form:

```
const name = 'Manuel';
const job = 'Developer';
const role = 'Author';

const user = {
  name: name,
  job: job,
  role: role,
};
```

We are using a lot of repetition here. **Shorthand property name syntax** in **ES2015** prevents this and allow us to use only the variable name if the name of the object property is the same. This reduces our code to:

```
const name = 'Manuel';
const job = 'Developer';
const role = 'Author';
```

```
const user = {
  name, job, role
};
```

Yep, since **ES2015** both of these methods of defining an object will lead to the same result. Of course, shorthand property syntax can be mixed with standard property syntax:

```
const name = 'Manuel';
const job = 'Developer';

const user = {
  name,
  job,
  role: 'Author'
};
```

Classes

Classes are a concept most will know from object oriented languages such as Java. However, with **ES2015** classes have been added to JavaScript. In the past, object orientation could only be mocked by using the prototype property of a function and defining its methods and properties. Compared to many other object oriented languages though, it felt overly complicated and wordy in JavaScript.

Since **ES2015**, classes can be defined by using the keyword `class`. While React equally uses principles of **functional programming**, it also depends heavily on ES2015 classes to instantiate **React Class components**. Before ES2015 it was possible to define React components using `createClass()` but it has since been deprecated and should no longer be used.

A class consists of a name, an optional **constructor** that gets called at creation of a class instance as well as an unlimited number of class methods.

```
class Customer {
  constructor(firstName, lastName) {
    this.firstName = firstName;
    this.lastName = lastName;
  }

  getFullName() {
    return this.firstName + ' ' + this.lastName;
  }
}
```

```
const firstCustomer = new Customer('Max', 'Mustermann' );
console.log(firstCustomer.getFullName());
```

Result:

 Max Mustermann

Additionally, classes can be extended using `extends`:

```
class Customer extends Person {}
```

Or:

```
class MyComponent extends React.Component {}
```

Using the inbuilt `super()` function the component can call the **constructor** of its parent class. In terms of React, the use of `super()` is only necessary if new classes have been added and if a constructor is present. If this is the case, `super()` is called and its `props` are passed to the constructor of the React.Component.

```
class MyComponent extends React.Component {
  constructor(props) {
    super(props);
  }
}
```

If we omit this, `this.props` would be undefined and the props within the component could not be accessed. In most cases we do not need to define our own constructors though, as React provides **lifecycle methods** which are preferable over the use of a constructor.

Rest and spread operators and destructuring

Another great simplification has been the introduction of the so-called rest and spread operators for objects and arrays. Strictly speaking, the use of these is not yet supported for objects in ES2015 because the specifics are still under discussion. However, this will change with ES2018 when they get added to the ECMAScript specification. First, the rest and spread operators were added to arrays in ES2015. Using Babel though, we can harness the power of these operators in our work with objects today. As you will see, many React projects will make heavy use of these.

But enough of this. What are they exactly? Let's start with the spread operator.

Spread operator

The spread operator allows us to "unpack" values. Pre-ES2015 one had to extract arguments from an array to pass them to a function via `Function.prototype.apply()`:

```
function sumAll(number1, number2, number3) {
    return number1 + number2 + number3;
}

var myArray = [1, 2, 3];
sumAll.apply(null, myArray);
```

Result:

ⓘ 6

Using the spread operator which consists of three dots (...) we can "unpack" these arguments or "spread" them.

```
function sumAll(number1, number2, number3) {
    return number1 + number2 + number3;
}
var myArray = [1, 2, 3];
sumAll(...myArray);
```

As we can see, `apply()` is not necessary anymore. However, spreading arguments is not only useful and limited to function arguments. It can also be used to easily combine two arrays into one:

```
const greenFruits = ['kiwi', 'apple', 'pear'];
const redFruits = ['strawberry', 'cherry', 'raspberry'];
const allFruits = [...greenFruits, ...redFruits];
```

Result:

```
['kiwi', 'apple', 'pear', 'strawberry', 'cherry', 'raspberry']
```

A new array is created which not only contains all values from greenFruits but also all values from redFruits. But there's more: a new array is also created for us — not just a reference to the old arrays. Thinking back to the previously mentioned **read-only** mentality in React, this will prove useful for the work with props. The spread operator can also be used to create a simple copy of an array:

```
const users = [ 'Manuel', 'Chris' , 'Ben'];
const selectedUsers = [...users];
```

selectedUsers is a copy of usersand all of its values. If we change the usersarray, no complications for selectedUsers occur.

Let's shift our focus to objects. Using the spread operator with objects is very similar to using it with arrays. However, instead of using every single value, every property that is enumerable in the object (roughly those that are used during a for(… in …) loop) will be used.

The spread operator is a great choice to create objects:

```
const globalSettings = { language: 'en-US' , timezone: 'Berlin/Germany' };
const userSettings = { mutedUsers: [ 'Manuel'] } ;
const allSettings = {...globalSettings, ...userSettings}  ;
console.log (allSettings);
```

Result:

```
{
  language: 'en-US' ,
  timezone: 'Berlin/Germany',
  mutedUsers: [ 'Manuel'],
}
```

The properties of each object can be found in the allSettings object. However, the spread operator is not limited to two objects. We can combine any number of objects into a new object. Even the combination of single properties is possible:

```
const settings = {
  ...userSettings,
  showWarnings: true ,
}
```

If there are object properties with the same name in any two objects, the property in the object declared last will be used:

```
const globalSettings = { language: ' en-US', timezone: 'Berlin/Germany' };
const userSettings = { language: ' de-DE' };
const allSettings = {...globalSettings, ...userSettings};
console.log (allSettings);
```

Result:

```
{
    language: 'de-DE',
    timezone: 'Berlin/Germany',
}
```

The userSettings object which has been declared after the globalSettings object overrides the language property by providing a key which is identical to that in the globalSettingsobject. The spread operator works in a similar fashion to the newly introduced Object.assign() method in ES2015 which is also used in in ES2015+ applications from time to time.

However, it is important to make a distinction here: Object.assign() mutates an existing object whereas the spread operator creates a new object. In terms of writing React components and their props, we want to avoid creating mutations, but for the sake of completion, let us look at a brief example anyway.

Combining objects with Object.assign()

Object.assign() takes any number of arguments and combines them into a single object:

```
const a = { a:  1 };
const b = { b: 2 };
const c = { c:  3 };
console.log(Object.assign(a,   b, c));
```

Result:

```
{a: 1, b: 2, c: 3}
```

The function returns an object in which all three of the objects that have been passed to Object.assign() have been combined. But is this really a new object? **No!** In order to prove this, let's print a, b, and c to the console:

```
console.log (a);
console.log (b);
console.log (c);
```

Result:

```
{a: 1, b: 2, c: 3}
{b: 2}
{c: 3}
```

As can be seen from the example above, `Object.assign()` did not create a new object for us. It merely added the properties of the second and the third object to the first. In terms of **pure functions** and **immutable objects** this is far from ideal and should be avoided.

There's a trick to ensure that objects can be combined via `Object.assign()` but also be created in a new object. Passing an empty object literal `{}` as the first argument to the function like this:

```
Object.assign({}, a, b, c);
```

... will achieve exactly what we want. It passes all the object properties of a, b and c while keeping the previous objects a, b and c intact.

Destructuring assignments

Before introducing the **rest operator** to you which is closely related to the **spread operator**, I want to talk about **destructuring assignments** (or **destructuring** for short).

Destructuring allows the extraction of one or more elements from any object or array and to assign it to a new variable. It is another great syntax extension that has been gifted to us with the introduction of ES2015.

Destructuring Arrays

Let's imagine that we want to extract the medalists of a 100m run and write them to a new variable. ES5 allows us to express this in the following:

```
const athletes = [
  'Usain Bolt' ,
  'Andre De Grasse ' ,
  'Christophe Lemaitre ',
  'Adam Gemili',
  'Churandy Martina' ,
  'LaShawn Merritt' ,
  'Alonso Edward' ,
  'Ramil Guliyev' ,
];

const gold = athletes[0];
const silver = athletes[1];
const bronze = athletes[2];
```

Thanks to **destructuring,** we can simplify this greatly and reduce the expression to a single statement:

```
const [gold, silver,  bronze] = athletes;
```

The array elements at index 0, 1 and 2 are now all to be found in the variables for `gold`, `silver` and `bronze`. The result is the same as in the previous example, however the second version is much shorter and a lot more succinct.

We can use array destructuring anywhere where the array has been initialized on the right side, even if it is contained in the `return` value of a function.

```
const getAllAthletes = () => {
  return [
    'Usain Bolt' ,
    'Andre De Grasse ' ,
    'Christophe Lemaitre ',
    'Adam Gemili',
    'Churandy Martina' ,
    'LaShawn Merritt' ,
    'Alonso Edward' ,
    'Ramil Guliyev' ,
  ]
}

const [gold, silver, bronze] = getAllAthletes()
```

As can be seen above, the array function returns an array with all the athletes. We can use destructuring directly once it is called and do not need to save the `return` value in a temporary variable.

If we want to omit elements from the array, their values can literally be omitted.

```
const [, silver,  bronze] = athletes;
```

In this example, we do not declare a variable gold and only save the silver and bronze medalists to our variables.

But **array destructuring** is not limited to assigning variables with `let` and const. There are many other cases that prove useful such as passing function arguments in the form of an array.

```
const logWinners = (athletes) => {
  const gold = athletes[ 0];
  const silver = athletes[1 ];
  const bronze = athletes[2 ];
  console .log(
    'Winners of Gold, Silver and Bronze are' ,
```

```
    gold,
    silver,
    bronze
  );
}
```

But this can be simplfied:

```
const logWinners = ([gold, silver, bronze]) => {
  console.log(
    'Winners of Gold, Silver and Bronze are' ,
    gold,
    silver,
    bronze
  );
}
```

We are passing the array to our `logWinners()` function and instead of defining a variable to each and every medalist winner we can combine our efforts and simply use the destructuring method.

Destructuring objects

The concept of destructuring is not only limited to arrays. Objects can also be assigned to variables if they share the same naming.

The semantics are very similar to those of arrays, with the difference that values are not being assigned based on position but based on their property name. Moreover, curly brackets are used instead of square brackets.

```
const user = {
  firstName: 'Manuel',
  lastName: 'Bieh' ,
  job: 'JavaScript Developer',
  image: 'manuel.jpg' ,
};
const { firstName } = user;
```

`firstName` now contains the value of `user.firstname`.

Object destructuring is among the most widely used features in React components. It allows for writing single props into new variables and to use them in JSX in an uncomplicated fashion.

Let's look at the following example of a Function component:

45

```
const UserPersona = (props) => {
  return (
    <div>
      <img src={props.image} alt="User Image" />
      {props.firstName} {props.lastName}
      <br />
      <strong>{props.job}</strong>
    </div>
  );
};
```

Having to repeat props in front of every property hinders readability of the component. Instead, we can use object destructuring and create a variable for each property of the props once.

```
const UserPersona = (props) => {
  const { firstName, lastName, image, job } = props;
  return (
    <div>
      <img src={image} alt="User Image" />
      {firstName} {lastName}
      <br />
      <strong>{job}</strong>
    </div>
  );
};
```

That already looks tidier and improves readability of the code, but we can simplify this further. Remember that it was possible to destructure arrays when they were being passed as a function argument. The same applies for objects. Instead of using the props argument, we can directly use **destructuring assignment**:

```
const UserPersona = ({ firstName, lastName, image, job }) => (
  <div>
    <img src={image} alt="User Image" />
    {firstName} {lastName}
    <br />
    <strong>{job}</strong>
  </div>
);
```

As a nice side effect, we can simplify this further as the implicit return from the **arrow function** allows us to omit the curly brackets and the explicit return. We are left with just 5 lines of **JSX.**

This syntax is very common in Function components but you can find a similar destructuring assignments in the beginning of the `render()` method of **Class components**:

```
render() {
  const { firstName, lastName, image, job } =   this.props;
  // more Code
}
```

Of course it is entirely up to you if you make use of destructuring or whether you continue to use `this.props.firstname` in your function. However, the former has developed into some sort of best practice and can be found in most React projects as it aids readability and makes it easier to understand it.

Renaming properties when destructuring

Sometimes it is necessary to rename properties. Either because a variable with the same name has already been declared or because a variable with the current property name would be invalid. Both of these are valid concerns and ES2015 offers a solution for these.

```
const passenger = {
  name: 'Manuel Bieh',
  class: 'economy' ,
};
```

The above `passenger` object contains a property named class which is a valid property name. However, it is not valid as a variable name. Direct destructuring is not possible in this case and would lead to an error:

```
const { name,  class } = passenger;
```

  Uncaught SyntaxError: Unexpected token }

In order to rename the variable, the invalid property name needs to be followed by a colon and the new name. This would pass as a valid **destructuring assignment**:

```
const { name, class: ticketClass } = passenger;
```

The value of the `class` property is written into the new variable `ticketClass` which, as opposed to `class`, is a valid name for a variable. The name of the passenger can easily be destructured into a variable with the name name.

Defaults in destructuring assignments

It is also possible to use defaults with **destructuring**. If you are trying to destructure a property of an object in which it does not exist, you can define a default to use instead. Instead of using a colon as we did for reserved names, we use the equals sign followed by the default value we want to pass:

```
const { name = 'Unknown passenger' } = passenger;
```

If no property called name was present in the object or its value was undefined, name would result in Unknown passenger in this example. If however an empty string is passed or null, the default would **not** be used.

Combining renames and defaults

Now it's getting interesting because combining renaming and default naming is possible. It might not be the simplest code to follow first but syntactically it is correct. Let use our previous passenger object again to illustrate this point. First, we define the name property to be renamed to passengerName and then pass it the default value of Unknown passenger if no property name is found on the object. We also want to keep using ticketClass instead of the reserved class and assign the value economy to it, should it not exist as a property on the object.

```
const {
  name: passengerName =  'Unknown passenger',
  class: ticketClass = 'economy' ,
} = passenger;
```

If the newly named variables passengerName and ticketClass are not present in the object to be destructured, the values Unknown passenger and economy are assigned. We do however need to ensure that the object itself is not null, otherwise the JavaScript interpreter will throw an error:

```
const {
  name: passengerName =  'Unknown passenger',
  class: ticketClass = 'economy' ,
} = null;
```

 Uncaught TypeError: Cannot destructure property `name` of 'undefined' or 'null'.

There is an untidy yet highly practical trick to ensure that the object we are working with is not null or undefined. The **logical OR operator** can be used to declare a fallback object if our

48

actual object is `null` or `undefined`.

```
const {
    name: passengerName =  'Unknown passenger',
    class: ticketClass = 'economy' ,
} = passenger || {};
```

With the addition of `|| {}` we express that if the `passenger` object is **falsy**, an empty object should be used instead. Arguably, it would be "cleaner" to check if `passenger` is an object first and only then to continue and destructure it. The **logical OR operator** provides a handy and concise alternative for our tool set though and should be sufficient in most cases.

Destructuring and the **spread operator** can be used together too:

```
const globalSettings = { language: 'en-US'  };
const userSettings = { timezone: 'Berlin/Germany' };
const { language, timezone } = { ...globalSettings, ...userSettings };
```

In this example, the **spread operator** is resolved first and a new object with all the properties of `globalSettings` and `userSettings` is created. Then, using **destructuring** variables are being assigned.

Rest operator

The rest operator takes care of the remaining elements in an array or object after **destructuring** or the remaining arguments of **function arguments**. Its name is pretty self-explanatory — it deals with the **"rest"** of the elements. Similar to the **spread operator**, the **rest operator** is preceded by three dots .... However, it will not be found on right side of an assignment but on the **left**. Moreover, only **one** rest operator can be used in each expression (also in stark contrast to the **spread operator**).

Let's investigate the **rest operator** in function arguments. Assume, that we want to write a function that can take any number of arguments — it doesn't matter whether 2, 5 or 25 arguments are being passed. ES5 offers the keyword `arguments` to us with which we can access an array of all the function arguments within our function:

```
function Example() {
    console .log(arguments );
}
Example(1 , 2, 3, 4, 5);
```

Result:

Arrow functions however do not offer this functionality anymore and will throw an error if you attempt to access the **arguments**.

```
const Example = () => {
  console.log(arguments );
};
Example(1 , 2, 3, 4, 5);
```

Result:

The **rest operator** offers a neat solution to this problem: it writes all the remaining function arguments which we have not already extracted into their own variables into one more variable with any given name:

```
const Example = (...rest) => {
  console.log(rest);
};
Example(1 , 2, 3, 4, 5);
```

Result:

But this does not only work for a single function argument but also if you previously defined some other parameters. The **rest operator** will quite literally take care of the **rest**:

```
const Example = (first, second, third, ...rest) => {
  console.log('first:', first);
  console.log('second:' , second);
  console.log('third:', third);
  console.log('rest:' , rest);
};
Example(1 , 2, 3, 4, 5);
```

Result:

50

We could say that the **rest operator** "collects" the remaining elements from a **destructuring** operation and saves them to variable which is indicated just after the three dots. Even though, we have named this variable `rest` in our previous examples, you can give it any valid name.

The **rest operator** is not limited to functions but can also be used in **array destructuring**:

```
const athletes = [
  'Usain Bolt' ,
  'Andre De Grasse' ,
  'Christophe Lemaitre' ,
  'Adam Gemili',
  'Churandy Martina' ,
  'LaShawn Merritt' ,
  'Alonso Edward' ,
  'Ramil Guliyev' ,
];
const [gold, silver, bronze, ...competitors] = athletes;
console.log(gold);
console.log(silver);
console.log(bronze);
console.log(competitors);
```

Result:

```
(i)   'Usain Bolt'
      'Andre De Grasse'
      'Christophe Lemaitre'`
      [
        'Adam Gemili',
        'Churandy Martina',
        'LaShawn Merritt',
        'Alonso Edward',
        'Ramil Guliyev'
      ]
```

... as well as in **object destructuring**:

```
const user = {
  firstName: 'Manuel',
```

51

```
  lastName: 'Bieh' ,
  job: 'JavaScript Developer',
  hair: 'Brown' ,
};
const { firstName, lastName, ...other } = user;
console .log(firstName);
console .log(lastName);
console .log(other);
```

Result:

> (i)   Manuel
>
>   Bieh
>
>   { job: 'JavaScript Developer', hair: 'Brown' }

All the values not being explicitly written into a variable during **destructuring**, can be accessed via the **rest variable** which we have declared above.

Template Strings

Template strings in ES2015 offer yet a third alternative to write a string. Strings can already be declared by using either single exclamation marks (`'Example'`) or double exclamation marks (`"Example"`). Since ES2015, backticks can also be used to declare a string: `` `Example` ``.

There are two variations of **template strings**. There are the usual **template strings** which can contain JavaScript expressions as well as **tagged template literals** in their extended form.

Tagged template literals are much more powerful than regular **template strings** as their output can be modified with the help of a special function. However, for our usual work with React this is not our primary concern.

If you wanted to mix them with JavaScript expressions or values, you would normally use plain old **string concatenation** pre-ES6 times.

```
var age = 7;
var text = 'My daughter is '  + age + ' years old' ;
```

```
var firstName = 'Manuel';
var lastName = 'Bieh' ;
var fullName = firstName + ' '  + lastName;
```

Template strings allow us to include **JavaScript expressions** in this variation of a string. In order to do this, you wrap the expression you want to include in this form: `${ }`. Let us look at our previous examples but rewrite them using **template literals**:

```
const age = 7;
const text = `My daughter is ${age} years old`;


const firstName = 'Manuel';
const lastName = 'Bieh';
const fullName = `${firstName} ${lastName}`;
```

It is important to note that we are not limited to using variables as shown above. Equally, you can use any JavaScript expressions (i.e. function calls), in this case:

```
console.log(`Today's date is: ${new Date().toISOString()} `);
console.log(`${firstName.toUpperCase()}   ${lastName.toUpperCase()} `);
```

Promises and async/await

Promises are not an exclusively new concept in JavaScript, however with ES2015 they been standardized and can be used without any other additional libraries for the first time. Promises allow for asynchronous development by linearizing with callbacks. A promise takes in an **executor function** which again takes two arguments, namely `resolve` and `reject`, and can take any of three states: `pending`, `fulfilled` or `rejected`. The initial state of a promise is always pending. Depending on the operation of the executor function being successful or unsuccessful, meaning `resolve` or `reject`, the status of the of the promise will change to either `fulfilled` or `rejected`. You can react directly to these two states with `.then()` or `.catch()` respectively. If `resolve` is being passed to the executor function, the `then()` part will execute. If `reject` is called, **all** `then()` calls are skipped and the `catch()` block is executed instead.

An executor function **has** to execute one of the two functions it has been passed, otherwise the promise will be stuck in an *unfulfilled* state. This can lead to unexpected and false behavior and can even cause memory leaks within an application.

To reiterate the difference between promises and callbacks, let us have a look at the following example:

```
const errorHandler = (err) => {
  console.error('An error occured:', err.message);
};

getUser(
```

```
    id,
    (user) => {
        user.getFriends((friends) => {
            friends[ 0].getSettings((settings) => {
                if (settings.notifications ===  true) {
                    email.send(
                        'You are my first friend!' ,
                        (status) => {
                            if (status === 200 ) {
                                alert('User has been notified via email!');
                            }
                        },
                        errorHandler
                    );
                }
            }, errorHandler);
        }, errorHandler);
    },
    errorHandler
);
```

The asynchronous getUser() function is called to obtain user information with their id. Using its getFriends() method, we can obtain a list of all of their friends. To collect the first friend's (friends[0]) user settings, the getSettings() method is called. If this friend has allowed email notifications, an email is sent to them. We react asynchronously to the response of the mail server.

Despite this example being relatively simple, the code is nested **6 layers** deep — and we are not even taking care of explicit error handling or edge cases. Working with callbacks can become cumbersome and confusing quickly, especially once callback functions will trigger further callback functions, as in our example. It comes as no surprise that this is often called **callback hell** or the **pyramid of doom**.

Let us rewrite this and assume that our fictional API methods will each return a promise:

```
const errorHandler = (err) => {
    console .error( 'An error occured:', err.message);
};

getUser(id)
    .then((user) => user.getFriends())
    .then((friends) => friends[ 0].getSettings())
    .then((settings) => {
        if (settings.notifications ===  true) {
            return email.send( 'You are my first friend!' );
```

```
    }
  })
  .then((status) => {
    if (status === 200 ) {
      alert( 'User has been notified via email' );
    }
  })
  .catch(errorHandler);
```

Each step is being followed by then() to react to the previous promise. Although the same end result is reached by this piece of code, we are only nesting 2 layers deep and readability is improved immensely.

It is relatively simple to refactor code based on callbacks into one that is using promises. In order to demonstrate this, I will show you an example of the Geolocation API and its getCurrentPosition() method. For those of you who do not know it: the method exists on the navigator.geolocation object and opens a dialog in the browser asking the user for permission to use their current location. The method expects two callbacks as arguments, namely the success callback and the error callback. The first callback, the success callback, is being passed an object with the user's location if they have previously agreed. The second callback, the error callback, is being passed an error object. This can occur because the user has not given permission to use their current location or due to a location not being possible for other reasons.

```
navigator.geolocation.getCurrentPosition(
  (position) => {
    console.log(
      `User position is at ${position.coords.latitude}, ${
        position.coords.longitude
      }`
    );
  },
  () => {
    console.log('Unable to locate user' );
  }
);
```

The callback can be transformed into a promise:

```
const getCurrentPositionPromise = () => {
  return new Promise ((resolve, reject) => {
    navigator.geolocation.getCurrentPosition(resolve, reject);
  });
};
```

Yep, that's it! Now we can access the user's location like the following instead of using callback syntax:

```
getCurrentPositionPromise()
  .then((position) => {
    console.log(
      `User position is at ${position.coords.latitude}, ${
        position.coords.longitude
      }`
    );
  })
  .catch(() => {
    console.log('Unable to locate user' );
  });
```

A few of the newer JavaScript Browser APIs have already followed this new implementation. If you want to learn about promises and how they work in detail, I suggest you to read the the following article on the MDN web docs[19]. The explanation and reasoning for promises should only serve as an introduction to a much more interesting feature though, namely:

Asynchronous functions with `async` / `await`

Asynchronous functions with `async` and `await` can be seen as the next step in the asynchronous evolution in the JavaScript ecosystem and been added to the JavaScript specification in ES2016. While still using promises under the hood, async/await make them invisible and allow us to write asynchronous code that resembles synchronous code. No more callbacks and then() or catch().

In order to use it, prepend the asynchronous function with the `await` keyword. However, to use `await` the async keyword needs to be applied in the function call in which `await` is used. It tells the JavaScript interpreter that we are using an asynchronous function and omitting it would throw an exception.

Bringing it back to our previous example of the user that wants to send an email to their first friend, we can rewrite it using these asynchronous functions:

```
(async () => {
  try {
    const user = await getUser(id);
    const friends = await user.getFriends();
    const settings = await friends[ 0].getSettings();
    if (settings.notifications ===   true) {
      const status = await email.send( 'You are my first friend!' );
      if (status === 200 ) {
```

```
        alert( 'User has been notified via email' );
      }
    }
  } catch (err) {
    console.error( 'An error occured:', err.message);
  }
})();
```

For me personally asynchronous functions with `async` and `await` have been one of the most notable changes in JavaScript in the past few years. They facilitate working with asynchronous data greatly, especially compared to complex and confusing callbacks. Even promises, which were already a massive improvement over callbacks, look almost complex compared to async / `await`.

Import syntax and JavaScript modules

Modules in JavaScript are a bit of special topic. They did not exist officially but there have been many attempts to introduce JavaScript modules in the past. If you have been part of the development scene for a while, you might remember **AMD** (Asynchronous Module Definition) and if you have worked with Node.js before you should have come across CommonJS Modules (i.e. `module.exports` and `require('./myModule')`). There has been a lot of debate centering on which module standard should become the de-facto standard, what the syntax is supposed to look like and how the implementation should work on the side of the interpreter. In the end, consensus was reached on using `import` and `export` keywords to let the modules communicate with each other.

Babel was first to implement a solution that was based on the previous standard of the specification. This implementation had to change in between though as updates were made to the standard. When webpack entered the scene, it implemented yet another mechanism to manage resolving and loading of JavaScript modules which is based on the now approved final standard. Just like TypeScript.

After **10** years, we have finally reached consensus for the specification and JavaScript engines are busy implementing it. This sounds rather complicated. It surely has been in the past. However, nowadays most agree and developers finally found clarity. But there are a few gotchas still which is why we should still rely on Webpack, Babel or TypeScript to work with modules. But more on that later.

We have talked a lot about the history of modules now. But how do imports work and what even are modules?

Modules in JavaScript

The primary goal of modules is to encapsulate JavaScript scope for each module. In this case, a module is actually a single **file**. ****As long as you are not explicitly limiting their scope by using an *IIFE* (*Immediately Invoked Function Expression*), each function, each variable etc that you declare in JavaScript is available globally. Modules prevent this by only making the code inside it available **in the module itself**. This can avoid complications such as two libraries using the same variable. Moreover, modules encourage reusable code without being scared of using already existing variables or overriding functions that have already been declared.

Modules can **export:** functions, classes or variables that have been declared within them. Other modules can then import these exports if necessary. In order to export these functions and variables, a special export keyword is used. To import these, you might recognize a pattern here, there is an import keyword. Exporting can take two forms: **named exports** and **default exports**.

Named Exports

Assume that we have created a module - calc.mjs - that provides a number of functions for us to make more complicated calculations. For example, the module could contain the following:

```
export const double = (number) => number * 2 ;
export const square = (number) => number * number;
export const divideBy = (number, divisor) => number / divisor;
export const divideBy5 = (number) => divideBy(number,   5);
```

We announce an **export** by using the keyword. Then, declaring a variable and assigning it an arrow function with one or more parameters and directly returning the result we could use this function elsewhere in another module. Alternatively, we can achieve the same with two separate steps:

```
const double = (number) => number * 2 ;
export double;
```

Using the import keyword, we can now use these functions elsewhere in our application. To do this, we use import followed by the exports that we want to import in curly brackets as well as from and the path to module.

```
import { double, square, divideBy5 }  from './calc.mjs' ;

const value =  5;
console .log(double(value));  // 10
```

```
console.log(square(value));   // 25
console.log(divideBy5(value)); // 1
```

Theoretically, a file can have **as many exports as you want**. Beware though, they have to have different names and an already exported name **is not allowed to be exported again**.

Default Export

In addition to the so-called **named exports** from the example above, there is also the singular `default` export. This is a special form of an export that is only allowed to be used within a module **once** and declared by using `default`. If a variable or function has been marked as `default` it is possible to import it without curly brackets. The **default export** can alleviate the need for importing a lot of named exports by bundling them into a single default.

```
export const double = (number) => number * 2 ;
export const square = (number) => number * number;
export const divideBy = (number, divisor) => number / divisor;
export const divideBy5 = (number) => divideBy(number,  5);

export default {
  double,
  square,
  divideBy,
  divideBy5,
};
```

To use any of the above functionality, our application would only need to import the module itself — meaning the **default export** — and assign it to a variable:

```
import Calc from './calc.mjs' ;

console.log(Calc.double(value));   // 10
console.log(Calc.square(value));   // 25
console.log(Calc.divideBy5(value)); // 1
```

In most cases, it is useful for each module to have a **default export**. Especially in many component based libraries like React or Vue.js it is common to only define one export per module, which should be the **default export**. Even if this is not necessary from a syntactical point of view, it has become the standard for working with React.

```
export default class MyComponent extends React.Component {
  // ...
}
```

59

Inconsistencies: Browser vs Node.js

If you paid attention, you might have noticed that we imported a file named `calc.mjs` (not `calc.js`) above. This convention has been agreed upon in a lengthy process to ensure that JavaScript modules can be used in Node.js.

So if you want to write universal JavaScript that can be run on the server with Node.js but also client-side in the browser, you **have to** use the `.mjs` file ending for all your files. Especially, if you want to achieve this without tools such as Babel, Wepback or TypeScript.

Loading modules works a little different in Node.js compared to the browser. While the browser does not care which file ending a module has (as long as the server sends it back with the Content-Type `text/javascript`), Node.js requires the `.mjs` file ending to classify JavaScript modules.

To use JavaScript modules in the browser, the `type` attribute needs to be set to `module` in the corresponding `<script></script>` element:

```
<script src="./myApp.mjs" type="module"></script>
```

Those browsers that support `type="module"`, also support the `nomodule` attribute to indicate a fallback for browsers that do not support modules and safely ignore it.

```
<script src="./myApp.mjs" type="module"></script>
<script src="./myApp.bundle.js" nomodule></script>
```

A browser supporting modules would simply load `myApp.mjs` while all other browsers would serve a bundled `myApp.bundle.js` (for example generated with Webpack).

But that's not all: Node.js has its own, very special mechanism to find and load files. Modules that do not have a relative file path, i.e. not start with `./` or `../`, will be looked for in `node_modules` or `node_libraries` for example. Node.js also loads an `index.js` by default if it finds a directory with the name you specified.

```
import MyModule from 'myModule';
```

Node.js would look for an export in a directory such as `./node_modules/myModule` in this case and load an `index.js` that is inside of it. Alternatively, it would look for the file in the `main` field of the `package.json`. The browser on the other hand cannot try a bunch of different file paths to find a file because each and every search would result in an expensive network request and many costly 404 responses.

On top of that the module that you want to import from, also called the **Import Specifier** (that's the part just after the `from`), is protected in the browser. It has to consist of either a valid URL

60

or a valid file path.

Imports like this are not possible in browsers to date:

```
import React from 'react';
```

If we want to use JavaScript modules server-side as well as client-side, we will have to keep using module bundlers like Webpack for now. The proposal for **Package Name Maps** which is supposed to solve this problem is only in the early stages of discussion and will probably appear in a later version of ECMAScript.

Summary

ES2015 and the following versions of the ECMAScript standard have given us a lot of new functionality that did not exist in JavaScript before. It is hard to imagine working without these — especially when using React. The most notable new features are:

- Variable declarations with `let` and `const`
- **Arrow functions** — to create functions that do not bind their own `this`
- **Classes** — they are the basis of **React Class components** and facilitate a multitude of things
- **Rest and Spread operators** — which increase the read- and writability of data in arrays and objects immensely
- **Template strings** — to facilitate working with JavaScript expressions in Strings
- **Promises** and **Asynchronous functions with `async`/ `await`** — which enhance working with asynchronous data and make it much easier
- **Import** and **Export** — for encapsulating reusable JavaScript on a module basis

JSX – an Introduction

JSX as an important building block in React development

Before diving deeper into the development of components, I want to first talk about **JSX**. As mentioned earlier, JSX makes up a large portion of the code written in most React components and thus a large amount of React in general. In my opinion, JSX is one of the reasons why React has been so widely and readily adopted by the developer community. Nowadays, even other frameworks or libraries like Vue.js offer the possibility to use JSX to supercharge their components.

At first glance JSX does not look very different from HTML or XML. As in XML or in XHTML, every opening element also needs to have a matching closing element `</div>` or has to be self-closing (`<img/>`). In contrast to XML and XTHML though, JSX can include **JavaScript expressions** making it extremely powerful.

JSX elements are transformed into nested `React.createElement()` calls at a later step in our build process. Remember that I mentioned in the introduction that React creates a tree-like structure of elements – this happens here.

This all sounds a lot more complicated than it actually is though. Let's look at an example with the following HTML snippet:

```
<div id="app">
  <p>A paragraph in JSX</p>
  <p>Another paragraph</p>
</div>
```

If we use this snippet of HTML in **JSX**, Babel will later transpile it into the following executable JavaScript:

```
React.createElement(
  'div',
  { id: 'app' },
  React.createElement( 'p', null, 'A paragraph in JSX' ),
  React.createElement( 'p', null, 'Another paragraph' )
);
```

The first argument for the `createElement()` call denotes the tag name of the DOM element's string representation or another JSX element (in this case this would only be a function reference).

The second argument of the `createElement()` call are the **props** of an element. Props are comparable to HTML attributes but are much more flexible than regular HTML attributes. They are not limited to strings but can also include arrays, objects or even other React components as their value.

All other arguments are the so-called *"children"* of the element. In our example above, the `div` contains two children: two paragraphs (`<p>`). These in turn do not have any other props though (`null`) and only contain a text string (`A paragraph in JSX` and `Another paragraph`) as their children.

If anyone is a little confused at this point or finds JSX a little intimidating, I can assure you that writing JSX will become second nature to you in no time. It will feel like writing HTML markup. I still deem it very important to understand how JSX works under the hood, especially to grasp slightly more complex examples in the future.

Expressions in JavaScript

What exactly does it mean for us to be able to use JavaScript expressions in JSX?

A JavaScript expression is not much more than a piece of code that will generate a "value" or returns a "result" as a result of its operation. Put simply, anything that you can write on the **right** hand side of a variable declaration (so after the = sign):

```
1 + 5;
```

... is an expression whose value is 6.

```
'Hel' + 'lo';
```

... is another expression that **concatenates** the two strings `Hel` and `lo` into a single value `Hello`.

Instead, we could use any of the following as all **JavaScript data types** can be used as an expression:

```
6
'Hello'
[1,2,3,4]
{a: 1, b: 2, c: 3}
true
null
```

The ES2015 **Template String Syntax** is yet another expression. Even though we are using backticks (`` ` ``) they are just a plain string in the end:

```
`Hello ${name} `;
```

However, this is **not** an expression:

```
if (active && visibility === 'visible' ) { … }
```

This is because I could **not** simply write code like this:

```
const isVisible =  if (active && visibility === 'visible' ) { … }
```

Every JavaScript interpreter would rightly complain because of invalid syntax.

If we omit the `if` in this snippet, we are left with a **Logical AND operator** which is indeed an expression and returns a value (in this case true or `false`):

```
const isVisible = active && visibility === 'visible'  ;
```

The ternary operator (? :) is also an expression:

```
Condition ?  true :  false;
```

Expressions are not limited to boolean values, numbers or strings but can also include objects, arrays or even functions and arrow function calls. You will certainly see them again in the future.

Example for an arrow function:

```
(number) => {
  return number * 2 ;
};
```

All of this will become important very soon. To put the cherry on top, I will tell you now that expressions can in turn include other JSX — you can play this game forever.

Let's look at a few other examples of JSX that contain valid JavaScript expressions to really drive home these concepts:

Simple mathematics

```
<span>5 + 1 = {5 + 1}</span>
```

Ternary operator

```
<span>Today is { new Date().getDay() === 1 ? 'Monday' : 'not Monday' }</span>
```

Ternary operator as a value of a prop

```
<div className={user.isAdmin ?  'is-admin' : null}>…</div>
```

Array.map() with JSX as its return value (which in turn contains an expression)

```
<ul>
  {['Tintin', 'Milou' ].map((name) => (
    <li>{name}</li>
  ))}
</ul>
```

Number values in props

```
<input type= "range"  min={0} max={100} />
```

All of these are great examples of using expressions to ensure JSX is much more than just HTML.

What else you should know

For those of you who have paid close attention, you may have noticed a few things depending on the level of your JavaScript knowledge. In some examples, parentheses appear in seemingly odd places. The parentheses, "(" and ")", need to be wrapped around any JSX which spans more than one line — so not quite so random anymore.

You can usually just put your JSX in parentheses without problem. Many people actually prefer this practice as all JSX is uniformly treated the same way, but only multi-line JSX actually requires parentheses.

If an **expression** instead of a **string** should be used inside our props (as in the example "Ternary Operator as a value of a prop"), we should use curly brackets ("{" and "}"). These indicate to React that an expression is contained within them as opposed to a plain string which would be indicated by single or double quotes.

For each object, **two** opening and closing braces need to be used. The outer braces introduce the expression whereas the inner ones represent the braces of the object contained within.

```
<User data={{ name: 'Manuel', location: 'Berlin' }} />
```

Similarly, array literals also need to be included within a set of braces. The outer one representing the expression and the inner brackets denoting the array.

```
<List items={[1, 2, 3, 4, 5]} />
```

Some of you may have noticed that the prop `className` was used in the example. The DOM Element API of the browser lets us access the `class` attribute of an element by using `Element.className` . React does just the same and borrows from the properties of the DOM Element class.

Some attribute names deviate from the regular JavaScript equivalents in JSX as they use reserved words. In the example, `class` is a reserved word which is why we use `className` instead. Same applies to `for`. The `for` is usually the JavaScript keyword for starting a loop but can also be used to inform a `<label>` which input field it belongs to. Instead of using `for`, JSX code can employ the HTMLLabelElement Interface[20] `htmlFor` .

```
<fieldset>
    <input type="text" id="name" />
    <label htmlFor="name">Name</label>
</fieldset>
```

This pattern applies to all major HTML attributes. All HTML attributes that should be set need to adhere to the following rules `tabindex` is `tabIndex`, `readonly` to `readOnly`, `maxlength` becomes `maxLength` .

The development mode of the browser usually reminds everyone that the regular HTML attributes should be renamed though and thus makes it easy to avoid these mistakes before they happen.

 Warning: Invalid DOM property `class`. Did you mean `className` ?

For those of you who want to really understand which HTML attributes are supported in React, this list will help (fasten your seat belts - it's going to be long):

```
accept acceptCharset accessKey action allowFullScreen alt async
autoComplete autoFocus autoPlay capture cellPadding cellSpacing
challenge charSet checked cite classID className colSpan cols content
contentEditable contextMenu controls controlsList coords crossOrigin
data dateTime default defer dir disabled download draggable encType
form formAction formEncType formMethod formNoValidate formTarget
frameBorder headers height hidden high href hrefLang htmlFor
httpEquiv icon id inputMode integrity is keyParams keyType kind label
lang list loop low manifest marginHeight marginWidth max maxLength
media mediaGroup method min minLength multiple muted name noValidate
nonce open optimum pattern placeholder poster preload profile
radioGroup readOnly rel required reversed role rowSpan rows sandbox
scope scoped scrolling seamless selected shape size sizes span
spellCheck src srcDoc srcLang srcSet start step style summary
tabIndex target title type useMap value width wmode wrap
```

The same applies to SVG elements. You can also use these in JSX as SVGs are valid XML. The documentation for SVG attributes and which of these are supported is easily at least three times as long than the one for plain HTML modules. Take a look if you want to know more: https://reactjs.org/docs/dom-elements.html#all-supported-html-attributes

Inline styles

Of course there are exceptions: the style attribute is one of them. While inline styles in plain HTML are written as strings with their original CSS property names, React uses JavaScript properties and an object instead of a string.

For comparison - this is regular HTML:

```
<div style="margin-left: 12px; border-color: red; padding: 8px"></ div>
```

And this is the equivalent in JSX:

```
<div style={{ marginLeft: '12px' , borderColor: 'red', padding: '8px' }} />
```

Events form another exception. Events are an extensive topic and thus will be dealt with in an own chapter later.

Comments in JSX

JSX also allows the use of comments, albeit with a different look to their HTML counterparts:

```
<!-- This is an example for an HTML comment -->
```

Instead the comments are contained within braces and will be opened in the form of a JavaScript multi-line comment:

```
{
    /* This is a JSX comment */
}
```

Comments can easily span multiple lines of course. In contrast, the usual one-liner JavaScript comments introduced with the double slash (//) cannot be used in JSX meaning even short one-line comments need to be written with the above (/* */).

And this is it! All these examples and explanations should have laid the groundwork for understanding and working with JSX, enabling you to follow along in the upcoming chapters.

Summary

- Multi-line JSX has to be surrounded by parentheses
- JSX includes JavaScript expressions. These have to be contained in braces and can then be used in props
- To use HTML elements, the DOM Element Interface writing standard has to be used (`htmlFor` instead of `for`, `className` instead of `class`)
- CSS inline styles have to be written as a JavaScript object
- Comments are put within braces and use multi-line comment Syntax: {/* */}

Rendering of Elements

In the previous chapters I have used them a few times without explaining them: what actually are **React elements**?

React elements are the smallest building blocks in a **React application**. They describe what is going to be rendered on the screen. Although they sound similar to DOM elements, they differ in one important point: React elements are only simple objects — thus they are easy to create and performant. Calling `React.createElement()` to create a **React element** does not trigger a DOM operation.

> (i) React **elements** are often confused with React **components** and used interchangeably. This is not correct though. **Elements** make up the building blocks of **components**. We are going to talk about **components** in great depths in the following chapters, but you should read and understand this chapter about **elements** first.

We have already learned how we can create a **React element**. **JSX** allows us to save many lines of code by avoiding lengthy `React.createElement()` calls. But how do we render an element to the screen, i.e. show it in the browser?

In order to achieve this, we are making use of the `render()` method of `ReactDOM`. Additionally, we need a **root node** or a **mount node** to render a **React element**. This node works as a placeholder and informs React where the element should be rendered to. Theoretically, there can be many different root nodes in the HTML document. React controls these independently and keeps track of the different mount nodes. So instead of having one large **React application**, you could easily choose to have many smaller (or larger) **apps** in a single HTML document. In most situations, you are likely to only have a **single root node** for your **React application**.

But let's get to the important parts: how to render a **React element**. Pass the **element** you want to render as the first argument to `ReactDOM.render()` and then pass the **root node** as the second argument, which is the DOM node that the **element** will be rendered into.

Imagine that we want to render a `div` with the id `root` in the HTML document, which will work as our **root node**:

```
<!DOCTYPE html>
<html>
  <head>
```

```
      <title></title>
    </head>
    <body>
      <div id="root"></div>
    </body>
  </html>
```

The call matching this is the following:

```
const myFirstElement =  <div>My first React Element</div> ;
ReactDOM.render(myFirstElement,  document.getElementById('root' ));
```

If you execute this code in the browser, you will see <div>My first React element</div **inside** of the root div.

React elements are **immutable** meaning that they do not change. Once the element has been created, it represents a particular state in the user interface. The official React documentation metaphorically speaks of a single frame in a film. If we wanted to update the user interface of our application, we would need to create a **new React element** with the updated and changed data — don't be afraid, it sounds more complex than it actually is!

React is clever enough to figure out which parts of an application have changed and will only update those parts that have actually been updated, thanks to a clever comparison algorithm. **React elements** and their children will be compared to the previous version and only invoke a DOM operation if a change is present. If used correctly, React's **reconciliation process** can drastically improve the performance of our application as regular DOM updates are very costly and negatively impact performance. Depending on the changes in the specific **React element**, you might not even need to update a full DOM element every time and often only a few attributes need to change.

But let's look at that in practice:

```
function showTime() {
  const time = new Date().toLocaleTimeString();
  const timeElement = (
    <div>
      <p>It is now {time} o' clock. </p>
    </div>
  );
  ReactDOM.render(timeElement,  document.getElementById('root' ));
}
setInterval(showTime, 1000 );
```

Once again a **React element** was created. Once it is invoked in `ReactDOM.render()` , it will tell us the time. Because we only care about punctuality, we pass the element and the `ReactDOM.render()` call into a function which is called every 1000ms.

Inspecting the elements in the **Chrome Dev Tools** reveals: with each `ReactDOM.render()` call only the time itself is updated. The remaining elements as well as the DOM nodes or even parts not impacted of the shown text remain the same:

```
DevTools - iz1ks.codesandbox.io/                          —    □    ✕

  ⬆  ⬚  |    Elements      Console    »        ⊗ 1    ⋮

...<!doctype html> == $0
  <html lang="en">
  ▶ <head>...</head>
  ▼ <body>
      ▼ <div id="root">
          ▼ <div>
              ▼ <p>
                  "Es ist jetzt "
                  "20:47:55"
                  " Uhr"
                </p>
            </div>
        </div>
      </body>
  </html>
```

React only updates the time, nothing else.

We've just met one of the most fundamental principles of React in practice: React's **declarative** way of creating user interfaces. Instead of telling our app in an **imperative** fashion to update itself every second, we **declaratively** define in the **React element** that we want to see the current time in a particular place at each re-render.

Implementing this said functionality without React might look something like the following:

```
function changeTime() {
  const time = new Date().toLocaleTimeString();
  const target = document.getElementById('root' );
  target.textContent = 'It is now ' + time + " o' clock";
}
setInterval(changeTime, 1000 );
```

The main advantage of **declarative** programming is that we only **describe states** and mention how something should render instead of deciding on each and every step and how to reach our final state. Especially complex applications benefit greatly from declarative approaches, as both readability and simplicity are drastically improved and makes applications less error prone.

 In practice, `ReactDOM.render()` is only called once. Mostly when opening a page. We have only used `render()` repeatedly in the examples to illustrate how **ReactDOM** and **React elements** work together

Components (instead of elements) trigger a re-render if their state changes or if they have been passed new props, but let's look at components in the next chapter!

Components in React

The two types of React components

We've already implemented our first `Hello World` component in the section "Into the deep end". While this component taught us the basics of **React** and **React components**, it was a simplistic example and did not make use of everything React offers.

Components are relatively easy to explain: they allow us to de-construct complex user interfaces into multiple parts. Ideally, these parts are reusable, isolated and self-contained. They can deal with any input from the outside, so-called **props** (from "properties"), and describe what's going to be rendered on the screen by whatever they define in the `render()` method.

We can cluster components into two different versions: **Function components**, which are expressed in the form of a function, and **Class components**, which build upon the newly introduced ES2015 classes. Until recently the term **Stateless Functional component** was very common, as state could only be managed in class components before the introduction of React Hooks. We are going to take a deep dive into **Hooks** and how state is managed from React 16.8.0 onward in a later chapter.

Function Components

The simplest way to define a React component is through a **Function component**. You might have guessed it, function components are just regular JavaScript functions:

```
function Hello(props) {
    return <div>Hello {props.name} </div>;
}
```

To be classified as a valid **React component** the function has to fulfill two criteria. It has to either return an explicit `null` (undefined is not allowed) or a valid `React.element` (in the form of JSX) and receives a `props` object. But even the `props` object can be optional and take in `null` as an argument.

Class Components

The second method of defining a **React component** has already been shown to you in a previous chapter! But let's mention it once again — I am talking about **Class components**. These are based upon the ES2015 classes and extend `React.Component` or

React.PureComponent . Don't worry if you do not know what a PureComponent is for now, we are going to look at them soon. Class components have at least one method named render():

```
class Hello extends React.Component {
  render() {
    return <div>Hello {this.props.name} </div>;
  }
}
```

There is one big pitfall to look out for: **Function components** take in their **props** as function arguments. **Class components** on the other hand cannot take in arguments and can only access their **props** via the instance method this.props.

Both of these components will render the exact same result!

> ⓘ One thing to keep in mind is to always name your components according to the standard. Both function and class components require their displayName(so their actual component name) to start with a **capital letter**. In between the rest of the characters, capital and lower case letters can be used interchangeably as long as the first letter is **capitalized**.
>
> If you mistakenly name your React component something along the lines of section, React would interpret it as the corresponding DOM element which is of course something we would like to avoid. Section on the other hand would be a valid name for a component and would thus be differentiated from the regular DOM element.

I am going to consciously avoid going into detail about state in this chapter. State is a very complex topic and is thus getting a chapter of its own. I would advise you to work through this chapter first to understand how components work, and then delve deeper into state in the next chapter.

Special case: PureComponent

The **Pure component** is a special form of the **Class component**. It inherits from React.PureComponent and works similarly to a React.Component with the difference that React only renders a Pure component if its **props** or **state** have changed compared to the previous render phase. It is often used to optimize performance.

This is achieved by performing a "shallow" comparison to identify whether the **references** are identical to the previous render. It does not matter if the **values** themselves did not change, a

Pure component will still re-render if the references have changed.

This sounds a little abstract. Let's look at another two examples to illustrate the point:

```
const logFunction = (message) =>   console.log(message);

class App extends React.Component {
  render() {
    return <MyComponent  logger={logFunction} /> ;
  }
}
```

We have defined a function called logFunction outside of the class in this example.
MyComponent receives a prop called logger with a **reference** to the logFunction. The **identity**
of the **reference** will stay the same after a re-render. A **Pure component** would not re-render if
its state did not change as the props are identical to that of the previous render.

However, in the following example a **Pure component** *would* be rendered:

```
class App extends React.Component {
  render() {
    return <MyComponent  logger={(message) => console.log(message)} />;
  }
}
```

While we still pass the same function to MyComponent, we create a new function identity with
each new render. Therefore, the "shallow comparison" will no longer match between the
previous and new props; a re-rendering is triggered.

The same applies to Objects and Arrays:

```
<MyComponent
  logConfig={{ logLevel: 'info'  }}
  logEntries={[ 'Message 1', 'Message 2']}
/>
```

This would also trigger a re-render as the logConfig object or array would be replaced with
each new render.

"Pure" Function Components

Class components are derived from the Component or PureComponent class. By defining this
class we are deriving from, we choose whether the component should re-render with each new
change in a component which is higher up in the hierarchy. Regular **Function components** do
not offer this functionality as they are merely JavaScript functions. Since **React 16.6.0** React

offers a new wrapper function called React.memo() which also allows us to optimize our re-renders in **Function components**. We wrap the call around the function in question.

```
const MyComponent = React.memo((props) => {
  return <p>I only re-render if my props change</p> ;
});
```

Using React.memo(), the **Function component** works similarly to the **Class component** equivalent which is derived from the React.PureComponent .

Curious already? Play around with the demo to deepen your understanding:

```
import React from 'react';
import ReactDOM from 'react-dom';

class ClassComponent extends React.Component {
  render() {
    return <p>Class Component: {new Date().toISOString()} </p>;
  }
}

class PureClassComponent extends React.PureComponent {
  render() {
    return <p>Pure Class Component: {new Date().toISOString()} </p>;
  }
}

const FunctionComponent = () => {
  return <p>Function Component: {new Date().toISOString()} </p>;
};

const MemoizedFunctionComponent = React.memo(() => {
  return <p>Memoized Function Component: {new Date().toISOString()}</p> ;
});

class App extends React.Component {
  state = {
    lastRender: new Date().toISOString(),
  };

  componentDidMount() {
    this.interval = setInterval(() => {
      this.setState({ lastRender: new Date().toISOString() });
    }, 200);
  }
```

```
  componentWillUnmount() {
    clearInterval( this.interval);
  }

  render() {
    return (
      <div>
        <p> App: {this.state.lastRender} </p>
        <ClassComponent />
        <PureClassComponent />
        <FunctionComponent />
        <MemoizedFunctionComponent />
      </div>
    );
  }
}

ReactDOM.render(<App /> , document.getElementById('root'));
```

The App component triggers a re-render every 0.2 seconds without new **props** being passed. The question of all questions is: Which components are being re-rendered and which are not?

Component composition — multiple components in one

We have only really included DOM elements in our example components so far, but **React components** can also include other React components. By defining the component in the same scope or by using CommonJS or ES-Modules imports with`require()` or `import`, other components can be used in the same scope.

Example:

```
function Hello(props) {
  return <div>Hello {props.name} </div>;
}

function MyApp() {
  return (
    <div>
      <Hello name="Manuel" />
      <Hello name="Tom" />
    </div>
  );
}

ReactDOM.render(<MyApp />, document.getElementById('app'));
```

`<MyApp />` returns a `<div>` which contains the `Hello` component which is used to greet both Manuel and Tom. The result:

```
<div>
  <div>Hello Manuel</div>
  <div>Hello Tom</div>
</div>
```

Important: A component can only ever return *one* **root element**. This can either be:

- a single React element:

```
<Hello name= "Manuel />
```

- in nested form - as long as only a single element is on the outer layer:

```
<Parent>
  <Child />
</Parent>
```

- a DOM element - which in turn can also be nested and include other elements:

```
<div>…</div>
```

- … or it can be self--closing:

```
<img src= "logo.jpg"  alt= "Bild: Logo"  />
```

- or simply:

```
null;
```

… but **never** `undefined`.

Since **React 16.0.0** we are also allowed to return:

- an array which contains valid return values:

```
[<div key="1">Hello</div>,  <Hello key= "2"  name= "Manuel"  />];
```

- a simple string

```
'Hello World' ;
```

- or a so-called "Fragment" - a special "component" which does not appear in the rendered output and can act as a container if we otherwise violated the rule of only ever returning one root element:

```
<React.Fragment>
  <li>1</li>
  <li>2</li>
  <li>3</li>
</React.Fragment>
```

Since **transpiling** with **Babel version 7**, fragments can also be expressed in their short form which contain an empty opening and closing element:

```
<>
  <li>1</li>
  <li>2</li>
  <li>3</li>
</>
```

Components can be composed into anything you like. It makes sense to break up large and complex components into many smaller and easier to read components to improve readability and make them reusable. This process often happens organically as you program as you will come to a point at which you will notice that breaking up your components would become useful.

Dividing components — keeping an overview

Let's have a look at an example of a Header component which includes a logo, a navigation and a search bar. This is a common example which you will come across all the time in web development:

```
function Header() {
  return (
    <header>
      <div className="logo">
        <img src="logo.jpg" alt="Image: Logo" />
      </div>
      <ul className="navigation">
        <li>
          <a href="/">Homepage</a>
        </li>
        <li>
          <a href="/team">Team</a>
        </li>
```

```
      <li>
        <a href="/services">Services</a>
      </li>
      <li>
        <a href="/contact">Contact</a>
      </li>
    </ul>
    <div className="search-bar">
      <form method="post" action="/search">
        <p>
          <label htmlFor="q">Search:</label>
          <input type="text" id="q" name="q" />
        </p>
        <input type="submit" value="Search" />
      </form>
    </div>
  </header>
);
}
```

We have just learned that React components can easily be composed of smaller other React components. This way of breaking up components is highly encouraged in React. So what could we do with the above code snippet to make it easier for ourselves? That's right: we can break up our relatively big component into multiple smaller ones which all only do one thing — and do it well.

First, the logo can easily be used elsewhere on the page which is a totally valid assumption. Second, the navigation might not only appear in the header but might also be included in the sitemap. Last, the search bar might eventually not only be used in the header but also on its own dedicated search results page.

Transferring this approach to our code, we achieve the following result:

```
function Logo() {
  return (
    <div className="logo">
      <img src="logo.jpg" alt="Image: Logo" />
    </div>
  );
}

function Navigation() {
  return (
    <ul className="navigation">
      <li>
```

```
        <a href="/">Homepage</a>
      </li>
      <li>
        <a href="/team">Team</a>
      </li>
      <li>
        <a href="/services">Services</a>
      </li>
      <li>
        <a href="/contact">Contact</a>
      </li>
    </ul>
  );
}


function SearchBar() {
  return (
    <div className="search-bar">
      <form method="post" action="/search">
        <p>
          <label htmlFor="q">Search:</label>
          <input type="text" id="q" name="q" />
        </p>
        <input type="submit" value="Search" />
      </form>
    </div>
  );
}


function Header() {
  return (
    <header>
      <Logo />
      <Navigation />
      <SearchBar />
    </header>
  );
}
```

Even if the code has become longer, we have created a number of improvements.

Simpler collaboration

All components can and should be saved in their own files so other team members or even complete teams can own one or more components. This will spread ownership across teams and make responsibilities clearer. Moreover, it reduces the risk of accidentally overwriting a colleague's file or having to continually deal with merge conflicts in Git. Teams become *consumers* of other teams' components which offer a simple interface of their component with possible props.

Single responsibility principle

Our components now all have clearly defined responsibilities. Each component only fulfills a single task which can be inferred from its name. For example, the logo will be displayed and look the same wherever I use it in my application. If the search bar ever needs amended, one can simply search for the SearchBar.js code and modify the code according to specifications and it will update everywhere it is used. The header component is used as a overarching component whose responsibility it is to hold all the components of the header and inject them wherever the header is used.

Reusability

Last but not least, we have also increased the reusability of our components. If I wanted to use the logo not only in the header but also in the footer (as already mentioned), nothing prevents us from also using it in the footer component. Multiple different pages with different page layouts can all still use the very same header component if we choose to include it. The consumer of a single component does not even need to know which other components it is composed of. It is sufficient to import the component and it will deal with its own dependencies.

Props — receiving data in a component

I have talked about **props** a lot already in this book. I think it is about time to reveal the secret and explain what they are.

Props enable components to receive any form of data and access it within the **component**. Let us think back to our **Function component**. We passed the **props** to our function as a regular argument. **Class components** work in a similar fashion with the difference that the **props** are passed to the component via the Class **constructor**. They are only available to it via `this.props` as opposed to a plain function argument as was the case with the function component. React takes care of this all in the parsing stage of the `createElement()` calls.

But remember: whenever a component receives new **props** from the outside, it triggers a re-render of the component! We can explicitly prevent this from happening by using the `shouldComponentUpdate()` **lifecycle method**. We are going to look at **lifecycle methods and state** in the following chapter. For now just keep in mind that if a **component** receives **props** from the outside it will cause the **component** as well as its children to re-render.

Props inside a component are read-only

Regardless of the way in which **props** enter a component, they are **always read-only** inside the component and can and can only be read but not modified. People generally speak of **immutability** or **immutable objects** in this case. In order to work with changing data, React uses **state**. But let's focus on **props** for now.

Functions that do not modify their input and do not have any external dependencies are commonly referred to as **pure functions** in function programming. The reasoning behind this is relatively simple: if anything changes outside of the function, the function itself should not depend on the changes, as its functionality is closed in itself and well encapsulated, thus being free of **side effects**. All important parameters are simply passed to the function resulting in the same output with the same input each and every time.

To put it in other words: it does not matter which variables change their value outside of the function or how often other functions are called elsewhere. If a **pure function** receives the same parameters as before, it will result in the same output as before — each and every time.

Why is this important though? React follows this principle of **pure functions** inside its components. If a component is passed the same props from the outside and the state remains the same, the output of the component should always be the same.

Pure functions in detail

As **pure functions** form a fundamental principle of React, I would like to explain them a little more with the help of some examples. Much of this will sound more theoretical and complex than it will actually be once its used in practice. However, I'd still like to explain them to increase your understanding.

Example for a "pure function"

```
function pureDouble(number) {
   return number * 2 ;
}
```

Our first function is passed a number, doubles it and returns the result. It does not matter whether the function is being called 1, 10 or 250 times: if I pass the number 5 as a value I will receive a 10 every time. Same input, same output.

Example of an "non-pure function"

```
function impureCalculation(number) {
   return number + window .outerWidth;
}
```

This second function is no longer *pure* as it will not reliably return the same output every time, even if its input is identical to the one before. At the moment, my browser's window size is 1920 pixels wide. If am calling this function with the value 10 as the argument, I will get back 1930 (10 + 1920). If the window size is decreased to 1280 pixels though and the function is called again with the same argument of 10 I will receive a different result (1290). Hence, this is not a **pure function**.

It is possible to change this function into a "pure" function by passing the window width as another argument:

```
function pureCalculation(number, outerWidth) {
  return number + outerWidth;
}
```

The function is still dependent on my window width, however by calling pureCalculation(10, window.outerWidth) the result will be "pure" as if the same input is passed, the same output is generated each and every time. This will become easier to understand once the function is reduced to its fundamental properties:

```
function pureSum(number1, number2) {
  return number1 + number2;
}
```

Same Input, same output.

Another example of an impure function

Assume that we want to implement a function that receives an object with parameters as its input:

```
var car = { speed: 0 , seats: 5 };
function accelerate(car) {
  car.speed += 1;
  return car;
}
```

This function is also impure as it modifies its entry value. During the second function call, we already work with a totally different value compared to the previous call.

```
console.log(accelerate(car));
// {speed: 1, seats: 5}

console.log(accelerate(car));
// {speed: 2, seats: 5}
```

How do we transform our example into a "pure" function? By ensuring that our values are not modified and creating a new object based off the entry value which is returned by the function:

```
var car = { speed: 0  };
function accelerate(car) {
  return {
    speed: car.speed +  1,
  };
}
```

New result:

```
console.log(accelerate(car));
// {speed: 1}

console.log(accelerate(car));
// {speed: 1}
```

And yes, it's "pure"! Same input, same output.

You might wonder at this point, why I even bother telling you all this. After all, you have come to learn React (at least I would wonder at this point why I am supposed to understand all of this).

React is an extremely liberal library: It does not enforce much and leaves a lot of freedom and choice for its developers. However, one thing is really important and React takes this quite seriously: **components and their relation to props have to behave in the same way as "pure functions". If the same props are passed, the same output needs to generated.**

If you do not pay attention and ignore this guideline, React might behave strangely and we might have to deal with unexpected and undesirable side effects — and trust me, you do not want to deal with such bug fixes. I mean, the desire to develop professional interfaces in a short amount of time is what led you to pick up this book in the first place. You wanted to learn about a tool that can facilitate that, and React can do that, as long as you abide by this one rule.

At the same time though, this principle has a nice side effect. By embracing "pure functions" React components are easier to test.

That's nice and all that, but what exactly does "read-only inside of a component" mean? After studying "pure functions", this is explained quickly. It does not matter how our props are accessed — if it is via the props argument in a **Function component**, via the constructor() in a **Class component** or at any other point in a **Class component** via this.props. The most important thing to remember is this: I do not want to, and also should not under any circumstances, change the value of the **props** I pass in.

Outside of the component, it is an entirely different story. We can change values as we please (provided that we do not use another component to change our current component's props which just had these passed in).

This is not possible

```
function Example(props) {
    props.number = props.number +  1;
    props.fullName = [props.firstName, props.lastName].join(' '   );
    return (
        <div>
            ({props.number}) {props.fullName}{' '}
        </div>
    );
}

ReactDOM.render(
    <Example number={5} firstName="Manuel" lastName="Bieh" />,
    document.getElementById('app')
);
```

Result:

 TypeError: Cannot add property number, object is not extensible

I try to directly access and change the `number` and `fullName` props inside of my example component. But of course, this does not work as we have just learned that props are always **read-only**.

However, this is possible

Sometimes, it might still be beneficial to derive a new value from some props that have been passed in. This is not a problem at all. Since React 16.3.0 we have been given a dedicated function called `getDerivedStateFromProps()` which I want to explain in a bit more detail in another chapter.

If I only want to show the value that can be derived from the props that I have passed in as part of the component I can only change the output based on the props:

```
import React from 'react';
import ReactDOM from 'react-dom';

function Example(props) {
```

```
  return (
    <div>
      ({props.number + 1}) {[props.firstName, props.lastName].join(' ')}
    </div>
  );
}

ReactDOM.render(
  <Example number={5} firstName="Manuel" lastName="Bieh" />,
  document.getElementById('app')
);
```

Result

```
<div>(6) Manuel Bieh</div>
```

In this case, only the output based on the `props` was modified but not the props themselves.

This is also possible

But how can we actually change props outside of a component? So far, we have only talked about how components should not be changed *within* the component.

It is best to explain this with yet another example, even if it is a little abstract in this case:

```
import React from 'react';
import ReactDOM from 'react-dom';

let renderCounter = 0;
setInterval( function() {
  renderCounter++;
  renderApp();
}, 2000);

const App = (props) => {
  return <div>{props.renderCounter} </div>;
};

function renderApp() {
  ReactDOM.render(
    <App renderCounter={renderCounter} />,
    document.getElementById('app')
  );
}

renderApp();
```

Let's go through this one by one. First of all, we set the variable `renderCounter` to its initial value of 0. This variable will count how often our `App` component renders, or to be more precise: how often we call `ReactDOM.render()` which will cause the `App` component to re-render.

Second, we start an interval which invokes the `renderApp()` function every 2000 milliseconds. But the interval not only executes the function every 2 seconds, it also increments our `renderCounter` variable by 1 each time. It is actually quite exciting what's happening here: we are modifying our `renderCounter` prop from **"the outside"**.

The component itself is untouched and stays completely "pure". If it is being called with:

```
<App renderCounter={ 5} />
```

it will give us this result:

```
<div>5</div>
```

It does not matter how many times the component was actually rendered, the result will be the same. **Same input, same output.**

Inside of the function, we keep embracing "purity". We do not modify the entry value and we do not have any direct external dependencies to the outside which could influence our rendering. The value itself is only changed outside of the component and passed into the component as a new value. We do not actually need to go into much more detail at this point. The only thing that matters is that our component will render the same output given the same inputs. As you can see above, this is true in this case. We do not need to concern ourselves with who changes props outside of the component, how often this happens or in which form as long as we do **not** change the props *inside* of the component. So far so good.

Props are an abstracted function argument

Put simply, props are actually not very different from our regular function arguments. They can appear in different forms just as their counterparts. Similar to regular JavaScript functions or constructors, they can accept anything as an argument which would also be allowed to be passed in to those functions and constructors. Simple strings, objects, functions or even other React elements (which also boil down `createElement()` calls) can be valid props.

```
<MyComponent
  counter={3 }
  text= "example"
  showStatus={ true}
  config={{ uppercase: true }}
  biggerNumber={Math .max(27, 35)}
```

```
  arbitraryNumbers={[ 1, 4, 28, 347, 1538 ]}
  dateObject={ Date }
  dateInstance={ new Date()}
  icon={
    <svg x="0px" y= "0px" width= "32px" height="32px" >
      <circle fill="#CC3300" cx="16" cy="16" r="16" />
    </svg>
  }
  callMe={() => {
    console.log('Somebody called me' );
  }}
/>
```

Let's look at this example to illustrate the point I have just made. Most of these props do not make a lot of sense in the grand scheme of things but they all represent valid JSX and props which can be passed to a component. They are extremely powerful and versatile and can take a lot of different forms.

Props are not limited to one nested layer

Components can easily pass through props to child elements further down the component tree. While it can be helpful to break up bigger components into lots of little ones and pass some of the props to them, it can become cumbersome and complex really quickly. It is hard to tell in this instance where a prop originated from and where it was first used, making it even harder to change the value of a prop.

```
function User(props) {
  return (
    <div>
      <h1>{props.name}</h1>
      <UserImage image={props.image} />
      <ListOfPosts items={props.posts} />
    </div>
  );
}


ReactDOM.render(
  <User name={user.name} image={user.image} posts={user.posts} />,
  document.getElementById('app')
);
```

Summary

Components have to act as **pure functions** and return the same result if the same props were passed.

- Props inside a component should be treated as **read-only**
- Components can receive an **arbitrary number of props**
- In JSX, props are passed similarly to how data is passed in HTML attributes
- In contrast to HTML, JSX allows for multiple forms of values. If the values are not of type string, they will be surrounded by **braces**
- Props can take in any **JavaScript expressions** as their value
- Once received, props can be passed down as many levels as required

State and Lifecycle Methods

We have mentioned it in places and now we are finally going to look at it in greater detail — **state** and the so-called **lifecycle methods**.

As mentioned in the previous chapter, components can: hold, manage, and change their own **state**. But **if the state within a component changes, it always triggers a re-render of the component**. This behavior *can* be avoided by opting for a `PureComponent` as we have learned in the previous chapter, which might be useful in some cases. The foundational logic remains though. A state change leads to a re-render of a component and all of its children, except from those cases in which the children are actually a `PureComponent` or its call is surrounded by a `React.memo()` call.

Relying on state to change our interface is extremely useful. It means that we do not need to rely on manually calling `ReactDOM.render()` to update our interface, and that components manage their own re-renders independently.

State is tightly connected to the so-called **lifecycle methods.** These comprise a number of optional methods which can be called at different times and for different uses cases in **Class components**. For example, there are **lifecycle methods** for when a component is first mounted, if a component receives new props or if the state within a component changes.

Since **React 16.8.0, Function components** can also manage their own state through the use of **Hooks**. Hooks can also react to certain lifecycle events but we will not describe them in detail at this point. This chapter will focus primarily on Class components and their associated lifecycle methods. Hooks on the other hand will receive their own dedicated chapter later in the book as they can still be considered a relatively new and extensive topic.

Our first stateful component

State inside a Class component can be accessed via the instance property `this.state`. It is encapsulated to the **component** and neither parent or child components can access it.

To define a component's initial state we can choose three ways. Two of these are relatively simple, the third is a little more advanced. We're going to cover the latter when we learn about the **lifecycle method** `getDerivedStateFromProps()` .

Initial state can be defined by setting `this.state`. This can either be done via the constructor of a **Class component**:

```
class MyComponent extends React.Component {
  constructor(props) {
    super(props);
    this.state = {
      counter: props.counter,
    };
  }
  render() {
    // ...
  }
}
```

... or by defining state as a **ES2017 class property**. This is much shorter but still requires the **Babel plugin** @babel/plugin-proposal-class-properties (pre-Babel 7:   babel-plugin-transform-class-properties):

```
class MyComponent extends React.Component {
  state = {
    counter: this.props.counter,
  };
  render() {
    // ...
  }
}
```

Class Property Syntax is supported out-of-the-box by **Create React App**. As most projects today rely completely or in part on the CRA setup, this syntax is already widely used and common to see in most projects. If you encounter a project where this is not the case, I'd urge you to install it and use this Babel plugin as it reduces the length of your code and is easily set up.

Once **state** is defined, we can **read** its value via this.state. While it is possible to mutate this.state directly, it is actively discouraged.

Changing state with this.setState()

To change state within components, React offers a new method for use inside of **Class components**:

```
this.setState(updatedState);
```

Whenever state is supposed to change within the component, this.setState() should be used to achieve this. By calling this.setState() React knows to execute **lifecycle methods** (for example `componentDidUpdate()`) and thus **re-render** the component. If we were to change state directly, for example by using `this.state.counter = 1;` , nothing would happen initially as the render process would not be triggered. React would not know about its change in state.

The `this.setState()` method might look a little complex at the start. This is also due to the fact that old state is not simply replaced by new state, triggering a re-render, but because many other things take place behind the scenes. Let's take a look at it step by step.

The function itself can take **two different types of arguments**. The first being an **object** containing the new or updated state properties and the second being an **updater function** which again returns an object or `null` if nothing should change. If you happen to have the same property name in your object as you do in state, the state value will be **overwritten** while all other properties will **remain the same**. To reset properties in state, their values need to be explicitly set to `null` or `undefined`. The new state that is being passed is thus **never replaced** but **merged together** with the existing state.

Let us have another look at our example above in which we defined state with a `counter` property whose initial value was `0`. Assuming that we want to change this state and add another `date` property to pass the current date, we can construct the new object like so:

```
this.setState({
  date: new Date(),
});
```

If an **updater function** was used instead, our function call would look like this:

```
this.setState(() => {
  return {
    date: new Date(),
  };
});
```

... or even shorter:

```
this.setState(() => ({
  date: new Date(),
});
```

Finally, our component contains the new state:

```
{
  counter: 0,
```

```
    date: new Date(),
  }
```

To guarantee that only the most current state is always accessed, an **updater function** should be used which contains the current state as a parameter. Many developers have already made the mistake of trying to access this.state right after calling setState() only to realize that their state is still old.

 React "collects" many sequential setState()calls and **does not immediately invoke them** to avoid an unnecessary amount of re-renders. Sequential setState()calls which are called right after each other are executed as a **batch process**. This is important to keep in mind as we cannot reliably access new state with this.state just after a setState()call.

Assume that we would like to increment the state counter three times in quick succession. Intuitively, we might feel compelled to write the following code:

```
this.setState({ counter:  this.state.counter +  1 });
this.setState({ counter:  this.state.counter +  1 });
this.setState({ counter:  this.state.counter +  1 });
```

If the first initial state was 0, what will the new state be? What do you think? 3? Nope. It's 1! But why? React uses its **batching mechanism** to cluster these setState() calls together in order to avoid a jarring user interface which continually updates. The above code snippet could be translated into the following code if it was written in **functions**.

```
this.state = Object.assign(
    this.state,
    { counter:  this.state.counter +  1 },
    { counter:  this.state.counter +  1 },
    { counter:  this.state.counter +  1 }
);
```

The counter property overwrites itself after each batch update but always uses this.state.counter as its base reference for incrementing by 1. After all state calls having executed, React calls the render() method again.

If an **updater function** is used instead, the current state is passed as a parameter and access is given to the state when the function is actually called:

```
this.setState((state) => ({ counter: state.counter +   1 });
this.setState((state) => ({ counter: state.counter +   1 });
```

```
this.setState((state) => ({ counter: state.counter +    1 });
```

This example uses an **updater function** which always updates the current state's value. The value of this.state.counter is 3 in this case, as we expected, because the state parameter which we provide to the updater function is accessing the current state. While this is possible in theory, it is not exactly recommended. Values should be collected first and then batch processed in a single setState() call. This avoids unnecessary re-renders with potentially outdated state.

In some situations it might be necessary to access the value of the modified state. Luckily, React offers the possibility to provide a second parameter in the setState() call. This parameter is a callback function which is called **after** the state has updated so that we can safely access the state we have just modified.

```
this.setState(
  {
    time: new Date().toLocaleTimeString(),
  },
  () => {
    console.log('New Time:',  this.state.time);
  }
);
```

Lifecycle Methods

React offers a number of so-called **lifecycle methods** that can be called at different times in a **component's lifecycle**. These can be implemented in React **Class components**.

The lifecycle of a component starts as soon as it is **instantiated or mounted**, so when it is found in the render() method of a parent component being part of the returned component tree. The component's lifecycle ends if it is removed from the tree of components supposed to be rendered. Additionally, there are **lifecycle methods** that react to **updates** or **errors** as well as being "unmounted".

Overview of lifecycle methods

The following shall be a comprehensive overview of the **lifecycle methods** that are currently available, clustered by the phases in which they occur in a component's lifecycle.

Mount phase

These methods are only called **once** when the component is first rendered (or put simply: added to the DOM).

- `constructor(props)`
- `static getDerivedStateFromProps(nextProps, prevState)`
- `componentWillMount(nextProps, nextState)`   (deprecated in React 17)
- `render()`
- `componentDidMount()`

Update phase

If new props are being passed to a component, or if state changes within the component, these update methods will be called. Alternatively, an explicit `forceUpdate()` method could be invoked.

- `componentWillReceiveProps(nextProps)`   (deprecated in React 17)
- `static getDerivedStateFromProps(nextProps, prevState)`
- `shouldComponentUpdate(nextProps, nextState)`
- `componentWillUpdate(nextProps, nextState)`   (deprecated in React 17)
- `render()`
- `getSnapshotBeforeUpdate(prevProps, prevState)`
- `componentDidUpdate(prevProps, prevState, snapshot)`

Unmount phase

This phase only has one matching method which is called as soon as the component is removed from the DOM. It can be useful to tidy up event listeners and `setTimeOut()` or `setInterval()` calls which had been added during mounting of the component:

- `componentWillUnmount()`

Error handling

Another method to deal with errors has been added to React with React 16. This method can be called to catch errors that occur during the rendering process in a lifecycle method or in the constructor of a **child component**.

- `componentDidCatch()`

Components which implement `componentDidCatch()` are commonly called **error boundaries** and help to visualize an alternative to the erroneous tree of components. It could be a high-level component (with regard to its position in the component hierarchy) that displays an error page and asks the user to reload. But equally, it could also be a low level component which only renders a little error message next to a button, triggered by an erroneous action attached to the button.

Lifecycle methods in practice

Let's have a look at how **lifecycle methods** behave in a simple component. The code implements a component which updates its own state every second and displays the current time. As soon as the component **mounts** an interval is started which updates the state of our component in the `componentDidMount()` method. A re-render is triggered and the current time is shown again.

```
import React from 'react';
import ReactDOM from 'react-dom';

class Clock extends React.Component {
  state = {
    date: new Date(),
  };

  componentDidMount() {
    this.intervalId = setInterval(() => {
      this.setState(() => ({
        date: new Date(),
      }));
    }, 1000);
  }

  componentWillUnmount() {
    clearTimeout( this.intervalId);
  }

  render() {
    return <div>{this.state.date.toLocaleTimeString()}</div> ;
  }
}

ReactDOM.render(<Clock /> , document.getElementById('root'));
```

We see that the **lifecycle methods** `componentDidMount()` and `componentWillUnmount()` are being used in the above example. **Default state** is defined with the property date and holds an instance of the date object. When the component **mounts** (`componentDidMount()`) the `setInterval()` interval is started and its id is saved within the instance property `this.intervalId`. As the interval invokes the `setState()` method every second, the component regularly triggers a re-render meaning the `render()` method is called again and shows the current time again.

Generally, the interval function is independent of the React component apart from the fact that it calls the `setState()` method of the component. Depending on how deeply interlinked the function and the component are, React determines if function calls should be stopped or not once the component is no longer needed. In the case of the `setInterval()` function, React does not, and we have to take care of stopping the component ourselves. Luckily React provides a method which enables us to do just that: `componentWillUnmount()` .

This method is called just before React removes the component from the DOM and can be used to cancel any XMLHttpRequests that might still be running, to remove event listeners or to cancel a running interval — and that is just what we need here. Shortly before the component is removed, the `clearTimeOut()` is invoked and we pass the function the interval id which we previously saved in in the instance property.

If we ever forget this during development mode, React will remind us if we try to call `this.setState()` on an already removed component:

 Warning: Can't call setState (or forceUpdate) on an unmounted component. This is a no-op, but it indicates a memory leak in your application. To fix, cancel all subscriptions and asynchronous tasks in the componentWillUnmount method.

in Clock

As opposed to previous examples, we only call `ReactDOM.render()` once. The component takes care of the rest and initiates the render process once its **state** has updated. This is the normal procedure when developing applications with React. A single `ReactDOM.render()` call is enough for the app to manage itself, allow interaction with the user and react to state changes and re-render the interface.

The combination of state and props

We have seen a number of examples of components which process props, as well as **stateful** components which manage their own local state, but there is a lot more to discover. Only the combination of lots of different components make React as powerful as it is when it comes to user interface development. A component can have its own **state** and also pass it to child components via **props**. This not only enables us to strictly separate business and layout logic but also allows us to develop components which are ultimately task-based and only represent a small part of our application.

The separation of business and layout components is often referred to by two different terms: **smart** components (business logic) and **dumb** components (layout). As you can guess, **smart components** should not be tied to the layout of the user interface at all, whereas **dumb**

components should be free of any logic or side effects. Dumb components should only focus on the plain display of static values.

Another example of multiple components interacting with each other:

```
const ShowDate = ({ date }) => <div>Today is {date}</div>;

const ShowTime = ({ time }) => <div>It is {time}.</div>;

class DateTime extends React.Component {
  state = {
    date: new Date(),
  };

  componentDidMount() {
    this.intervalId = setInterval(() => {
      this.setState(() => ({
        date: new Date(),
      }));
    });
  }

  componentWillUnmount() {
    clearInterval(this.intervalId);
  }

  render() {
    return (
      <div>
        <ShowDate date={this.state.date.toLocaleDateString()} />
        <ShowTime time={this.state.date.toLocaleTimeString()} />
      </div>
    );
  }
}

ReactDOM.render(<DateTime />, document.getElementById('root'));
```

Arguably this example is a little bit artificial but it illustrates the point. We can see how multiple components interact with each other. The DateTime component is our **logic component (smart component)** and takes care of "getting" the time and updating it. The **layout** component on the other hand deals with the actual display of the date (showDate) and the time (ShowTime) via the props it has been passed. The layout component is implemented as a simple **Function component** as a **Class component** would have been unnecessarily complex and produced too much overhead.

The role of lifecycle methods in combination with components

In the beginning I mentioned a few other **lifecycle methods** apart from componentDidMount() and componentWillMount() . React also recognizes these if they have been implemented within a **Class component**.

In order to understand these different **lifecycle methods** better, let's create an example component in which we include the **lifecycle methods** in debug messages. This will help us to see them in the browser console. To be more precise, the example actually consists of two components: one of them being a parent component, the other being a child component which receives props from its parent component (which it simply ignores in this case).

```
import React from 'react';
import ReactDOM from 'react-dom';

const log = (method, component) => {
  console .log(`[${component} ]`, method);
};

class ParentComponent extends React. Component {
  state = {};

  constructor(props) {
    super(props);
    log('constructor', 'parent');
  }

  static getDerivedStateFromProps() {
    log('getDerivedStateFromProps' , 'parent');
    return null;
  }

  componentDidMount() {
    log('componentDidMount', 'parent');
    this.intervalId = setTimeout(() => {
      log('state update' , 'parent');
      this.setState(() => ({
        time: new Date().toLocaleTimeString(),
      }));
    }, 2000);
  }

  shouldComponentUpdate() {
    log('shouldComponentUpdate' , 'parent');
    return true;
```

100

```
    }

    getSnapshotBeforeUpdate() {
      log('getSnapshotBeforeUpdate' , 'parent');
      return null;
    }

    componentDidUpdate() {
      log('componentDidUpdate' , 'parent');
    }

    componentWillUnmount() {
      log('componentWillUnmount', 'parent');
      clearInterval( this.intervalId);
    }

    render() {
      log('render', 'parent');
      return <ChildComponent time={this.state.time} />;
    }
  }

class ChildComponent extends React.Component {
    state = {};

    constructor(props) {
      super(props);
      log('constructor', 'child');
    }

    static getDerivedStateFromProps() {
      log('getDerivedStateFromProps', 'child');
      return null;
    }

    componentDidMount() {
      log('componentDidMount', 'child');
    }

    shouldComponentUpdate() {
      log('shouldComponentUpdate', 'child');
      return true;
    }

    getSnapshotBeforeUpdate() {
      log('getSnapshotBeforeUpdate', 'child');
```

```
    return null;
  }

  componentDidUpdate() {
    log('componentDidUpdate', 'child');
  }

  componentWillUnmount() {
    log('componentWillUnmount', 'child');
  }

  render() {
    log('render', 'child');
    return <div> {this.props.time} </div>;
  }
}

ReactDOM.render(<ParentComponent /> , document.getElementById('root'));
```

Both of these components reliably lead to the following result:

```
[parent] constructor
[parent] getDerivedStateFromProps
[parent] render
[child] constructor
[child] getDerivedStateFromProps
[child] render
[child] componentDidMount
[parent] componentDidMount
[parent] state update
[parent] shouldComponentUpdate
[parent] render
[child] getDerivedStateFromProps
[child] shouldComponentUpdate
[child] render
[child] getSnapshotBeforeUpdate
[parent] getSnapshotBeforeUpdate
[child] componentDidUpdate
[parent] componentDidUpdate
[parent] componentWillUnmount
[child] componentWillUnmount
```

Wow! There is a lot happening here. Let us go through this one by one, starting with the mounting phase.

constructor(props)

102

The first method to be called is the `constructor` of the `ParentComponent` component. React processes components in the tree from "the outside to the inside". The further up the component is in the component hierarchy, the earlier it will be instantiated. Afterwards, its `render()` method is called. This is necessary as React would not know otherwise which child components actually need processed and included in the component tree. React only runs the **lifecycle methods** for those components which have actually been included in the `render()` method of their parent component.

The constructor is passed the **props** of the component as a parameter and can transmit them to its parent component (mostly `React.Component` or `React.PureComponent`) via `super(props)`. If omitted, `this.props` in the constructor would be undefined leading to unexpected bugs and behavior.

In most cases today, it is not necessary anymore to declare the constructor. The Babel plugin **"Class properties"** can be used instead to implement instance methods as well as state as their own class properties. If it is not, the constructor is the place to define the initial state (for example `this.state = { }`) and bind the instance methods to their respective class instances with `.bind()` (for example `this.handleClick = this.handleClick.bind(this)`). This is necessary as instance methods would otherwise lose their context within the component as their event listeners are used inside JSX and `this` would not point to the instance of the component anymore.

static getDerivedStateFromProps(nextProps, prevState)

The constructor is followed by the static `getDerivedStateFromProps()` method. As can be inferred from its name, this is a **static** method and as does not have access to the component instance via `this`. Its primary goal is to calculate the **next state** of the component based on the props it has been passed and its last state. It is returned as an object. If no changes need applied to the state, `null` is returned instead. The method's behavior is identical to that of `this.setState()` and only updates those parts of the state which are part of the returned object. Those properties are merged along with the **last state** into a **new state**.

The method itself has been a controversial topic, succeeding the now **deprecated lifecycle method** `componentWillReceiveProps` . Other than the previous method, it does not have access to the component instance. The React core team has explained that the former can lead to unexpected behavior in asynchronous rendering of components and has thus marked it "unsafe". The same applies to `componentWillMount()` and `componentWillUpdate()` . While the term might be associated with security breaches, it actually means something a little different. Components using this lifecycle method could lead to bugs and other side effects after React version 17.

`getDerivedStateFromProps()` should not introduce any side effects (for example it should not trigger any XHRequests) and only **derive** the new state of the component instance based on its current props. In contrast to the constructor, this method is is not only called during the mounting phase of the component but also if the component receives new props. In order for that to happen the props do not have to have changed their content.

render()

Once a component has been created and its state has been derived, React calls the `render()` method which describes our user interface and the child components to render. The above example only contains one child component: the `ChildComponent`.

We now rinse and repeat. The `constructor()`, `getDerivedStateFromProps()` and then the `render()` method of our child component is called just the same as was the case in the `ParentComponent`. The Child component in our example does not have any other children implying that no other elements are rendered. If it did, their lifecycle methods would also be run until React would find a component which does not return any other React components anymore. It would simply contain DOM elements like div, p, section and span etc (and of course any combination of these), `null` or an array which in turn would not contain any other components.

componentDidMount()

The `componentDidMount()` method enters the scene once such a component is reached. It is called as soon as a component and all of its children have been rendered. From now on, we can also access the DOM Node of the component if necessary or start intervals or timeouts or initiate network requests via XHR/fetch. The `componentDidMount()` method is the best place for these.

As opposed to the constructor, this method is called from "the inside to the outside" determining the method's way of first processing child components and then their parent components. We can see this in action in our above example. The log clearly shows that first the `componentDidMount()` of the `ChildComponent` is called and only then `ParentComponent's` `componentDidMount()` is invoked.

In the above example, we started a `setTimeOut()` within the `ParentComponent` which modifies the state of our component every 2000 milliseconds. It demonstrates which lifecycle methods are being called during the update of a component. Any other changes on the state of the mounted component are no longer part of the mounting phase but part of the update phase. This phase is entered after the first 2000 milliseconds once the `ParentComponent` modifies its own state via `this.setState()`.

shouldComponentUpdate(nextProps, nextState)

Whenever a component updates, whether that is due to state change within the component or because it receives new props from the outside, shouldComponentUpdate() is called. But beware: there is a difference depending on whether the props or the state changed: if a component receives new props from the outside, getDerivedStateFromProps() is called shortly beforehand.

The shouldComponentUpdate() method enables us to inform if a costly re-render is actually necessary. The method receives the **next props** and the **next state** as a parameter and can determine, based on those, whether a re-render should take place. The method either has to return true to trigger the re-render or false which will prohibit the calls of componentDidUpdate() , getSnapshotBeforeUpdate() as well as render().

In many more complex applications, the update cycle is only triggered because a change has happened somewhere in the parent component but is irrelevant for the child components. In these cases, shouldComponentUpdate() can be helpful as to optimize the rendering performance by preventing further re-renders.

If we were to return false from our ParentComponent's shouldComponentUpdate() method, our logging output would be much shorter. Lines 14-18 would simply be missing. The component itself would not re-render, the render() method would not be called and the ChildComponent would also not re-render as well as update itself.

However, in our code example true is returned which in turn calls the render() method of the ParentComponent. This triggers another re-render of the ChildComponent which receives new props which mirror the ParentComponent updated state. And just like that we find ourselves in the update cycle of the ChildComponent.

Similar to what has already happened in the mount cycle, getDerivedStateFromProps() derives a new state based on the new props. Afterwards shouldComponentUpdate() is called. This is where we can check whether the component's relevant props have actually changed and if they did not, we could prohibit the re-render by returning false from shouldComponentUpdate() . If we did not do that, the obligatory call of the render() method would follow. Let's look at the next **lifecycle method** that would occur next in our component lifecycle.

getSnapshotBeforeUpdate(prevProps, prevState)

This method is relatively new and has only been introduced in React 16.3.0 along with getDerivedStateFromProps() to better deal with asynchronous rendering in React. It receives the **last props** and the **last state** and has access to the current state of the HTML DOM before React applies any modifications from the last render() cycle.

If we want to remember the current scroll position in a long list or table to be able to jump to the previously inspected item after an update, getSnapshotBeforeUpdate() can be really useful. It can return any value or null and its return value can be passed to componentDidUpdate() as a third parameter.

In my experience, getSnapshotBeforeUpdate() is rarely used. It might even be the least used out of all the **lifecycle methods** as we rarely need to access DOM elements directly. Most problems that used to be solved by manipulating the DOM API in an imperative fashion, can now be solved directly in the abstract component tree with JSX.

`componentDidUpdate(prevProps, prevState, snapshot)`

componentDidUpdate() forms the last method of the update cycle. It is called after getDerivedStateFromProps() has derived the new props, shouldComponentUpdate() has returned true and after getSnapshotBeforeUpdate() has created the last snapshot of the latest condition of the DOM.

The method receives the **last props** as well as the **last state** — meaning the last props and last state just before the component was updated. If the component contains a getSnapshotBeforeUpdate() method, its return value will be passed as a third parameter.

Similar to componentDidMount() , componentDidUpdate() is also resolved from the "inside to the outside". First, the componentDidMount() methods of the child components are called, then those of the parents. componentDidUpdate() is the perfect place to trigger side effects, for example starting XHRs if certain properties of the components have changed. This can easily be checked with a simple comparison between the current props and the last props (which we have received as a parameter) or the current state and the last state.

It is safe to access the **current DOM** during this method as React will have applied all the changes resulting from modified JSX in the render() method.

And with componentDidUpdate() the **update cycle** has also come to a finish. While the **mounting cycle** is only ever run once, namely when the component **first** renders, the update cycle can be triggered an infinite number of times: as soon as the component changes its state or receives new props.

`componentWillUnmount()`

I admit that I have cheated in the logs of our example. componentWillUnmount() is only ever run if a component is completely removed from the DOM. This has not happened in our example. A component counts as "unmounted" after it has been explicitly removed by calling ReactDOM.unmountComponentAtNode() (this is particularly important for mount nodes) or if it is not implicitly returned from the render() method of its parent component anymore.

In those two cases, `componentWillUnmount()` will be called but of course only if it has been manually implemented. This is true for most **lifecycle methods** apart from `render()`. The `componentWillUnmount()` **lifecycle method** is an essential tool to "clean up" our application. It is the place where functions can and **should** be called to ensure that no traces are left behind. "Traces" can refer to timeouts we are still waiting on (`setTimeout`) or intervals which are still running (`setInterval`) but also DOM modifications which have taken place outside of our component JSX, as well as network requests which are still ongoing (XHR/Fetch calls) or simply event listeners which were added to the DOM via the API method `Element.addEventListener()` .

Event listeners are a good topic to end this chapter on. As opposed to working with the regular DOM API, the use of `addEventListener()` is almost not necessary anymore in React as React introduces its own event system to aid readability and consistency.

Diagram of lifecycle methods

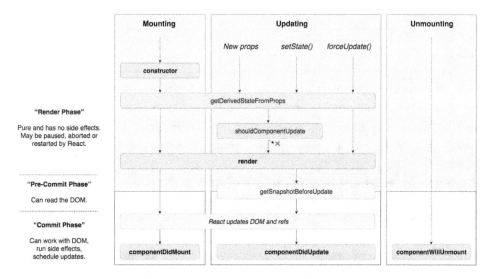

Diagram depicting the different lifecycle methods and the phases in which they are run (CC0 Dan Abramov)

Event Handling

The interaction between a user and the interface is a fundamental part of developing applications with complex user interfaces — especially with regard to **events**.

I click a button and something happens. I write text into an input field and something happens. I select an element from a list and something happens. In vanilla JavaScript, the browser provides us with the addEventListener() and removeEventListener() methods. In React however, you can safely ignore them in most use cases. React provides its own system to define user interaction and does so with (don't be scared now) **inline events**.

These **inline events** resemble HTML attributes (for example <button onclick="myFunction" />) but work entirely differently.

I know this is a little frustrating. For years, web developers have labored away and learned that event listeners should be neatly separated from the markup - **separation of concerns** anyone? But React introduces a very different way of dealing with events.

Behind the scenes, React handles a lot of the hard work and also enables to us to safely and easily stay in the component context by allowing the definition of event handlers as **class methods**. Layout logic as well as behavioral logic is encapsulated in a single component meaning we do not have to jump between many different controllers or views.

Differences between The React event handlers and the native Event API

As mentioned previously, React and JSX events resemble HTML attribute definitions. But there are differences: events in React are defined with **camelCase** instead of **lowercase** meaning onclick is changed to onClick in React, onmouseover is now defined by onMouseOver and ontouchstart would be written as onTouchStart — you get the picture.

The first parameter that is passed to the event handler is not an object of type Event as could be assumed. Instead, React supplies its own wrapper for the native event object, named a SyntheticEvent . The wrapper is part of React's event system and also works as a sort of normalizing layer to ensure cross-browser compatibility and, as opposed to some other browsers, it strictly follows the event specifications of W3C[21].

In order to prevent the standard behavior of the browser during an event, we cannot simply return false from the event handler. React forces us to explicitly call preventDefault() - another fundamental difference to usage in the native Browser API.

Last but not least, let's look at the event attribute or, in React's case, the event **prop**. React uses a **function reference** instead of a plain string (which would be the standard in HTML) which mandates the use of curly brackets to inform JSX that a JavaScript expression is used.

This would look similar to:

```
<button onClick={validateInput}>Validate</button>
```

For comparison, this is how a similar event would look in HTML:

```
<button onclick="validateInput" >Validate</ button>
```

While this might seem alienating to use function references as a prop, it offers a lot of advantages. We gain cross-browser compatibility basically "for free"! React neatly registers events in the background with addEventListener() and also safely and automatically removes them as soon as the component *unmounts*. How convenient!

Scopes in event handlers

Usually the use of ES2015 classes in React mandate that event handlers have to be defined as methods of the current class component. However, class methods **are not automatically bound to the instance**. Let's unpack what this means: initially this will be undefined in all of our event handlers.

Here is an example to reiterate this:

```
class Counter extends React.Component {
  state = {
    counter: 0 ,
  };

  increase() {
    this.setState((state) => ({
      counter: state.counter +  1,
    }));
  }

  render() {
    return (
      <div>
        <p> {this.state.counter} </p>
        <button onClick ={this.increase} >+1</button>
      </div>
    );
```

```
    }
  }
```

An onClick event is added to increment the counter by one each time the user presses a button labelled +1. But when the user clicks the button, instead of seeing the actual counter, they will receive an error message:

 TypeError

Cannot read property 'setState' of undefined

Why is that? The answer is **scoping!** Whenever we click the button in the increase() event handler, we actually operate outside of the component instance. This means we cannot access this.setState() resulting in our above error. While it might seem annoying, it is not actually something React has thought up but it's actually standard behavior for ES2015 classes. But fear not, there are a number of techniques to combat this:

Method binding in the render() method

Probably the most trivial solution is to *bind* the method inside of the render() method. We add a .bind(this) to the reference of the class method:

```
<button onClick={ this.increase.bind( this)}>+1</button>
```

The method is now invoked in the **scope of the component instance** and our counter starts to increment the count as intended. While you might come across this method quite a few times, it is not entirely recommended and has one obvious advantage. With every call of the function, a new function is created "on-the-fly" which is different to the one before. A simple check using shouldComponentUpdate() to compare this.props.increase === prevProps.increase would yield false every single time and possibly even lead to re-render of the component. Even if the function has not changed at all. Therefore, using this method is actually considered a **performance bottleneck** and should thus be avoided.

Method binding in the constructor

Another neater solution to bind a method to a class instance is to bind it when initializing a class in the constructor:

```
class Counter extends React.Component {
  constructor(props) {
    super(props);
    this.state = {
```

```
      counter: 0 ,
    };
    this.increase = this.increase.bind( this);
  }
  // [...]
}
```

This way, the method is only bound to the instance **once** and possible checks to compare the method's likeness would always yield `true`. Thus, expensive `shouldComponentUpdate()` calls can easily be avoided. However, using this method of binding the method to the class instance is not without problems either: if the component in question does not yet use a constructor, it will now certainly have to. In order to do this, we need to call the `super(props)` method to pass the **props** of the component to the `React.Component` parent class. In the end, we end up writing the name of the method twice. Once on its own, and once to define and bind its `this`.

Using this method allows us to avoid potential performance bottlenecks, even if it is a little bit more verbose, but it could still be considered somewhat messy and cumbersome. We will now look at an even easier way to bind a method to a class instance.

Class properties

Beware: in order to use the method I am about to explain, you need to have installed the babel plugin `@babel/plugin-proposal-class-properties`. But as most React setups already include this by default, I will assume that we can use **class properties** safely and without error. If this is not the case for some reason, event handler methods should always be bound in the constructor.

But how exactly do we bind our method via a **class property**? To be entirely correct: we are cheating. Instead of defining a real class method as shown in the above example, we define a **public class property** which is passed an **arrow function**:

```
class Counter extends React.Component {
  state = {
    counter: 0 ,
  };
  increase = () => {
    this. setState(( state) => ({
      counter:  state.counter + 1 ,
    }));
  }
}
```

The most important factor hides within the first line. Instead of:

```
increase() { … }
```

We write:

```
increase = () => { … }
```

Problem solved!

As mentioned earlier, we define a **real class method** within our first example whereas we assign a property within the class with same name an **arrow function** as a **value**. As it is not binding its own `this`, we access the `this` of the class instance instead.

Events outside of the component context

While you can certainly also implement native browser events in React, you should try to use React's own event system whenever possible. It offers cross-browser compatibility, follows the W3C standard for browser events and also optimizes when possible.

From time to time however, it is necessary to define events outside of the component context. Some classic examples are `window.onresize` and `window.onscroll`. React's event system does not support global events outside of the component context but if you want to define native browser events you can do so in the `componentDidMount()` method. You should pay attention though, whenever an event listener is added with `addEventListener()` , these **need to removed** once you're done with them.

The `componentWillUnmount()` method is the perfect place to do this. While it might seem annoying, global events can cause **performance bottlenecks** or even **memory leaks** if not removed properly as they would be added again each time a component is mounted and called multiple times.

The `SyntheticEventObject`

React does not pass a native object to its event handlers but an object of type `SyntheticEvent`. Its primary purpose is to ensure cross-browser compatibility. If you ever feel an urge to access the original event though (I actually never felt the need to), React provides it to you via the object property `nativeEvent`.

But that is not the only way the `SyntheticEvent` object and native event object differ: the `SyntheticEvent` object is **short-lived** and **nullified** shortly after the event callback has been called (mainly for performance reasons). Accessing properties of the event object is not possible anymore once outside the original event handler.

What does that mean in detail? Let's look at another example:

```
class TextRepeater extends React.Component {
  state = {};

  handleChange = (e) => {
    this.setState((state) => ({
      value: e.target.value,
    }));
  };

  render() {
    return (
      <div>
        <input type="text" onChange={this.handleChange} />
        <p> {this.state.value} </p>
      </div>
    );
  }
}
```

An onChange event is registered that is added into a paragraph once the value in the text field has changed. In order to access the provided value, the Event object provides a property called target. You might have encountered it already as it has been used in jQuery and vanilla JavaScript too. The target allows us to access the element on which the event has been performed, the text field in our case. This in turn contains a value property which we can use to write the current value of the text field into state.

We are running into a bit of a problem though: this.setState() uses an **updater function** or more precisely a callback. However, it happens outside of the event handler scope meaning the SyntheticEvent has already been reset or e.target does not exist anymore.

 TypeError

Cannot read property 'value' of null

The easiest solution for this problem is to define an object literal instead of an updater function:

```
handleChange = (e) => {
  this.setState({
    value: e.target.value,
  });
};
```

While this would certainly solve the problem, it would not help us much. We still encounter the first problem when trying to access the properties of the SyntheticEvent object if, for example, it was wrapped within a setTimeout() callback. We need to come up with another solution.

Writing values into variables

In most situations it is sufficient to write certain values that should later be accessed in a callback into their own variable. The callback does not try to access the SyntheticEvent anymore but only the variable which has been assigned a value from the SyntheticEvent.

```
handleChange = (e) => {
  const value = e.target.value;
  this.setState(() => ({
    value: value,
  }));
};
```

This works! Bonus points for using **object destructuring** and the **object property shorthand**.

```
handleChange = (e) => {
  const { value } = e.target;
  this.setState(() => ({ value }));
};
```

Persisting SyntheticEventswith e.persist()

While it is not used much in practice, it is theoretically possible to use the SyntheticEvent object's persist() method to keep a reference to the event in question. This could possibly be useful when trying to pass a SyntheticEvent object to a callback function **outside** of the event handler.

If you ever come across this situation though, it might be worth to consider whether that code of the callback function should actually live in the event handler itself. Our example function would look like this:

```
handleChange = (e) => {
  e.persist();
  this.setState(() => ({
    value: e.target.value,
  }));
};
```

First, the `e.persist()` method is invoked. Second, the **updater function** can safely access `e.target` and its `value` property.

Summary

- **Always** use event props in JSX to define events: `onChange`, `onMouseOver`, `onTouchStart`, `onKeyDown`, `onAnimationStart` etc (even if it seems a little odd at first).
- Event handlers have to be explicitly bound to the class instance if other class methods like `this.setState()` are accessed. **Public Class Properties** and **Arrow Functions** are the more elegant ways to do this.
- Avoid defining your own events with `addEventListener()` API. If at all necessary, do not forget to remove the event when unmounting your component with `removeEventListener()`.
- `SyntheticEvent` objects are „nullified". Beware of using callback functions outside of the event handler. The event object might not exist anymore at the time of calling the callback.
- `event.persist()` can force React to prevent resetting the event object to `null`.

Forms

Forms play a special role among the other DOM elements in React, and work a little different, as they already have some sort of **state**. This state is not related to React.

The state of a text field results from the value entered, the state of a checkbox or a radio button results from being selected or not, and `<select></select>` lists hold the state of one or more `<option></option>` elements that are selected. React does not change any of these values. If you feel comfortable using the form state, you can keep using it without issues and nothing changes for the development of your components.

React calls these components **uncontrolled components** as React does not concern itself with the state management of these components. State handling is either completely independent of React or only in the direction of DOM form state to React state, but **never the other way round**. A form element does not know about updates in React state and will keep showing the same value or status (in the case of checkboxes, selects and radio buttons) as before.

Controlled components, in contrast, are deeply linked to React State. An update in the React state will have an effect on the value or the status of the form element and vice versa. While **controlled components** are harder to implement, they are "safer" to use as it is less likely that both states differ from each other.

Uncontrolled Components

Uncontrolled components can take two different forms. First, plain form elements can be rendered which are processed server-side and do not interact with React at any time. The form is completely static so to say. React does **not intervene** if this is what is desired, and allows the developer to **freely** choose an approach.

But uncontrolled components could also still interact with React, which is the second form of an **uncontrolled component**. This variation of an uncontrolled component writes changes of the form element **into React state** either to validate data in the background or to render the data in a different place. Changes that have been made to the state in React in different parts of the application do not directly influence the form fields.

An example for an uncontrolled component:

```
class Uncontrolled extends React.Component {
  state = {
    username: '',
```

```
    isValid: false,
  };

  changeUsername = (e) => {
    const { value } = e.target;
    this.setState(() => ({
      username: value,
      isValid: value.length >  3,
    }));
  };

  submitForm = (e) => {
    e.preventDefault();
    alert(`Hello ${ this.state.username}`);
  };

  render() {
    return (
      <form method="post" onSubmit={this.submitForm}>
        <p>Your username: {this.state.username}</p>
        <p>
          <input type="text" name="username" onChange={this.changeUsername} />
          <input type="submit" disabled={!this.state.isValid} />
        </p>
      </form>
    );
  }
}
```

The user can enter their username into a simple text field. The uncontrolled component is notified of a change via the onChange event and can process the username further if necessary. As React only reacts **passively** and is simply notified of changes in the text field, we still refer to these types of components as **uncontrolled components**.

In most cases, it is sufficient to define these type of **uncontrolled components** if forms are not overly complex. However, we have to remember that the react state and DOM state are completely **decoupled** from each other and only work **in one direction**. Once the onChange event has been triggered, the React state can update safely. However, the text field would not update if changes to values of the React state had been made elsewhere in the application (for example due to a response in an asynchronous request).

A form field is said to be **controlled** as soon as a value attribute is set. From this point on, React expects the developer to synchronize the React state with the form field state. If we only want to set an initial value without converting the complete component into a **controlled component**, React allows us to define a defaultValue attribute instead of the usual value attribute, the equivalent being defaultChecked for checkboxes and radio buttons. The element itself will stay **uncontrolled** but show an initial value or status.

Controlled components

In order to portray state changes within form fields, as well as transferring changes made by users in form fields into state, a **controlled component** is needed. React fully takes care of the state handling of these form elements. We transfer a value to the value attribute which we receive from the state and also derive the changed value and pass it back to the state.

React state is seen as a **single source of truth** (or a similar state container like Redux). The only relevant value is the one that can be found in React state and the corresponding input in a form will constantly reflect this value in the state.

Let's take a look at an example to illustrate this better:

```
class Controlled extends React.Component {
  state = {
    username: '',
    isValid: false,
  };

  changeUsername = (e) => {
    const { value } = e.target;
    this.setState(() => ({
      username: value,
      isValid: value.length >  3,
    }));
  };

  submitForm = (e) => {
    e.preventDefault();
    alert(`Hallo ${ this.state.username}`);
  };

  render() {
    return (
      <form method="post" onSubmit={this.submitForm}>
        <p>{username}</p>
        <p>
          <input
            type="text"
            name="username"
            onChange={this.changeUsername}
            value={this.state.username}
```

```
            />
            <input type="submit" disabled={!this.state.isValid} />
          </p>
      </form>
    );
  }
}
```

At first glance the `Controlled` component does not look very different from the Uncontrolled component. The defining difference that turns this component into a `controlled` one rather than `uncontrolled` lies in line 29. The `value` attribute of this `<input />` indicates to React that it should now **control** the form element and that changes to the input field should be reflected in the state. In order to pass changes to the React state, it is important to define the `onChange` handler to keep the form field and React state in sync. Failing to do that, will result in input fields that do not update and is — perhaps unsurprisingly — a mistake made relatively often.

There are a few other things to consider. The `value` attribute is only ever allowed to be a **string** but never `undefined` or `null`.

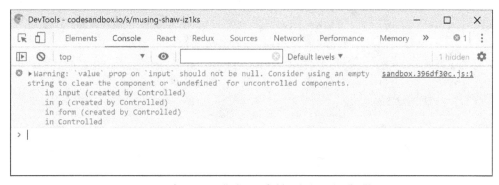

Warning for a controlled input field with the value "null"

The `select` elements that have the `multiple` attribute are an exception to the rule. The `value` attribute in this case needs to be an **array** (rather than a string).

Noticed anything? I spoke of a `value` attribute for a `<select>` field. But normally an `<option>` is selected by setting its `selected` attribute in HTML. React works a little different and controls the value with another `value` attribute. The same applies to the `<textarea>` element (which usually indicates its initial value with the `textContent` attribute).

React unifies the mechanism for changing values by enforcing a `value` attribute for the `input`, `textarea` and `select` elements (with the exceptions of `checkbox` and `radio` inputs). This attribute always has to be a **string** or, in the case of a `select` with a `multiple` attribute, an **array of strings**.

Changes made to the form elements always need to be sent back to **React state**. This can become cumbersome, especially when dealing with checkboxes or radio buttons which do not only change a value but a status (checked).

The following example of a controlled component should provide an exhaustive list of all basic types of HTML form elements. Any other input elements not listed like email, date and range work exactly the same.

```
class FullyControlledComponent extends React.Component {
  state = {
    text: '',
    textarea: '',
    checkbox: false,
    singleSelect: '',
    multipleSelect: [],
  };

  changeValue = ({ target: { name, value } }) => {
    this.setState(() => ({
      [name]: value,
    }));
  };

  changeCheckbox = ({ target: { name, checked } }) => {
    this.setState(() => ({
      [name]: checked,
    }));
  };

  changeSelect = ({ target: { name, value, selectedOptions, multiple } }) => {
    if (multiple) {
      value = Array.from(selectedOptions).map((option) => option.value);
    }

    this.setState(() => ({
      [name]: value,
    }));
  };

  render() {
    return (
      <form>
        <input
          type="text"
          name="text"
          value={this.state.text}
```

```jsx
        onChange={this.changeValue}
      />

      <textarea
        name="textarea"
        value={this.state.textarea}
        onChange={this.changeValue}
      />

      <input
        type="checkbox"
        name="checkbox"
        checked={this.state.checkbox}
        onChange={this.changeCheckbox}
      />

      <input
        type="radio"
        name="radio"
        value="1"
        checked={this.state.radio === '1'}
        onChange={this.changeValue}
      />
      <input
        type="radio"
        name="radio"
        value="2"
        checked={this.state.radio === '2'}
        onChange={this.changeValue}
      />

      <select
        name="singleSelect"
        value={this.state.singleSelect}
        onChange={this.changeValue}
      >
        <option value="">Please select</option>
        <option value="1">One</option>
        <option value="2">Two</option>
      </select>

      <select
        name="multipleSelect"
        value={this.state.multipleSelect}
        onChange={this.changeSelect}
        multiple
```

```
      >
          <option value="1">One</option>
          <option value="2">Two</option>
        </select>

        <pre>{JSON.stringify(this.state, null, 2)}</pre>
      </form>
    );
  }
}
```

The core of the form is formed by three event handlers that cater to the different types of form elements: `changeValue` , `changeCheckbox` and `changeSelect` .

These are triggered by the `onChange` events in their corresponding form elements and are passed an object of type `SyntheticEvent` . We access properties of the `target` property of the `SyntheticEvent` via **ES2015 object destructuring** in order to update React state.

For elements of type `<input type="text" />` , `<input type="radio" />` and `<textarea />`, we pick `name` and `value`, for `<input type="checkbox" />` elements `name` and the `checked` property are important, whereas `select` elements also need to provide a `name` and whether a selection is offered to the user or a multiple select (with `value` or `selectedOptions`). We can find out whether we're dealing with a simple or multiple select by inspecting the `multiple` property with `e.target` .

Changing of values

If a value is modified, as is the case with text inputs and radio buttons, the corresponding React state is set to the value provided by the user, triggered by the `onChange` event. Controlled components now mandate the following procedure:

1. When the user inputs text, the value changes.
2. The `onChange` event is triggered and processed by the event handler.
3. The event handler sets state using the new value.
4. React re-renders the user interface and sets `this.state` to the new value.
5. The user sees their newly provided value on the screen.

This is **business as usual** for the user and they will not notice that the form works differently behind the scenes and does not reflect usual browser behavior. React fully takes care of the logic in the background and painted a new "frame" in the user interface.

Changing state in checkboxes and radio buttons

Checkboxes (`<input type="checkbox" />`) work in a similar fashion but their value will remain the same. Checkboxes change their state rather than their value by providing the boolean `true` or `false` in its `checked` property. If the `checked` property is controlled by React, the form field is said to be controlled. One can check whether the checkbox is activated (`true`) or not (`false`) by inspecting `e.target.checked` in the event handler which passes this information to React state. React then takes care of the re-render and showing the status of the checkbox to the user.

Radio buttons on the other hand are a kind of a hybrid element. Similarly to checkboxes, radio buttons are seen as controlled if their `checked` attribute is managed by React. However, there are often multiple radio buttons containing the same name but different values within the same document. It would not make sense to set the values of these names to either `true` or `false` as we are interested in the actual value of the selected radio button. Thus, the value of the radio button is written into state. We can check whether the selected value in the state is the same as the value of the field with `checked={this.state.radio === "1"}` . We set `checked` to true in this case if the value of the radio button `radio` is equal to 1.

Changing state with simple or multiple selects

Let's start with a simple use case: a simple `<select>` list modifies its value just like a text field, then triggers a re-render and finally shows the selected value in the freshly painted user interface. Multiple selects form an exception though.

Other than their counterparts, a simple select list or a simple text input, multiple select lists do not expect a string value but an **array of strings.** Annoyingly, we have to construct this array ourselves as `e.target.value` only ever contains a single value, even if multiple options are possible. The `e.target.selectedOptions` property, an object of type `HTMLCollection` , can help us and contains a list of `<option>` elements which are currently selected. This object can easily be transformed into an array using the static array method `Array.from()` added in ES2015. Using `Array.map()` we can furthermore iterate over this array and return a new array containing all the relevant values:

```
Array.from(selectedOptions).map((option) => option.value);
```

The newly created array is then written into state as a new value. But before that we check using `e.target.multiple` whether we are actually dealing with a `<select>` with multiple choices as it is only this `<select>` which expects an array as a value.

Alternatively, we could have passed the `changeValue` method to the simple select and the `changeSelect` method to the select with multiple choices. Because each select would have received its own event handler, we could have avoided the additional check of checking for a `multiple` select. However, following the procedure I have shown above will make your code more resilient to change requests as the type can be easily changed in the future. In the end it is up to you though.

Special cases within controlled components

I have used the `name` attribute as the key in the above example to save their value in state. This can come in handy while working with server-side React and if forms are automatically generated and processed. It is not a requirement though: theoretically neither a `name` attribute nor the exact match of the state name and the `name` attribute is needed.

Saved values can also be nested and require to have more than one form within a component (But **attention**: React Anti-pattern). It is also not necessary to use React's own state to portray a **controlled component**. In practice, many developers choose to use an external state container such as **Redux, Unstated** or **MobX**.

Summary

(i) Forms in React can take a controlled or uncontrolled form.

Uncontrolled components are usually sufficient for simple forms, however it is recommended to have React control your form components to ensure a **single source of truth**. To achieve this, the `value` or `checked` attribute needs to be controlled by React while the developer needs to manually react to changes.

In contrast to regular HTML forms, React expects the value of textareas, selects and inputs to be in a `value` attribute.

Lists, Fragments, and Conditional Rendering

You have learned a lot about React so far. You now know why we need **props**, what **state** is and how it differs from **props**. You have learned how to implement a React component as well as to differentiate between a React **component** and a React **element**. You also learned how to use **JSX** to accurately depict the tree of elements that is being rendered and how you can leverage **lifecycle methods** to react to changes in your data. All of these lay the groundwork for simple React applications.

But there are a few details that we have not yet examined (or not explained in detail). However, these details will become more relevant the more complex our applications get.

Lists (as in working with data arrays), so-called **Refs** (which are references to the DOM representation of a React element), **Fragments** (a special component that does not leave traces or elements in the output) and **Conditional Rendering** based on props and state are part of these details and will be examined in this section.

They are too important to not mention them in the Basics section of the book but each topic on its own does not quite warrant its own chapter. Let's look at them now.

Lists

Lists refer to plain JavaScript arrays — in this instance: **simple** data that can be iterated over. They are essential for React, even plain JavaScript development, and it is hard to imagine developing without them. **ES2015+** offers many nice declarative methods such as `Array.map()`, `Array.filter()` or `Array.find()` that can even be used as expressions in JSX (if surrounded by curly brackets {}).

I have mentioned expressions in JSX and how to use them already in the chapter on JSX. But let's recap briefly: Arrays can be used as an expression in JavaScript and therefore also be included in JSX. If surrounded by curly brackets, they will be treated as child nodes during the transpilation step.

But there's more: `Array.map()` enables us to not only work with data but it can return modified items which in turn can also contain JSX. This adds further flexibility and allows us to transform data sets into React elements.

Let's assume that we want to show list of cryptocurrencies. The array containing the data has the following form:

```
const cryptos = [
  {
    id: 1,
    name: 'Bitcoin',
    symbol: 'BTC',
    quotes: { EUR: { price: 7179.92084586 } },
  },
  {
    id: 2,
    name: 'Ethereum',
    symbol: 'ETH',
    quotes: { EUR: { price: 595.218568203 } },
  },
  {
    id: 3,
    name: 'Litecoin',
    symbol: 'LTC',
    quotes: { EUR: { price: 117.690716234 } },
  },
];
```

First, we will aim to show this data as a simple unordered list in HTML. A resulting component could look similar to this:

```
const CryptoList = ({ currencies }) => (
  <ul>
    {currencies.map((currency) => (
      <li>
        <h1>
          {currency.name} ({currency.symbol})
        </h1>
        <p> {currency.quotes.EUR.price.toFixed(2)} € </p>
      </li>
    ))}
  </ul>
);
```

The component could then be used like this:

```
<CryptoList currencies={cryptos} />
```

The result is an unordered list with list items containing the crypto currency and their price. However, we also encounter an error in the console:

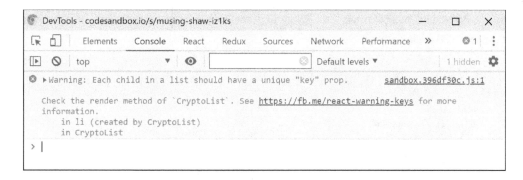

React expects a key prop for all of the values returned by arrays or iterators. The primary reasoning behind this rule is to make it easier for React's **Reconciler** (the React Comparison algorithm) to identify and compare list elements. The **Reconciler** can spot whether an array element was added, removed or modified if the key prop has been given. This prop needs to be a unique identifier which only appears **once in the array**. Normally, the id of a data set is used for this.

In our example, we can take the id of each item. Amended, the example now looks like this:

```
const CryptoList = ({ currencies }) => (
  <ul>
    {currencies.map((currency) => (
      <li key={currency.id}>
        <h1>
          {currency.name} ({currency.symbol})
        </h1>
        <p> {currency.quotes.EUR.price.toFixed(2)} € </p>
      </li>
    ))}
  </ul>
);
```

The key only has to be unique **within the iterator compared to its sibling elements but not inside the component**. We can easily use the CryptoList component elsewhere using the same key - even within the same component. Just don't use the key again in the same loop.

If your data set does not contain an easily distinguishable id, the **index** of the array can be used as a **last resort.** This is not recommended though and can lead to unexpected behavior in the rendering of user interfaces and also impact performance.

It is important that the key prop is always **present in the top-level component or array element within the iterator** but not in the JSX returned by the component.

To illustrate this point further, I'm going to transform the above list item into its own
CryptoListItem component.

```
const CryptoListItem = ({ name, symbol, quotes }) => (
  <li>
    <h1>
      {name} ({symbol})
    </h1>
    <p>{quotes.EUR.price.toFixed(2)} € </p>
  </li>
);
```

What do we notice? The key prop which we added beforehand is no longer present. Our `map()`
call would now look like this:

```
const CryptoList = ({ currencies }) => (
  <ul>
    {currencies.map((currency) => (
      <CryptoListItem
        key ={currency.id}
        name ={currency.name}
        symbol ={currency.symbol}
        quotes ={currency.quotes}
      />
    ))}
  </ul>
);
```

Although we actually render a `<li></li>` element under the hood, the `<CryptoListItem />`
needs to contain the key prop as it is the top level component within our `Array.map()` call in
this JSX snippet.

A little bit off-topic: We could even simplify the `CryptoList` component by using **Object spread
syntax**:

```
const CryptoList = ({ currencies }) => (
  <ul>
    {currencies.map((currency) => (
      <CryptoListItem  key={currency.id} {...currency} />
    ))}
  </ul>
);
```

This way, all properties of the currency objects are passed as props to the `CryptoListItem`
component.

If we didn't use an iterator such as `Array.map()`, a list would need to be explicitly defined like this:

```
const MyList = () => (
  <ul>
    {[<li key="1">One</li>, <li key="2">Two</li>, <li key="3">Three</li>]}
  </ul>
);
```

Fragments

Fragments are some sort of a special component and allow us to create valid JSX without leaving visible traces in the rendered markup. They are a solution to the "problem" of only ever returning a single element at the top in JSX. This is valid JSX:

```
render() {
  return (
    <ul>
      <li>Bullet Point 1 </li>
      <li>Bullet Point 2 </li>
      <li>Bullet Point 3 </li>
    </ul>
  );
}
```

But this isn't:

```
render() {
  return (
    <li>Bullet Point 1</li>
    <li>Bullet Point 2</li>
    <li>Bullet Point 3</li>
  );
}
```

In this example, multiple elements are being returned in the `render()` method without a surrounding element, leading to an error. We do not always want to create new elements though, especially if the surrounding element is found in a parent component and the child element is found in its own component.

On top of that, many elements (such as `table`, `ul`, `ol`, `dl`, ...) do not allow for `div` elements to be used as an intermediary wrapper (ignoring the fact that we would also litter the markup by using `div`s). As we are only permitted to ever return a single root element from a component,

Fragments can be incredibly useful. We could transform our example from above into the following:

```
render() {
  return (
    <React.Fragment>
      <li>Bullet Point 1 </li>
      <li>Bullet Point 2 </li>
      <li>Bullet Point 3 </li>
    </React.Fragment>
  );
}
```

The rule that every element returned by a loop needs to have a key prop, still holds. Using a **Fragment** this is still possible. Let's illustrate this further by examining another slightly more complex yet more realistic example:

```
import React from 'react';
import ReactDOM from 'react-dom';

const TicketMeta = ({ metaData }) => (
  <dl>
    {Object.entries(metaData).map(([property, value]) => (
      <React.Fragment key={property}>
        <dt>{property}</dt>
        <dd>{value}</dd>
      </React.Fragment>
    ))}
  </dl>
);

ReactDOM.render(
  <TicketMeta
    metaData={{
      createdAt: '2018-06-09',
      author: 'Manuel Bieh',
      category: 'General',
    }}
  />,
  document.getElementById('root')
);
```

The resulting output would be the following:

```
<dl>
  <dt>createdAt </dt>
  <dd>2018-06-09</dd>
  <dt>author </dt>
  <dd>Manuel Bieh</dd>
  <dt>category</dt>
  <dd>General </dd>
</dl>
```

It would simply not be possible to wrap a div or span or another element around the <dt></dt> or <dd></dd>. Trying to do that would result in this:

```
<dl>
  <div>
    <dt>createdAt </dt>
    <dd>2018-06-09</dd>
  </div>
  <div>
    <dt>author </dt>
    <dd>Manuel Bieh</dd>
  </div>
  <div>
    <dt>category</dt>
    <dd>General </dd>
  </div>
</dl>
```

... and is invalid HTML! A dl element only permits dt and dd as its child element. The **Fragment** helps us to alleviate these situations and creates valid JSX without creating invalid markup. It was only introduced in React 16.3 and meant that some React components were unnecessarily complex to deal with this problem to avoid violating JSX or HTML rules.

Fragment components can also be imported directly from React using a named import:

```
import React, { Fragment } from 'react';
```

Now, the notation of <Fragment> instead of <React.Fragment> can be used saving us multiple key strokes.

Using Babel 7 for transpilation, we can shorten the notation even further. An *empty* element can created using:

```
<>Fragment in shorthand syntax< />
```

This is a neat and tidy method to reduce the amount of fragments we need to explicitly define by name. But be careful: using the shorthand is not possible in loops as empty elements cannot contain any props. Elements in a loop require us to define a key prop thus forcing us to use `<React.Fragment>` instead.

Conditional rendering

Rendering components based on different conditions, **conditional rendering** for short, is a central concept in React. As React components are composed of JavaScript functions, objects and classes under the hood, conditions behave just as they would in regular JavaScript.

A React component renders a **state** of a **user interface** based on its **props** and its current **state**. In an ideal situation, this means that the component is free from **side effects**. To correctly deal with these different and changing parameters, using the render function to react to different conditions is a powerful feature. If my parameter is A, render this; if my parameter is B, render that. If I have incoming data in a list, show this data as an HTML list. If I do not have any data, show a placeholder instead.

If this sounds relatively simple, I can assure you, it is. But one should still be aware of knowing how to do conditional rendering in JSX. The `render()` function of **Class components** as well as **Functional components** can return a **React element** (also in form of JSX), a **string**, a **number**, `null` (if nothing should be rendered) or an **array** of these types.

There are a few methods of keeping the `render()` method nice and clean which I will explain now.

if/else

Probably the most simple and commonly known way to **conditionally render** is using `if/else`:

```
const NotificationList = ({ items }) => {
  if (items.length) {
    return (
      <ul>
        {items.map((notification) => (
          <li> {notification.title} </li>
        ))}
      </ul>
    );
  }
  return <p>No new notifications </p>;
};
```

This is a relatively simple use case. The `NotificationList` component receives a list of items in the form of props. If the list contains any entries at all, they are rendered as a list item of an unordered list. If however the list is empty, a message is returned informing the user that no new notifications are available.

Another more complex example: let's imagine we are working with a value that we want to make editable. Our component differentiates between the different modes of `edit` and `view`. Depending on which mode we are currently in, we either want to simply show text (**View mode**) or be able to see a text field containing the previously entered value (**edit mode**).

```javascript
import React from 'react';
import { render } from 'react-dom';

class EditableText extends React.Component {
  state = {
    value: null ,
  };

  static getDerivedStateFromProps(nextProps, prevState) {
    if (prevState.value === null ) {
      return {
        value: nextProps.initialValue ||   '',
      };
    }
    return null;
  }

  handleChange = (e) => {
    const { value } = e.target;
    this.setState(() => ({
      value,
    }));
  };

  setMode = (mode) => () => {
    this.setState(() => ({
      mode,
    }));
  };

  render() {
    if (this.state.mode === 'edit' ) {
      return (
        <div>
          <input
```

```
        type="text"
        value={this.state.value}
        onChange={this.handleChange}
      />
      <br />
      <button onClick={this.setMode('view')}>Done</button>
    </div>
  );
}

    return (
      <div>
        {this.state.value}
        <br />
        <button onClick={this.setMode('edit')}>Edit</button>
      </div>
    );
  }
}

render(
  <EditableText initialValue="Example" />,
  document.getElementById('root')
);
```

The relevant part can be found in the `render()` method of the component. The state is tested against its property value in `mode`. If `edit` is the current value in state, we directly return the input field with an "early return". If this is not the case, we assume that the "standard case" is taking place meaning that the current mode is `view`. The `else` part of this condition is not actually necessary here and would only add unnecessary complexity. Both times, the text is rendered with the difference that it is an editable `value` of an `input` field in one case, and a simple text node in the other. A button is included to switch between the different modes of `view` and `edit`.

Such `if`, `if/else` or `if/else if/else` constructs are common if you want to create output based on **state** and **props** within a component. I will explain them in more detail in just a moment.

null

No, this is not a mistake. Returning `null` is the most simple case of **conditional rendering**. If the `render()` method of a component returns `null`, nothing is rendered and also does not appear in the DOM. This can be useful for displaying error components that should only be displayed if the error has actually occurred.

```
render() {
  if (!this.state.error) {
    return null;
  }

  return (
    <div className ="error-message" >{this.state.error.message} </div>
  );
}
```

Using this form of a conditional check, we test whether the state contains an error property. If this is not the case, `null` is being returned. Otherwise, an error message containing the error in state is returned in a `div`. We achieve this by using a simple `if` condition similar to what we have used above.

Ternary Operator

The conditions that we have just seen are often used to deal with relatively big changes in a component. In many situations, we only want to differentiate between minor differences, for example setting a CSS class if a certain state is set. The ternary operator helps us to do just that. Let's refresh our knowledge. A ternary operator takes the following form: `condition ? met : not met`. For example: `isLoggedIn ? 'Logout' : 'Login';`

That's our first example for a ternary operator in JSX! It can be used within props but also in conditions to differentiate between different forms of output to render based on conditions. To make the example more concrete, we could use the info from above to include it in a button:

```
render() {
  const { isLoggedIn } = this.props;
  return (
    <button type="submit">{ isLoggedIn ? 'Logout' : 'Login' }</button>
  );
}
```

We will always return a button, but based on its `isLoggedIn` prop it can either include the message: **Logout** or **Login**.

Equally, the **ternary operator** can be used in props. Let's assume that we want to render a list of users in which some users have been deactivated. In this case, we want to be able to set a class to mark it using CSS. Markup that deals with this problem could look like this:

```
render() {
  const { user } = this.props;
  return (
```

```
    <div className ={user.isDisabled ? ' is-disabled' :  'is-active '}>{user.name}
</div>
  );
}
```

Users that have been deactivated are now marked with the is-disabled class, whereas active users are denoted with is-active.

Even complex JSX can be displayed using the **ternary operator**. As long as you follow the rule to use parentheses if the JSX spans multiple lines:

```
render() {
  const { country } =  this.props;
  return (
    <div>
      <p>State: </p>
      {country === 'de' ? (
        <select  name ="state" >
          <option  value= "bw" >Baden-Württemberg </option>
          <option  value= "by" >Bayern </option>
          <option  value= "be" >Berlin </option>
          <option  value= "bb" >Brandenburg</option>
          [...]
        </select>
      ) : (
        <input  type ="text"  name ="state"  />
      )}
    </div>
  );
}
```

In this example, a select list containing all German states is rendered if we previously selected de (for **Germany**) as our country. In all other cases a simple text input is shown to user in which they can enter their state freely. However, careful consideration should be given when to use the **ternary operator**: it can become a little hard to read quickly if complex JSX is used.

Logical AND (&&) and Logical OR (||)

The **logical operator** seems to resemble the **ternary operator** at first glance, but it is even shorter and more precise. As opposed to the **ternary operator**, a second "else" case is not needed. If the condition of the **logical AND operator** is not met, the expression simply returns undefined resulting in no visible markup for the user interface:

```
render() {
  const { isMenuVisible } =  this.props;
```

136

```
  return (
    <header>
      { isMenuVisible &&  <Menu /> }
    </header>
  );
}
```

In this example, we test against the value of the isMenuVisible prop and check if it is true. If that **is** the case, it will return the Menu component. If the result is false, undefined is returned and nothing else will be rendered to the screen.

In combination with the **logical OR operator**, we can emulate the behavior of the **ternary operator**:

```
render() {
  const { isLoggedIn } =  this.props;
  return (
    <button type="submit">{ isLoggedIn && 'Logout' || 'Login' } </button>
  );
}
```

The button will be labelled **Logout** if the isLoggedIn **prop** is true, or **Login** if the user is logged out.

Custom `render()` methods

Another way to increase the readability during complex **conditional rendering** is to move parts from the regular render() method to separate renderXY() methods. The regular render() method still forms the core of the component and decides which parts of the user interface to show to the user. Thus, this method should not become overly complex or contain any unnecessary logic.

It is not uncommon to move parts of long and complex render() methods into much smaller, more digestible chunks and implement these as custom class methods. If proper naming is used, this technique usually aids readability and understanding. Often these custom render() blocks are combined with if blocks:

```
class Countdown extends React. Component {
  renderTimeLeft() {
    // [...]
  }

  renderTimePassed() {
    // [...]
```

```
    }

  render() {
    const { currentDate, eventDate } =  this.props;
    if (currentDate < eventDate) {
      // currentDate is before eventDate so render countdown
      return this.renderTimeLeft();
    }
    // time is over so render how much time has passed since then
    return this.renderTimePassed();
  }
}
```

This **can** improve readability of the `render()` method but also increases the complexity of the component slightly. Many people recommend to move parts of the code into their own **Function components** instead though (myself included).

 As soon as you begin to consider moving parts of your code into custom `render()` methods within your component, you should think about moving these into their own separate **Function components**.

Custom Components with complex conditions

Instead of using multiple `render()` methods, we can create new **Function components**. These will receive **props** from their parent component and then take care of displaying their own data as an independent, self-governing and testable component.

Careful consideration should be given as to what data actually needs passed down to the new child component(s), and how to pass this data, as the component(s) should not contain too much logic or state.

Using custom components becomes useful once the `render()` method in one component has become too complex or if the same elements are used repetitively within a component.

Let's look at a form which consists of many similar text fields. Each of these text fields is embraced by its own paragraph, and contains a label and a `type` attribute. The label also needs to be equipped with an id that is unique to each field that it represents.

```
render() {
  return (
    <form>
      <p>
        <label for="email">
```

```
        Email
      </label>
      <br />
      <input type="email" name="email" id="email" />
    </p>
    <p>
      <label for="password">
        Password
      </label>
      <br />
      <input type="password" name="password" id="password" />
    </p>
    <input type="submit" value="Send" />
  </form>
  );
}
```

We only have two form fields in this example but in most projects you will find many more fields in way more complex forms. Even in this case, it might make sense to extract recurring fields into their own components to save ourselves keystrokes.

First, create a TextField component and then cut the recurring JSX from the form component into this one:

```
const TextField = ({ id, label, ...HTMLInputAttributes }) => (
  <p>
    <label for={id}>{label}</label>
    <br />
    <input {...HTMLInputAttributes} id= {id} />
  </p>
);


export default TextField;
```

This new component receives an id which is needed to link the label to the text input. Using **Object Rest/Spread**, we add all remaining props to the input element as attributes, transforming the component into the following:

```
render() {
  return (
    <form>
      <TextField name="email" label="Email" id="email" type="email" />
      <TextField name="password" label="Password" id="password" type="password" />
      <input type="submit" value="Send" />
    </form>
```

```
    );
  }
```

We have just transformed long and potentially hard to read markup into a clean and precise `render()` method which only consists of very few components. If we ever wanted to add a change which should affect all of our text fields (for example adding a class), this can be added with ease by only changing data in one place — in the new `TextField` component.

CSS and Styling

Styling is a topic of its own in React. React does not offer its own in-house solution to make styling easier, however the introduction of CSS-in-JS has shaken up the scene a little bit. Adopted widely and loved by some but hotly debated by others. With CSS-in-JS, the styling of components also moves into JavaScript to not break with the paradigm of component-based development. But let's start with the basics and explore the topic bit by bit.

Styling with the style attribute

The simplest way to style components in React is using the `style` attribute on regular HTML elements. It differs from regular HTML though. React components expect an **object** in the form of `property: value`. The property itself needs to be declared in JavaScript (not its regular CSS counterpart) form meaning `zIndex` instead of `z-index`, `backgroundColor` instead of `background-color` or `marginTop` instead of `margin-top`. If the values accept declarations in pixels, it is optional to explicitly define px as the corresponding unit:

```
<div style={{ border: '1px solid #ccc', marginBottom: 10 }}>
  A div with a grey border and a  10 pixel margin at the bottom
</div>
```

Values that are not used with a unit (for example `z-index`, `flex` or `fontWeight`) are not affected by this and can be used just like we are used to. React does not add px to these.

By using an object instead of a string, React keeps a consistent approach to dealing with styles. The regular `style` property of DOM elements `document.getElementById('root').style` is also an object and also ensures that we secure these by preventing XSS.

While using inline styling is not exactly recommended, it can be useful at times if the styling of an element depends on particular values in state.

Using CSS classes in JSX

It is much cleaner and nicer to use real CSS classes in JSX, just like we do in regular HTML with the difference being that we declare classes by using `className` instead of `class`:

```
<div className= "item" >...</div>
```

React renders normal syntax with our HTML equivalent:

```
<div class="item">...</div>
```

It is also quite common to concatenate values in the className prop dynamically:

```
render() {
  let className = 'item' ;
  if (this.state.selectedItem === this.props.itemId) {
    className += ' item--selected' ;
  }
  return (
    <div className ={className}>
      ...
    </div>
  );
}
```

In this example the value for className is item in each case. If the selected item is the current item, it also gets the class item item--selected .

The package classnames has become the de-facto standard to define classes based on a condition. It can be installed via the CLI:

```
npm install classnames
```

```
yarn add classnames
```

Now, we only need to import the package in those components where we want to use it:

```
import classNames from 'classnames' ;
```

This way, we are importing the function and give it the name of classNames . The function expects an arbitrary amount of parameters which can be a string or an object in the form of { class: true | false } . It works similar to what you might already expect: if the value in the condition is true, classNames employs a class with the same property name:

```
render() {
  return (
    <div className ={classNames( 'item', {
      'item--selected ': this.state.selectedId === this.props.itemId
    })}>
      ...
    </div>
  );
}
```

Objects can also be used to work with multiple properties. Multiple classes can be set if the condition is `true`:

```
render() {
  return (
    <div className ={classNames({
      'item': true,
      'item--selected ': this.state.selectedId === this.props.itemId
    })}>
      ...
    </div>
  );
}
```

If regular CSS classes are used, we should also ensure that the corresponding stylesheet is also linked in the HTML document. React does not usually take care of this on its own.

Modular CSS with CSS Modules

CSS Modules are some sort of predecessor to **CSS-in-JS** and combine a number of properties from CSS and JavaScript modules. As the name already suggests, the CSS is found in their own importable **modules**, which however contain pure CSS and are tied to one particular component. If we were to develop a component to display a profile picture in a file called `ProfileImage.js`, the **CSS Modules** approach often introduces another file with the name `ProfileImage.module.css` .When these CSS modules are imported, a cryptic classname is generated to ensure that the classname is only used in the single component. This aims to prevent that classnames are accidentally used by two different components.

CSS Modules are only a concept first of all, and do not dictate a particular approach or implementation. The implementation is achieved by tools such as `css-loader` for Webpack.

It's not actually necessary to enforce the file ending of `.module.css` (just regular `.css` would also be okay) but it has become convention in many well-known tools. **Create React App** also supports this convention out of the box without the need for further configuration by using the previously mentioned `css-loader` in the background (implemented in Webpack).

In these CSS files, regular and **standardized CSS** can be found. It can then be imported into a JavaScript module with ease:

```
import css from './ProfileImage.module.css';
```

We've just entered new territory: the variable `css` now containts an object with properties that relate to the classnames in our CSS modules. If there is a CSS class in the CSS file that has the name image, we can now access the property `image` on the CSS object. The resulting value in the rendered markup is a unique string such as `ProfileImage_image_2cvf73` .

We can pass these generated classnames to our components like this:

```
<img src={props.imageUrl} className={css.image} />
```

This code would result in the following rendered markup:

```
<img src ="..." className ="ProfileImage_image_2cvf73" />
```

If we used the class `image` in another component and also imported the css file with an `image` class, we wouldn not run into conflict as we would usually do in regular CSS. The *generated* classname would be different.

Everything that is allowed in regular CSS is also allowed in CSS Modules. The Cascade will remain intact:

```
.imageWrapper img {
  border : 1px solid red;
}

.imageWrapper:hover img {
  border-color : green;
}
```

This CSS snippet would be used in the following JSX structure:

```
const ProfileImage = () => {
  return (
    <div className ={css.imageWrapper} >
      <img src="..." />
    </div>
  );
};
```

CSS Modules aim to avoid conflicts in very isolated components while still allowing us to write regular CSS in CSS files without any JavaScript knowledge. They are a great solution for teams in which development is more separated into JavaScript and CSS and in which there are experts for both.

CSS-in-JS - Moving styles into JavaScript

I've already mentioned in the introduction that **CSS-in-JS** is a bit of a hotly debated topic. Opponents say that users of **CSS-in-JS** do simply not understand the cascade to write scalable CSS. Proponents on the other hand explain that the cascade is not the main reason for choosing **CSS-in-JS** but argue that a safer way is needed to write highly isolated components. I'm a bit more diplomatic myself and think that there's room and reasons for both. **CSS-in-JS** certainly has reason to exist. But what even is **CSS-in-JS**?

The **CSS-in-JS** approach mandates that the styles which are commonly found in CSS files are now moved into JavaScript. As was already the case in **CSS modules**, the primary goal is to create highly isolated components which are free of conflict making them easy to reuse throughout the application. However, as opposed to **CSS modules**, the styling in **CSS-in-JS** happens entirely in JavaScript. The syntax is very similar and it mostly feels like you're writing regular CSS.

CSS-in-JS is the umbrella term for the concept whereas the actual implementation is achieved by a number of different libraries. If you are looking for a great overview, I suggest you checkout out http://michelebertoli.github.io/css-in-js/[22] — this site covers over 60 different libraries that can help you to implement your own **CSS-in-JS** solution.

In the remaining parts of the chapter, I want to focus on **styled components** which is the most popular library with around 23,000 stars on GitHub. In order to use it, we need to first install it via the command line:

```
npm install styled-components
```

```
yarn add styled-components
```

Once installed, we are ready to import it and write our first **styled component**. Using the styled function, we define the HTML element that we want to style. **Template literal** syntax from ES2015 is used to define the CSS for our **styled component.**

In order to create a button which is black and yellow, we would need to write the following:

```
import React from 'react';
import ReactDOM from 'react-dom';
import styled from 'styled-components';

const Button = styled.button `
  background: yellow;
  border: 2px solid black;
  color: black;
  padding: 8px;
```

```
 `;

const App = () => {
  return (
    <div>
      <h1>An example of a styled component </h1>
      <Button>A black and yellow button without any function </Button>
    </div>
  );
};


ReactDOM.render(<App /> , document.getElementById('root'));
```

By using the notation const Button = styled.button **styled components** creates a new Button component and equips it with the CSS properties that we have defined within the **template literals**. Inside of the template literals, regular CSS can be used.

If we want to use pseudo selectors or elements, we can use these without their previous selector. For a :hover status, we can define the following:

```
const Button = styled.button `
  background: yellow;
  border: 2px solid black;
  color: black;
  padding: 8px;

  :hover {
    background: gold;
  }
`;
```

Props can also be accessed in **styled components**. By calling a function within the template string, all **props** of the element can be passed as the first parameter:

```
const Button = styled.button `
  background: yellow;
  border: 2px solid black;
  color: black;
  cursor: ${(props) => (props.disabled ?   'not-allowed' :   'pointer' )};
  padding: 8px;

  :hover {
    background: gold;
  }
`;
```

The cursor icon would change into a `not-allowed` symbol if the button had a `disabled` property. Moreover, **styled components** offers support for theming, server-side rendering, css animations and much more. For those of you who would like an in-depth explanation and overview, I suggest you check out the <u>thorough documentation</u>[23].

The main advantages of **CSS-in-JS** and **styled components** in particular are well summarized in the documentation:

- Critical CSS (meaning the CSS which is relevant for the current page) is automatically generated as **styled components** knows which components are used on each page and which styles they need
- By automatically generating classnames, the risk of conflicts is reduced to a minimum
- As all CSS is tied to a component, it is easy to spot redundant CSS. If a **styled component** is no longer used in the application, the CSS is no longer needed either and the component can be safely deleted.
- Component logic and component styling (CSS-in-JS) are found in the same spot, sometimes even in the exact same file. Developers do not need to spend a long amount of time anymore to find where exactly a styling change needs to take place.
- **Styled components** automatically generates CSS that contains vendor prefixes for all browsers.

Styled components is only one of many CSS-in-JS solutions. While it is probably the most well-known and most widely adopted, there are a number of great alternatives which can help you to find a solution which fits your project's specific needs. Other great and well-known alternatives are:

- <u>emotion</u>[24]
- <u>styled-jsx</u>[25]
- <u>react-jss</u>[26]
- <u>radium</u>[27]
- <u>linaria</u>[28]

III – Advanced Concepts

Higher Order Components

Higher Order Components (or **HOC** or **HOCs** for short) were, and still are, a central concept in React. They allow you to implement components with reusable logic and are loosely tied to **Higher Order Functions** from functional programming. These kind of functions take a function as a parameter and return another function. In terms of React, this principle is applied to components. **Higher Order Components** derive their name from those **Higher Order Functions**.

Let us look at an example to illustrate this concept better:

```
const withFormatting = (WrappedComponent) => {
  return class extends React.Component {
    bold = (string) => {
      return <strong>{string}</strong> ;
    };
    italic = (string) => {
      return <em>{string}</em> ;
    };
    render() {
      return <WrappedComponent bold={this.bold} italic={this.italic} /> ;
    }
  };
};
```

We have defined a function called `withFormatting` that takes in a React component. The function will return a new React component which in turn renders the component that was passed into the function and equips it with the props `bold` and `italic`. The component can now access these props:

```
const FormattedComponent = withFormatting(({ bold, italic }) => (
  <div>
    This text is {bold('bold')} and {italic('italic')}.
  </div>
));
```

Typically, **Higher Order Components** can be used to encapsulate logic. They relate closely to the concept of **smart** and **dumb** components. Smart components (which also encompass **Higher Order Components**) are used to display business logic, deal with API communication or behavioral logic. *Dumb components* in contrast mostly get passed static props and keep logic to a minimum (which is only used to for display-logic). For example, it might decide whether to show a profile image or, if it is not present, show a placeholder image instead. Sometimes, we also refer to **Container Components** (for *Smart* components) and **Layout Components** (for *Dumb* components).

But why do we categorize components this way? This strict divide into business logic and display logic enables component based development. It allows us to create layout components which do not know of possible API connections and only display data which is passed to them, no matter where it comes from. It also enables the business logic components to only concern themselves with business logic without caring about how the data is displayed in the end.

Assume we want to switch between a **list** and **map** view in a user interface. A **container component** will be in charge of gathering the data which is needed for the user and will pass them to the configurable **layout component**. As long as both components keep to the interface the developer has set up (think **PropTypes**), both components are easily interchangeable and can be tested and developed independently.

But enough of the theory. Let's look at an example. We are going to load a list of the 10 biggest cryptocurrencies and their current price. To obtain the data from the Coingecko API, we create a **Higher Order Component** which loads the data and passes it to the layout component:

```
const withCryptoPrices = (WrappedComponent) => {
  return class extends React.Component {
    state = {
      isLoading: true ,
      items: [],
    };

    componentDidMount() {
      this.loadData();
    }

    loadData = async () => {
      this.setState(() => ({
        isLoading: true ,
      }));

      try {
        const cryptoTicker = await fetch(
          'https://api.coingecko.com' +
            '/api/v3/coins/markets?vs_currency=eur&per_page=10'
        );
        const cryptoTickerResponse = await cryptoTicker.json();

        this.setState(() => ({
          isLoading: false,
          items: cryptoTickerResponse,
```

```
          }));
        } catch (err) {
          this.setState(() => ({
            isLoading: false,
          }));
        }
      };

      render() {
        const { isLoading, items } =  this.state;
        return (
          <WrappedComponent
            isLoading ={isLoading}
            items= {items}
            loadData= {this.loadData}
          />
        );
      }
    };
  };
```

Et voila! We have written an **HOC** to obtain the data of the crypto prices from coingecko.com. But the **Higher Order Component** itself is not enough to make this work: we also need to define a layout component to which we delegate the task of displaying the data.

In order to do that, we define a generic `PriceTable` component which does not know about which data exactly it displays: it could be current yoghurt prices from the local supermarket or cryptocurrency prices from a stock market. Thus, we have given it a very generic name, `PriceTable`:

```
const PriceTable = ({ isLoading, items, loadData }) => {
  if (isLoading) {
    return <p>Prices are being loaded. Please wait. </p>;
  }

  if (!items || items.length ===  0) {
    return (
      <p>
        No data available. <button  onClick ={loadData}> Try again!</button>
      </p>
    );
  }

  return (
    <table>
```

```
    {items.map((item) => (
      <tr key={item.id}>
        <td>
          {item.name} ({item.symbol})
        </td>
        <td> EUR {item.current_price}</td>
      </tr>
    ))}
    <tr>
      <td colSpan="2">
        <button onClick={loadData}>Reload</button>
      </td>
    </tr>
  </table>
  );
};
```

This component knows about three props: isLoading, to inform it which data is still being loaded, items, which represents an array of articles with their corresponding prices and loadData, a function which allows us to start another API request to obtain new data.

Both components act independently of one another. The PriceTable is not limited to showing cryptocurrency prices, and the withCryptoPrices component does not necessarily need to display its data in a PriceTable component. We managed to write two completely encapsulated and reusable components.

But how do we combine these two components now? We can simply pass the PriceTable component as a parameter to the withCryptoPrices HOC component. This will look like this:

```
const CryptoPriceTable = withCryptoPrices(PriceTable);
```

Whenever an instance of the CryptoPriceTable is rendered, the **Higher Order Component** will trigger an API request in the componentDidMount() lifecycle method and pass its result to the PriceTable component. The PriceTable then only needs to concern itself with displaying the data:

```
ReactDOM.render(<CryptoPriceTable /> , document.getElementById('root'));
```

This opens up a number of opportunities for us. First of all, both components are able to be independently tested. I will provide a bit more information in a later chapter about how exactly we can test layout components with snapshot testing.

We also have the opportunity to combine other layout components with the withCryptoPrices HOC. To illustrate this, we are going to display the prices in CSV format.

Our HOC will remain the same whereas the layout component can be implemented as such:

```
const PriceCSV = ({ isLoading, items, loadData, separator =   ';' }) => {
  if (isLoading) {
    return <p>Prices are loaded, please wait. </p>;
  }

  if (!items || items.length ===  0) {
    return (
      <p>
        No data available   <button onClick={loadData}> Try again </button>
      </p>
    );
  }

  return (
    <pre>
      {items.map(
        ({ name, symbol, current_price }) =>
          `${name}${separator}${symbol}${separator}${current_price}\n`
      )}
    </pre>
  );
};
```

And just like that we have implemented our very first own CSV layout component. We check again whether the data is being loaded, then whether items are present. This could also be extracted into another HOC component as HOCs can be nested as many times as you like. In the end, they are all just functions which are passed as parameters to yet another function.

At last, we can render the output: we iterate through the list of items, pick the relevant properties name, symbol and current_price via **Object Destructuring** and then wrap the individual lines with a pre element to correctly display the end of the line.

In contrast to the PriceTable component, we have introduced another optional prop: separator - to tell the render component how many separating symbols it should use to display the data. This separator prop can be passed as a simple prop (as is common in JSX):

```
const CryptoCSV = withCryptoPrices(PriceCSV);

ReactDOM.render(<CryptoCSV  separator="," />, document.getElementById('root'));
```

However, by introducing this change in the CSV component, another change needs to made in the withCryptoPrices HOC. So far only the isLoading, items and loadData props are passed to the child component (WrappedComponent):

```
return (
  <WrappedComponent
    isLoading ={isLoading}
    items= {items}
    loadData= {this.loadData}
  />
);
```

In order to pass the separator prop which was defined in `<CryptoCSV separator="," />` correctly to the `PriceCSV` component, we need to inform the **HOC** to also pass other remaining props to the `WrappedComponent` . You can either choose to explicitly pass other props or to only pass the **remaining** ones:

```
return (
  <WrappedComponent
    {...this.props}
    isLoading ={isLoading}
    items= {items}
    loadData= {this.loadData}
  />
);
```

`{...this.props}`can be used to pass the remaining props to the child component using Spread Syntax from ES2015+.

> ⓘ **Higher Order Components** are a great way to "centralize" logic and structure applications better. Logic can be easily extracted from layout components which would further complicate such components. Even though they have been a fairly new concept in React, the concept itself is a very old one.
>
> **Higher Order Components** are still widely used and there's nothing controversial about their usage. However, newer concepts to achieve the same or similar objectives have been introduced, of which many increase readability. These are **Functions as a Child**; the newer **Context API** which has been introduced in React in Version 16.3.0; and **Hooks** – which can be used inside of Function Components since 16.8.0. All of these will be explained in detail later.

Functions as a Child and Render Props

Functions as a Child (FaaC for short) and **Render Props** are treated separately in the official React documentation. However, **Functions as Children** are already mentioned in the **Render Props** section hinting at the fact that they are similar — if a little different. Thus, I would like to discuss them both at the same time. But what are they even?

Functions as a Child (also called **Functions as Children**) and **Render Props** are patterns which allow you to bundle business or application logic in some sort of overarching component - similar to a **Higher Order Component**. In contrast to a HOC though, a function is called which is passed the relevant data as a parameter (as opposed to returning a new component which receives data as props). The function takes the form of a child element of the relevant component in the **Function as Children** pattern (so this.props.children). The **Render Props** pattern on the other hand introduces the function as a prop with the name of render (or any other name).

We've learned that the value of a prop in JSX can be any valid JavaScript expression. As invoked functions can also return expressions, we can also use the return value of this function as a prop. Strings, Booleans, Arrays, Objects, other React elements and null can also be passed as props. children are a special form of props, meaning that both of these lines will result in the same output when rendered:

```
<MyComponent>I am a child element</MyComponent>
<MyComponent children="I am a child element" />
```

props.children can be used to access *I am a child element* in MyComponent.

We can use this principle and also pass functions which are invoked during render() within a component. This way, data can be passed from one component into the next. The principle is similar to that of **Higher Order Components**, but offers a little more flexibility. We do not need to connect our component with a Higher Order Component but can simply be included within JSX in our current component. Thinking back to our withFormatting HOC from the previous chapter, a similar approach could look like the following using a **Function as a Child (FaaC)**:

```
const bold = (string) => {
  return <strong>{string}</strong> ;
};

const italic = (string) => {
  return <em>{string}</em> ;
};
```

```
const Formatter = (props) => {
  if (typeof props.children !== 'function') {
    console.warn('children prop must be a function!');
    return null;
  }

  return props.children({ bold, italic });
};
```

We have defined two functions: the `bold` function and the `italic` function. `props.children` can then be called in a formatter function after checking whether the `children` props are actually a function. The function takes in an object with two properties: `bold` with the `bold` function as its value and `italic` with the `italic` function as its value. The invoked function is returned by the component.

Using this **Function as Children** component, a function in JSX is passed to the child element:

```
<div>
  <p>This text does not know about the Formatter function</p>
  <Formatter>{(({ bold }) => <p>This text {bold('does though')}</p>}</Formatter>
</div>
```

This increases flexibility as components no longer need wrapped by a Higher Order Function just to reuse functionality. In contrast to Higher Order Components, it is also possible to pass parameters directly from JSX into a function as a Child component and communicate with it.

Let's look at our second example again which we talked about in the chapter on Higher Order Components. This is what the rendered list of cryptocurrencies looks like as Function as a Child:

```
class CryptoPrices extends React.Component {
  state = {
    isLoading: true ,
    items: [],
  };

  componentDidMount() {
    this.loadData();
  }

  loadData = async () => {
    this.setState(() => ({
      isLoading: true ,
    }));
```

```
    const { limit } = this.props;

    try {
      const cryptoTicker = await fetch(
        `https://api.coingecko.com/api/v3/coins/markets?
vs_currency=eur&per_page= ${limit ||
          10} `
      );
      const cryptoTickerResponse =  await cryptoTicker.json();

      this.setState(() => ({
        isLoading: false,
        items: cryptoTickerResponse,
      }));
    } catch (err) {
      this.setState(() => ({
        isLoading: false,
      }));
    }
  };

  render() {
    const { isLoading, items } =  this.state;
    const { children } =  this.props;

    if (typeof children !== 'function') {
      return null;
    }

    return children({
      isLoading,
      items,
      loadData:  this.loadData,
    });
  }
}
```

At first glance, the example does not look much different to the one we have introduced in the previous chapter using Higher Order Components. But if you pay attention, you will notice some differences:

- No new component is generated and we can work directly with our current component
- The loadData method can access this.props to read the limit prop. This can then be used as a parameter in the API call

- The `render()` method does not return any component that was passed in anymore and calls the `children` function instead which it receives from its own props
- The `children` function receives the `isLoading` state and returns the items.

Using this component is similar to that from our previous example, with the exception that we can also pass an optional `limit` prop in this case:

```
<div>
  <h1>Current Crypto Currency Prices</h1>
  <CryptoPrices limit={5}>
    {({ isLoading, items }) =>
      isLoading ? (
        <p>Loading prices. Please be patient.</p>
      ) : (
        <ul>
          {items.map((item) => (
            <li>
              {item.name} ({item.symbol}): EUR {item.current_price}
            </li>
          ))}
        </ul>
      )
    }
  </CryptoPrices>
</div>
```

We can now combine the `PriceTable` component which expects three props with the `CryptoPrices` component (that returns the values needed in the `PriceTable`).

```
<CryptoPrices limit={ 5}>
  {({ isLoading, items, loadData }) => (
    <PriceTable isLoading={isLoading} items={items} loadData={loadData} />
  )}
</CryptoPrices>
```

Or even more succinct using spread syntax:

```
<CryptoPrices limit={ 5}>{(props) => <PriceTable { ...props} />}</CryptoPrices>
```

We have allowed for a great deal of flexibility in this example and do not explicitly need to tie a component to a HOC to enable logic (which saves us valuable time and effort).

But be careful: **Functions as a Child Components have limitiations that Higher Order Components do not have**. The data that is received by a **FaaC** component can also be used

within JSX. If we wanted to include highly abstract methods in logic components higher up in the component hierarchy, it would not be possible using **FaaCs**.

Render Props

But wait — what are **Render Props** and how to they differ from **Function as Children** components?

Put simply, they differ in the name of the prop. Some popular libraries eventually started using `render` as a name for a prop which expects functions as their values. In our `CryptoPrices` component, we would then use `render` instead of `children`:

```
<CryptoPrices limit={ 5} render={(props) =>  <PriceTable {...props} /> } />
```

Within the `CryptoPrices` component, we can write:

```
render() {
  const { isLoading, items } =  this.state;
  const { render } = this.props;

  if (typeof render !==  "function") {
    return null;
  }

  // Careful: render() does not have anything to do with the component with
  // the same name and gets injected via this.props.render
  return render({
    isLoading,
    items,
    loadData:  this.loadData
  });
}
```

It is personal preference to a degree. You do not need to give this prop the name of `render` and could theoretically choose any valid name. Any passed function will eventually turn the component into a "Render Prop".

It is possible to have an arbitrary number of props in such a component. If you were to implement a component which returns a table which includes a table head and a body, both receiving data from the data component, that would be no problem at all.

159

Render Props and FaaCs in combination with Higher Order Components

Here is a neat little trick: If you ever need a **Higher Order Component** but you only have a **FaaC** or **Render Prop** component, you can turn these into an HOC like this:

```
function withCryptoPrices(WrappedComponent) {
  return class extends React.Component {
    render() {
      return (
        <CryptoPrices>
          {(cryptoPriceProps) => (
            <WrappedComponent {...this.props} { ...cryptoPriceProps} />
          )}
        </CryptoPrices>
      );
    }
  };
}
```

However, you will not need to do this much in practice.

> ⓘ The **Function as a Child** pattern and the **Render-Props** pattern are both used to separate business logic and layout in different components. They are a more lightweight alternative to **Higher Order Components**, which cater to a similar use case.
>
> In contrast to a HOC, they can be easily used within the `render()` method of a component and do not need "linked" with another additional component making them more flexible and readable than **Higher Order Components**.

Context API

For a long time, the React **Context API** has been treated as somewhat of an afterthought. First only implemented as a prototype and treated experimentally, but later added to React in version **16.3**.

The Context API has been designed to distribute data from a component to so-called data *consumers* without explicitly passing props through the whole component tree. This is immensely useful for language settings as well as a global styling schema ("Theme").

The Context API consists of two main actors: The **Context Provider** as well as the **Context Consumer**. The **Provider** acts as a central instance for the corresponding data structure whereas the **Consumer** can *consume* this data at any point in the app. It forms some sort of "semi-global" data instance which is only valid in certain parts of the component hierarchy.

This does not mean that the data structure cannot be complex. It is not limited to strings or arrays but can consist of complex data. An application can have an unlimited amount of Contexts (for example one for the user-chosen language, one for the styling schema etc.) and Providers can be reused with different values. But let's take it one step at a time.

API

In order to create a new **Context**, React provides the `createContext` method:

```
const LanguageContext = React.createContext(defaultValue);
```

We have just created a new **Context** using this line of code. The Context now consists of a **Provider** and a **Consumer** component: `LanguageContext.Provider` as well as `LanguageContext.Consumer` .

The **Context** can now be used in the application by wrapping the contents of the tree within a Provider:

```
// LanguageContext.js
import React from 'react';
const LanguageContext = React.createContext( 'de' );
export default LanguageContext;


// index.js
import React from 'react';
import ReactDOM from 'react-dom';
```

```
import LanguageContext from './LanguageContext';

const App = () => (
  <LanguageContext.Provider   value={'en'}>
    {/* inside of this tree, the value of 'en' is available to other components
*/}
  </LanguageContext.Provider>
);


ReactDOM.render(<App /> , document.getElementById('#root'));
```

The `SelectedLanguage` component can now be used at any point within the application. If the value within the Provider changes, all **Consumer components** encompassed within the Provider will render again using the updated value.

A complete if a little artificial example is this:

```
import React from 'react';
import ReactDOM from 'react-dom';
import LanguageContext from './LanguageContext';
import DisplaySelectedLanguage from './DisplaySelectedLanguage';

const App = () => (
  <LanguageContext.Provider value="en">
    <header>Welcome!</header>
    <div className="content">
      <div className="sidebar" />
      <div className="mainContent">
        <DisplaySelectedLanguage />
      </div>
    </div>
    <footer>© 2019</footer>
  </LanguageContext.Provider>
);

ReactDOM.render(<App />, document.getElementById('#root'));
```

Although no **props** have been passed to the `DisplaySelectedLanguage` component, it still has knowledge of the currently selected language and will also demonstrate this accurately:

```
<p>The chosen language is en</p>
```

If the `value` within the Provider component changes, all Consumer components will re-render — if they are located within the current Provider's Context.

If we extend the example a little bit, we can easily add a little more structure to make a simple multilingual service.

The following example contains an object with translations to which we pass a rather complex object with multiple data types (consisting of an array, a string, a function to change the language as well as object with the original translations):

```jsx
import React from 'react';
import ReactDOM from 'react-dom';

const translationStore = {
  de: {
    greeting: 'Guten Tag!' ,
    headline: 'Heute lernen wir, wie Context funktioniert.'   ,
  },
  en: {
    greeting: 'Hello!',
    headline: 'Today we will learn how Context works.'   ,
  },
};


const defaultLanguage = 'de' ;

const defaultLanguageContextValue = {
  availableLanguages: Object .keys(translationStore),
  changeLanguage: () => {
    console .warn( 'Funktion changeLanguage() nicht implementiert!'  );
  },
  language: defaultLanguage,
  translations: translationStore[defaultLanguage],
};


const LanguageContext = React.createContext(defaultLanguageContextValue);

class Localized extends React. Component {
  changeLanguage = (newLanguage) => {
    this.setState((state) => ({
      translations: translationStore[newLanguage],
      language: newLanguage,
    }));
  };

  state = {
    ...defaultLanguageContextValue,
    changeLanguage: this.changeLanguage,
  };
```

```
    render() {
        return (
            <LanguageContext.Provider value={this.state}>
                {this.props.children}
            </LanguageContext.Provider>
        );
    }
}

const Greeting = () => (
    <LanguageContext.Consumer>
        {(contextValue) => contextValue.translations.greeting}
    </LanguageContext.Consumer>
);

const Headline = () => (
    <LanguageContext.Consumer>
        {(contextValue) => contextValue.translations.headline}
    </LanguageContext.Consumer>
);

const LanguageSelector = () => {
    return (
        <LanguageContext.Consumer>
            {(contextValue) => (
                <select
                    onChange={(event) => {
                        contextValue.changeLanguage(event.target.value);
                    }}
                >
                    {contextValue.availableLanguages.map((language) => (
                        <option value={language}>{language}</option>
                    ))}
                </select>
            )}
        </LanguageContext.Consumer>
    );
};

const App = () => (
    <Localized>
        <LanguageSelector />
        <p>
            <Greeting />
        </p>
```

```
      <p>
        <Headline />
      </p>
    </Localized>
  );
```

```
ReactDOM.render(<App />, document.getElementById('root'));
```

First of all, we define an object `defaultLanguageContextValue` which holds the default value of the newly generated Context object. This consists of:

- an object called `translationStore` which contains all available translations
- a standard language — German in this case (`de`) which is saved to a property called `language`
- an array named `availableLanguages` that lists all available languages of the `translationStore` object which we dynamically generate with `Object.keys()` — in our case: `["de", "en"]`
- a placeholder function (`changeLanguage()`) which is later replaced with an actual implementation in the `Localized` component. This helps us to avoid the case of incorrectly calling a function which is not yet implemented. Otherwise the warning: *"Function changeLanguage() is not implemented".*

The `changeLanguage()` function can only be implemented in the component itself as React cannot control the state (in this case languages and their translations) anywhere else other than **inside of a component**. We could save the current language settings inside of a global variable, however React would not re-render the component if something changed in this global variable as this value would neither be state nor props.

The `Localized` component serves as a wrapper component for our newly generated Context. We can save and modify the user's selected language here by changing the state accordingly. The `defaultLanguageContextValue` object is saved in the state of the component and the `changeLanguage()` method is also implemented here. This function receives a language (de or en) and modifies the state accordingly, and then it fetches the translations for the chosen language from the `translationStore` object and writes it to the state as new `translations`. If the user changes their language setting from German (default) to English, the function overrides all German translations currently in state with the English translations. By calling `this.setState()` a re-render is triggered and all Context Consumers within the component tree will be rendered with the updated value (which we pass to the Context Provider through the render() method in the component).

If this all sounds a little complicated so far, do not worry, it will become more intuitive once it is used in practice. I strongly advise you to try the above example yourself and play with the code.

However, there is a little gotcha in the above example: usually the state of a class component is defined first and only then properties and methods of this class will follow. In this example however, we did not follow this convention and implemented the changeLanguage() method first. Why? By defining changeLanguage() first, we ensure that this.changeLanguage will not be undefined. Only then, we construct the state property of our class.

The code snippet is still relatively complex — and unnecessarily complicated — too. We built our own component for both the headline and the greeting, to provide it with access to a Context Consumer which has access to the object containing the translations. However, we can optimize the code by constructing a generic component with which we can directly access the translations in the translations object. This component will be called Translated and receives a single prop: the property which we want to access in the translations object. In our example, this could either be greeting or headline.

```
const Translated = ({ translationKey }) => (
  <LanguageContext.Consumer>
    {(contextValue) => contextValue.translations[translationKey]}
  </LanguageContext.Consumer>
);
```

Our App component will now look like this:

```
const App = () => (
  <Localized>
    <LanguageSelector />
    <p>
      <Translated translationKey="greeting" />
    </p>
    <p>
      <Translated translationKey="headline" />
    </p>
  </Localized>
);
```

We can then safely eliminate the Headline and Greeting component from our example.

Attention: Especially when dealing with translations, it is not uncommon to denote the key for the translations with "key" . This would surely be a nice addition for our Translated component:

```
<Translated key="greeting" />
```

But key is a reserved word in React is used to identify elements in arrays and we can therefore not use it in this case. If you want to freshen up your knowledge about these, please refer to the chapter "Lists, Refs, Fragments and Conditional Rendering" in the "Basics" section and check in the section on "Lists".

Usage of Multiple Contexts

It is entirely possible to use multiple Context Providers within the same component hierarchy. Nesting them is not a problem. Even Providers of the same Context type can be nested inside of each other. The Context value of the *above* Provider is given to the Consumer components:

```
<MyContext.Provider value= "1">
  <MyContext.Provider value="2">
    <MyContext.Consumer>
      {(value) => <p>The value is {value}</p>}
    </MyContext.Consumer>
  </MyContext.Provider>
</MyContext.Provider>
```

The above example is completely valid. The output would be the following:

```
<p>The value is 2</p>
```

The **Consumer component** gets its data from the most adjacent **Context Provider** which is the one passing the value of "2".

Although it does not make sense to nest the *same* **Context Providers** within each other, it is not uncommon or incorrect to use *different* **Context Providers** within each other. An application can consist of a Theme Provider, a Language Provider and an Account Provider. The latter would take care of data handling for logged in users and manage access tokens or user-specific settings.

Abbreviation: contextType

While using Class components, we can employ a trick which allows us to avoid building another Consumer component bloating our component tree further.

In order to do this, we can use `contextType`: it can be assigned to a class component in the form of a static property. The Context value can then be accessed within the component via `this.context`. The value of the `contextType` property is created by `React.createContext()` which you need to call beforehand.

But be careful: It is only possible to assign **a single Context type** to a class. If we want to access two or more Contexts, we have to wrap the respective JSX in a Consumer component.

By using *Public Class Fields Syntax* from ES2015+, it is sufficient to define a static class property `contextType` and to assign it a Context.

If applied to our previous `Translated` component, the result would be:

```
class Translated extends React.Component {
  static contextType = LanguageContext;
  render() {
    return this.context.translations[ this.props.translationKey];
  }
}
```

The value of the current LanguageContext is assigned to the static `contextType` property of the component (which is no longer a Function component but a Class component). Its value can be read by accessing `this.context`.

Without using Public Class Fields Syntax (which I strongly encouraged in the previous chapters), the above code would look like the following:

```
class Translated extends React.Component {
  render() {
    return this.context.translations[ this.props.translationKey];
  }
}

Translated.contextType = LanguageContext;
```

The `contextType` would be defined outside of the component and no longer inside of it. In the end, it all boils down to personal taste, and does not have any real implications. We are only using another form of syntax which is only allowed in later versions of ECMAScript or provided by Babel via transpiling (by using the babel plugin `@babel/plugin-proposal-class-properties`).

Performance Gotchas

React massively optimizes **Context** under the hood in order to avoid unnecessary re-renders of components or avoid lengthy component hierarchies. Comparing the old value of the Context Provider with the new one, **Consumer components** are only re-rendered if the value in the **Context Provider** has actually changed.

While this sounds easy for a change, it does create a little gotcha which we need to look out for. It concerns the Context Provider whose value is recreated on-the-fly if we use it within the render() method. It is recommended to create the value of the Context outside of the render() method and pass a **reference** to the value instead of a **newly created value**.

Here is an example which you should NOT recreate:

```
class App extends React.Component {
  state = {
    color: 'red',
  };

  render() {
    return (
      <Provider value={{ color: this.state.color }}>
        <MoreComponents />
      </Provider>
    );
  }
}
```

We are creating a new object {color: this.state.color} with each call of the render() method. As React only checks if the reference of the value in the current render() is the same as the reference in the previous render() call (which is never the case as a new object is created on the fly each time), all Consumer components would re-render.

However, we can transform the above example to avoid this situation and make sure that React's performance algorithm can get to work:

```
class App extends React.Component {
  state = {
    color: 'red',
  };

  render() {
    return (
      <Provider value={this.state} >
        <MoreComponents />
      </Provider>
    );
  }
}
```

In this example, we are merely passing a *reference* to the state object of the component. As this remains intact during the re-renders of the component, it does not trigger a re-render if the content of the state did not change.

Refs

Refs allow us to directly access DOM elements that were created during the render process. Even if this is not necessary in most cases, it can be useful in handful of situations in which it is hard not to revert to using them. Examples are calculating the position or size of an element in order to display a tooltip based on them or to focus on a form field using `.focus()` once the component has loaded.

React has evolved over the years and so have the methods dealing with **Refs**. But they all have one thing in common. Refs are always defined by the `ref` prop of a DOM element in JSX, or to be more precise `createElement()`.

But a word of warning before we proceed. Even though **Refs** exist, they should be used sparingly and only if the declarative way of re-rendering components with updated state and props does not help us. Manipulation of attributes or attribute values or adding or removing classes, event listeners or changing properties like `aria-hidden` should always happen **declaratively** using props, state, JSX and re-rendering.

However, there are a few cases in which using Refs is acceptable or even necessary. These are:

- Setting focus on an input element (`input.focus()`) or calling methods such as `.play()` or `.pause()` on `video` or `audio` elements
- Invoking imperative animations
- Reading properties of elements currently in the DOM (e.g. `.getBoundingClientRect()`)

String Refs

The simplest and oldest form of refs are **string refs**. Nowadays, it is not recommended to use them anymore as they can impact performance and might be deprecated in the future. I wanted to mention them for the sake of completeness though as they are currently still part of the official API and as you might come across them during your work with React (especially if you are working with legacy code).

In order to define a **string ref**, you pass prop named `ref` to a DOM element and pass a value to that prop in **string** form. The corresponding DOM element is now accessible to us using the instance method `this.ref` **inside of the component**.

```
import React from 'react';
import ReactDOM from 'react-dom';

class ComponentWithStringRef extends React.Component {
```

170

```
  componentDidMount() {
    this.refs.username.focus();
  }

  render() {
    return <input type="text" ref="username" name="username" />;
  }
}

ReactDOM.render(<ComponentWithStringRef />, document.getElementById('app'));
```

We can use this.refs.username to gain access to the input field, and then focus it by calling this.refs.username.focus() .

Callback Refs

A more flexible alternative to **string refs** are the so-called **callback refs**. While being more flexible, their handling is slightly more cumbersome and needs to be managed explicitly. Using **callback refs**, it is possible to pass refs to a component's **child components** and access their corresponding DOM elements.

As the name might suggest, **callback refs** are declared using **callback form**. During **Mounting**, they only receive a single parameter: the DOM element or, if applied to a React component, its instance. We call the callback again during **Unmounting** but with null as a single parameter.

How you are using callback refs specifically is up to you, however it is a convention to save the reference to the DOM element as an instance property to be able to access it from anywhere inside the component.

Applying this to the above example, we end up with the following code:

```
import React from 'react';
import ReactDOM from 'react-dom';

class ComponentWithCallbackRef extends React.Component {
  usernameEl = null;

  componentDidMount() {
    this.usernameEl.focus();
  }

  setUsernameEl = (el) => {
    this.usernameEl = el;
  };
```

```
  render() {
    return <input type="text" ref={this.setUsernameEl}  name="username" /> ;
  }
}


ReactDOM.render(<ComponentWithCallbackRef />  , document.getElementById('app'));
```

Callback refs can also be used in child components and the **refs** can then also be accessed in their parent components. In order to do this, you pass the callback function of the child component a prop which is not allowed to be called `ref` (as this is a reserved word):

```
import React from 'react';
import ReactDOM from 'react-dom';

class UsernameInput extends React.Component {
  render() {
    return <input type="text" name="username" ref={this.props.inputRef} />;
  }
}


class ComponentWithRefChild extends React.Component {
  componentDidMount() {
    this.usernameEl.focus();
  }

  usernameEl = null;

  setUsernameRef = (el) => {
    this.usernameEl = el;
  };

  render() {
    return (
      <div>
        Username:
        <UsernameInput inputRef={this.setUsernameRef} />
      </div>
    );
  }
}


ReactDOM.render(<ComponentWithRefChild />, document.getElementById('app'));
```

If you were to name the prop ref, leaving us with `<UsernameInput ref={this.setUsernameRef} />` , you would end up with a reference to the UsernameInput

instance instead of its input element. If we used a **Function component**, `UsernameInput` would have been `null` as Function components cannot be instantiated.

However, if forwarding refs to child components is something you are trying to achieve, you are better off using the `forwardRef()` method. I will explain it at the end of this chapter.

Refs via createRef()

With React 16.3, we have seen the introduction of the top-level API method `React.createRef()`. It resembles the usage of **callback refs** but differs in a few cases. As was the case with **callback refs**, you also need to take care of ref handling yourself and it is still common practice to assign the **ref** to an **instance property**.

Instead of passing an almost identical method in the form of `(el) => { this.property = el }` each time, the reference is already created during the instantiation of the component which is then given to the `ref` prop of the element.

```
import React from 'react';
import ReactDOM from 'react-dom';

class ComponentWithCreatedRef extends React.Component {
  usernameEl = React.createRef();

  componentDidMount() {
    this.usernameEl.current.focus();
  }

  render() {
    return <input type="text" name="username" ref={this.usernameEl} />;
  }
}

ReactDOM.render(<ComponentWithCreatedRef /> , document.getElementById('app'));
```

While this looks very similar to **callback refs**, there is an apparent difference: you access the reference via `this.usernameEl.current` .

The reference to the element is not saved in the instance property which you assign the ref to, but in its `.current()` property. Apart from this, the behavior of `createRef()` is similar to that of callback refs. They can still be passed to child components via props and the DOM element can be accessed in the parent component.

To have a direct comparison — this was the use case with **callback refs**:

```
class MyComponent extends React.Component {
  usernameEl = null;

  render() {
    return (
      <input
        ref={(el) => {
          this.usernameEl = el;
        }}
      />
    );
  }
}
```

And this is the reference created with React.createRef() :

```
class MyComponent extends React.Component {
  usernameEl = React.createRef();

  render() {
    return <input ref={this.usernameEl} />;
  }
}
```

We are accessing the element via this.usernameEl.current .

Ref forwarding

Ref forwarding (references to a component or a DOM element) enables passing a reference through a component to a child component. In most cases, this will not be necessary but it can become of interest if you are creating reusable component libraries.

A **ref** is forwarded via React.forwardRef() and is passed a function as a parameter during this process. The ref itself passes props as well as the **ref** to it.

This sounds incredibly cumbersome, so let us look at an example instead. Let us first implement an Input component without a forwardRef:

```
import React from 'react';
import ReactDOM from 'react-dom';

const UsernameField = (props) => (
  <div className="myInput">
    <input ref={props.ref} {...props} />
  </div>
```

```
);

class App extends React.Component {
  usernameEl = React.createRef();

  componentDidMount() {
    console.log(this.usernameEl);
  }

  render() {
    return (
      <div className="App">
        <UsernameField ref={this.usernameEl} />
      </div>
    );
  }
}

ReactDOM.render(<App />, document.getElementById('root'));
```

In this case, `componentDidMount()` does not have access to our input field from the `UsernameField` component. Instead, the instance of the component would actually be the **ref** itself. As `UsernameField` is a **Function component**, we do not even have an instance of the component. The associatedconsole.log result would be: `{ current: null }` - not exactly ideal if we want to gain access to the input element in order to focus on it.

It is sufficient in this case to wrap the `UsernameField` component with a `React.forwardRef()` call. We can now amend the code of the `UsernameField` in the above example:

```
const UsernameField = React.forwardRef((props, ref) => (
  <div className ="myInput" >
    <input ref={ref} {...props} />
  </div>
));
```

We have thus informed React that it should forward the `ref` prop on the `UsernameField` in our App component to the component. It is passed the **ref** as a second parameter of the function and can pass this ref to any other element in the DOM or to another component.

If the **ref** is passed to a component lower in the component tree, the same restrictions apply: The relevant component either has to be a class component (then the reference would point to the instance of the class) or the component needs to conduct ref forwarding via `forwardRef()`.

Be careful with Higher Order Components!

Careful consideration and care needs to be taken with **refs** while implementing **Higher Order Components**. If there is doubt whether these HOC should be able to access forwarded Refs, they also need to be wrapped by a `forwardRef()` call.

Let's extend our example from above and assume that we want to create a **HOC** to show all of our form elements in a unified layout. Thus, a **HOC** `withInputStyles` is created which can wrap input elements in which it is possible to assign them a ref.

This procedure is a little complicated and I have found it a little complicated to explain this properly in written form without confusing the reader further. Instead, I invite you to inspect the following code closely and read its associated comments. As soon as the idea of **Higher Order Components** and **forwardRefs** begins to make sense, the example should be sufficient to understand the actual explanation. And if it is not clear from the get go: this case is so incredibly rare that you will not need it much in practice.

So let's look at the example of **forwardRef** and **Higher Order Components**:

```
import React from 'react';
import ReactDOM from 'react-dom';

const withInputStyles = (InputComponent) => {
  class WithInputStyles extends React.Component {
    render() {
      // We access the forwarded Ref in the props of the component
      const { forwardedRef, ...props } =  this.props;

      // ... and use it as the ref for the component wrapped by the HOC
      return (
        <InputComponent
          {...props}
          ref={forwardedRef}
          style={{ border: '2px solid black', padding: 8 }}
        />
      );
    }
  }

  // We return a forwardRef from the HOC
  return React.forwardRef((props, ref) => (
    // We pass the ref as the temporary prop "forwardRef"
    <WithInputStyles {...props} forwardedRef={ref} />
  ));
};
```

```
// Here, we pass the ref of our component to a regular React.forwardRef() call
const UsernameField = React.forwardRef((props, ref) => (
  <input ref={ref} {...props} />
));

// Here, we connect the HOC to the UsernameField component
const StyledUsername = withInputStyles(UsernameField);

class App extends React.Component {
  // Here we are creating the Ref as we usually do and to access it later
  usernameEl = React.createRef();

  componentDidMount() {
    this.usernameEl.current.focus();
  }

  render() {
    return (
      <div>
        <StyledUsername ref={this.usernameEl} />
      </div>
    );
  }
}
```

Error Boundaries

Whenever an error occurs and an exception is thrown in a React application, there is a strong possibility that the application display no longer works and that the user will only see a blank page. To avoid this behavior, React introduced so-called **Error Boundaries** in version 16.0.

An **Error Boundary** describes a component which can catch certain errors **in its children** and can also render an alternative component tree to protect users from experiencing a blank page. Error Boundaries always serve as a parent component of a component tree. If an exception is thrown in the component tree, the Error Boundary can intercept and handle the error. Try and think of error boundaries as a special form of a `try` / `catch` block for component hierarchies.

They can deal with mistakes that result from the handling of the following situations:

- Errors in **lifecycle methods**
- Errors in the `render()` method anywhere **inside** the Error Boundary
- Errors in the `constructor()` of a component

If React encounters an error in a lifecycle method, the `render()` method or in the constructor of a component, the Error Boundary can safely prevent it. It can display a fallback that can prompt the user to restart their application or inform them that something has gone wrong. Similar to Context components, Error Boundaries can be nested inside each other. If an error occurs, the implementation of the higher Error Boundary component takes precedence.

 Attention: Error Boundaries' primary goal is to prevent and deal with errors in the handling of user interfaces which would otherwise prevent further rendering of the application status. If you think about implementing form validation with Error Boundaries, please refrain from doing so as Error Boundaries were not intended for this use case and should not be used for that matter.

There are certain situations in which Error Boundaries do not work:

- in event handlers
- in asynchronous code (like `setTimeOut()` or `requestAnimationFrame()`)
- in server-side rendered components (SSR)
- in errors which occur in the **Error Boundary** itself

Error Boundaries will not work in these situations as it is either not necessary or not possible for them to deal with the problem at hand. If an event-handler throws an error, this might not necessarily impact its render and React can continue to show a working interface to the user. The only repercussion would be the missing interaction based on said event.

Implementing an Error Boundary

There are two simple rules when it comes to implementing an **Error Boundary**:

1. Only Class components can be turned into an **Error Boundary**
2. The class has to implement the static `getDerivedStateFromError()` method or the class method `componentDidCatch()` (or both of them)

Strictly speaking, we are already dealing with an **Error Boundary** from a technical point of view if one or both of the methods mentioned above have been implemented. All other rules that apply to regular Class components also apply to **Error Boundaries**.

Let's look at an implementation of an **Error Boundary**:

```
class ErrorBoundary extends React.Component {
  state = {
    hasError: false,
  };

  static getDerivedStateFromError(error) {
    return {
      hasError: true ,
      error,
    };
  }

  componentDidCatch(error, info) {
    console.log(error, info);
  }

  render() {
    if (this.state.hasError) {
      return <h1>An error has occured. </h1>;
    }

    return this.props.children;
  }
}
```

First of all, we define a new component. We have named this component `ErrorBoundary` but it is possible to give it any other name too. You can freely choose the name of the **Error Boundary** and only need to adhere to React's component naming conventions: components need to start with a capital letter and be a valid JavaScript function name.

For matters of simplicity and readability, I would urge you to choose clear and identifiable component names such as `AppErrorBoundary` or `DataTableErrorFallback` . This will allow other team members in your project to see which components are used to deal with errors at a glance.

In the above example we have set up state with a property of `hasError` and provided an initial value of `false` as errors usually do not occur during initialization.

Next, let's look at the static `getDerivedStateFromError()` method. Using this method, React is informed that the component in use is supposed to act as an **Error Boundary** and should come into effect if an error occurs in its children. The method itself is passed an `error` object which is the same as the object which is also passed to the `catch` block of the `try` / `catch` statement.

`getDerivedStateFromError()` works very similar to the `getDerivedStateFromProps()` method we have already encountered in the chapter on lifecycle methods. It can return a new object and thus create new state or leave all as is by returning `null`. In the above example, we have set the `hasError` property to `true` and also save the `error` object in our state. As the method itself is static though, it cannot access other methods in the component.

This method is called during the `render()` phase of a component when React compares the current component tree with its previous version and just before the changes are committed to the DOM.

The `componentDidCatch()` method has also been implemented. It receives an error object as its first parameter and React-specific information as its second. This information contains the *"Component Stack"* — crucial information which allows us to trace in which components we have encountered errors and more specifically how which children and children of children were involved. It will display the component tree up until an error will occur. If you want to use an external service to log these errors, this method is a good place to deal with side effects. `componentDidCatch()` is run during the *Commit* phase meaning just after React has displayed changes from state in the DOM.

As `componentDidCatch()` is not a static method, it would be entirely possible to modify its state via `this.setState()` . However, the React Team plans to prohibit this usage in the future which is why I do not recommend it at this point. It is safer to use the static `getDerivedStateFromError()` method instead to create a new state and react to errors once they have occurred.

Finally, we react to possible errors in the `render()` method. If the `hasError` property in state is set to `true`, we know that an error has occurred and can thus display a warning such as `<h1>An error occured.</h1>` . If on the other hand everything works as expected, we simply return `this.props.children` . How exactly the errors encountered are dealt with is up to the developer. For example, it might be sufficient to inform the user that certain information cannot be displayed at the moment if the error is only small. If however serious errors have been encountered, we should prompt the user to reload the application.

Error Boundaries in practice

We now know how to implement an **Error Boundary**: by adding either static `getDerivedStateFromError()` or `componentDidCatch()` to your components. **Error Boundaries** should not implement their own logic, should not be too tightly coupled to other components and be as independent as possible. It is at the developer's discretion to decide how granular the **Error Boundary** should be according to the specific use case.

It's a good idea to implement different and nested **Error Boundaries** to cater to a variety of errors: one Error Boundary that wraps around the whole application, as well as one that wraps only optional components in the component tree. Let's look at another example:

```
import React from 'react';
import ReactDOM from 'react-dom';

const App = () => {
  return (
    <ErrorBoundary>
      <ApplicationLogic />
      <ServiceUnavailableBoundary>
        <WeatherWidget />
      </ServiceUnavailableBoundary>
    </ErrorBoundary>
  );
};

ReactDOM.render(<App /> , document.querySelector('#root'));
```

Two **Error Boundaries** are used in the above example: `ErrorBoundary` and `ServiceUnavailableBoundary` . While the outer boundary will catch errors that might occur in the `ApplicationLogic` component, the `ServiceUnavailableBoundary` could catch errors in the weather widget and display a more granular error message like *"the service requested cannot be reached at the moment. Please try again later".*

If the `WeatherWidget` component throws an error, the `ServiceUnavailableBoundary` will catch it and everything that is currently used in the `ApplicationLogic` component will remain intact. If we did not include the `WeatherWidget` in its own **Error Boundary**, the outer **Error Boundary** would be used instead and the `ApplicationLogic` component would not be shown.

Generally, it is good practice to have at least one **Error Boundary** as high up as possible in the component hierarchy. This will catch most unexpected errors like a `500 Internal Server Error` page would do and can also log them. If needed, further **Error Boundaries** should be added to encompass useful logic in further component trees. This depends entirely on how error prone a specific area of the tree is (due to unknown or changing data) or if a specific area of the tree has been neglected.

> Since React version 16, components will be "unmounted" and removed from the tree if a serious error occurred or an exception was thrown. This is important as it ensures that the user interface does not suddenly stop working or returns incorrect data. It is especially critical to ensure if we were to work with online banking data. Imagine the consequences if we were to incorrectly send money to the wrong recipient or transfer an incorrect amount.
>
> In order to deal with these errors and risks properly, **Error Boundaries** were introduced. They allow developers to inform users that the application is currently in an erroneous state. As errors and mistakes can never be fully avoided in an application, using **Error Boundaries** is highly recommended.

Portals

Portals allow us to render components in DOM nodes which are *outside* of the parent-node of the current component hierarchy but still have access to the current component environment. A common example (but of course not the only one) is an overlay which is rendered in its own `<div>` outside of the actual application.

The portal remains in the context of the component that has created it and thus has access to all data that is also available to the parent component such as its props and state. However, they are placed in entirely different locations in the rendered HTML compared to the rest of the application. Being able to access props and state is crucial for **Portals**, as they allow us to access common context such as translations.

Creating portals

Creating a portal is relatively simple compared to other concepts we have learned about so far. The component intended to use the portal has to call the `createPortal()` method from ReactDOM and pass in a valid component as the *first* and an existing destination node as the *second* parameter.

The following example shows a common HTML snippet using portals:

```
<!doctype html>
<html>
<head>
<title>Portals in React</title>
</head>
<body>
<div id="root"><!-- this is where our React App is located --></div>
<div id="portal"><!-- this is where the content of the portal will be stored -->
</div>
</body>
</html>
```

While this snippet shows the corresponding React App:

```
import React from 'react';
import ReactDOM from 'react-dom';

const App = () => {
  return (
    <div>
```

183

```
        <h1>Portals in React</h1>
      </div>
    );
};


ReactDOM.render(<App /> , document.querySelector('#root'));
```

As our `<App />` is placed into the `div` with the id of `root`, the `<body>` of the app would now result in this HTML snippet:

```
<body>
  <div id="root" >
    <div>
       <h1>Portals in React</h1>
    </div>
  </div>
  <div id="portal"> <!-- this is where the content of the portal will be stored -->
</div>
</body>
```

Each additional component or each additional HTML element which is used in the JSX of our App component would end up in the `div` with the `id="root"`. If we are dealing with a **Portal** however, the code would resemble the following:

```
import React from 'react';
import ReactDOM from 'react-dom';


const PortalExample = () => {
  return ReactDOM.createPortal(
    <div>Portal says Hello </div>,
    document.querySelector( '#portal' )
  );
};
```

Here, we can see the `createPortal()` method in action: first, we indicate which type of JSX should be rendered and second, we pass in the type of container where the JSX should be rendered into. Let's place this `PortalExample` component into our App:

```
import React from 'react';
import ReactDOM from 'react-dom';


const App = () => {
  return (
    <div>
       <h1>Portals in React</h1>
```

184

```
            <PortalExample />
        </div>
    );
};


ReactDOM.render( <App />, document.querySelector('#root'));
```

The resulting <body> in the HTML document will look like this:

```
<body>
    <div id="root">
        <div>
            <h1>Portals in React </h1>
        </div>
    </div>
    <div id="portal">
        <div>Portal says Hello </div>
    </div>
</body>
```

The Portal is rendered into the #portal node instead of the #root node where all other content including the component itself is placed. A Portal is rendered once the component mounts and is removed from the DOM if the component containing the portal is removed from the component tree.

Portals and their relationship to their parent component

In order to further our understanding of portals, we are going to build — surprise surprise — a modal portal. The basis is formed by the same HTML which we have used in the introduction of portals before. There are two divs in the example: one in which our application is rendered and another in which we render the portal.

This time however, the modal will only open once a user has clicked a button. The portal will contain a button which allows the user to close the window. A state variable called modalIsOpen is used to alternate between the two states and is either true or false. The ModalPortal component will be rendered via an && conditional in JSX, thus it is only shown if this.state.modalIsOpen is true.

During the time in which the value of the state changes from false to true, the ModalPortal component is mounted and the ModalPopup is rendered into the <div id="portal"> with a slightly transparent background. Once the value changes from true to false again, the ModalPortal is removed from the App component in the component tree. React takes care to ensure that the ModalPortal component and its contents are not found on the page anymore.

185

In code form, we are left with the following example:

```
import React from 'react';
import ReactDOM from 'react-dom';


const ModalPortal = (props) => {
  return ReactDOM.createPortal(
    <div
      style={{
        background: 'rgba (0,0,0,0.7)',
        height: '100vh',
        left: 0,
        position: 'fixed',
        top: 0,
        width: '100vw',
      }}
    >
      <div style={{ background: 'white', margin: 16, padding: 16 }}>
        {props.children}
      </div>
    </div>,
    document.getElementById('portal')
  );
};


class App extends React.Component {
  state = {
    modalIsOpen: false,
  };

  openModal = () => {
    this.setState({ modalIsOpen: true });
  };

  closeModal = () => {
    this.setState({ modalIsOpen: false });
  };

  render() {
    return (
      <div>
        <h1> Portals in React</h1>
        <button onClick={this.openModal}> Open Modal</button>
        {this.state.modalIsOpen && (
          <ModalPortal>
            <p>This text is opened in a Portal. </p>
```

186

```
            <button onClick={this.closeModal} >Close Modal </button>
        </ModalPortal>
      )}
    </div>
  );
  }
}
ReactDOM.render( <App />, document.getElementById('root'));
```

We need to pay special attention to the `this.closeModal()` method. Even though this method is defined in the `App` component, it is called within the `ModalPortal` component in the context of the `App` component once a user has clicked on the button "Close Modal".

This method can also alter the state of component via `modalIsOpen` even though the component is not placed within `<div id="root">` as the rest of the components. Portals allow us to do this as the content is placed within the same component tree **within React**. The **resulting HTML** however, is different and the code is placed in a different `<div>` to the rest of the application.

Code Splitting

When developing projects with React, most people tend to also use a **bundler** such as **Webpack**, **Browserify** or **Rollup**. These tools ensure that all files and all imports are later bundled into a single big file which can be deployed in a relatively simple fashion without having to worry about relative links between files. This process is referred to as **bundling**. A **bundle** can easily grow and reach a size of a megabyte or more especially if many third party libraries are used. Large bundles are a big performance problem as bigger bundles take longer to be processed and downloaded by the browser as well as executing.

To combat large bundles, a technique called **Code Splitting** is used to counteract it. **Code Splitting** defines the process in which we separate our application into many smaller bundles which are all able to run on their own and load further bundles if necessary. A common separation is either splitting by dependencies (React, ReactDOM, ...) or having a bundle per route.

One of the simplest ways to make use of code splitting is to use **Dynamic Import Syntax**. It's currently in discussion at **TC39** and thus in the process of being standardized. But **Babel** and **Webpack** enable us to make use of Code Splitting today. It is necessary to install the babel plugin `@babel/plugin-syntax-dynamic-import` to make use of code splitting. **Create React App** as well as **next.js** and **Gatsby** support **Code Splitting** out of the box and do not need to be configured to allow it.

Using dynamic imports

We have briefly touched on import syntax in the chapter on ES2015+. Dynamic Import Syntax is an extension of this syntax and allows us to dynamically lazy load them. Dynamic imports are similar to a promise:

```
// greeter.js
export sayHi = (name) => `Hi ${name}!`;
```

```
// app.js
import('./greeter').then((greeter) => {
  console.log(greeter.sayHi('Manuel'));  // "Hi Manuel!"
});
```

When Webpack finds a dynamic import, it will automatically perform code splitting and put this file into its own so-called *Chunk*. These Chunks are loaded independently once they are needed within the application - thus the naming of **Lazy Loading.**

Lazy Loading of components with React.lazy()

Let's talk about **lazy loading in React**. To make the experience of performing **lazy loading** more enjoyable, React offers its own method from version **16.6** onward to dynamically lazy load components. It is combined with **Dynamic Import Syntax** and allows the developer to easily load certain components only when the application has started running thus further reducing the size of the bundle.

Even though a component might have been loaded via React.lazy(), it can be used in React just as a regular component. It can also receive props as well as refs, contain further elements or be self-contained. The React.lazy() method expects a function as its first parameter which will return a dynamic import. This import has to import a component which has been exported using default exports before.

```
// LazyLoaded.js
import React from 'react';

const LazyLoaded = () => (
  <p>This component is only loaded by the server once it is in use.  </p>
);
```

```
// app.js
import React, { Suspense } from 'react';
import ReactDOM from 'react-dom';

const LazyLoaded = React.lazy(() =>  import('./LazyLoaded.js' ));

const App = () => (
  <Suspense fallback= {<div>Application is loading</div> }>
    <LazyLoaded />
  </Suspense>
);
```

```
ReactDOM.render(<App /> , document.getElementById('root'));
```

This method allows us to easily optimize for the size of our JavaScript bundle and only load certain files from the server when they are actually requested by the user. During the time it takes loading and receiving the data from the server to being executed, we will see information informing us that <div>Application is loading</div>. This is only possible because we are using a feature which has also been added to React in version **16.6**: React.Suspense.

189

Display fallbacks with React.Suspense

Back in the day, the Suspense component on the React object was named **Placeholder**. This is a very accurate description of the task it fulfills: acting as a placeholder for components which have not yet been rendered and displaying alternative content in the meantime. These fallbacks can take many forms: they can be a message that parts of the application are still being loaded or take the form of a loading animation. The placeholder to display is passed to **Suspense** in the `fallback` prop and *has* to be defined. Any valid React Element can be used and passed as a prop. Strings such as `<Suspense fallback="Loading ...">[…]</Suspense>` are also a valid.

As long as the component which you want to lazy load has not fully loaded, all children of the Suspense element will be replaced with the indicated fallback. Additionally, no limits on the number of React.lazy() component imports have been enforced. The fallback placeholder will be shown until all components have loaded and can be displayed.

Nesting components is also possible and can be a great idea in certain scenarios. When there are parts of the site which are slightly less important and might interfere with the rendering of the primary user interface, it is recommended to wrap these parts of the application / the component tree in their own Suspense element. This will boost performance and drive the important parts of the application to load first.

A possible scenario to use Suspense in practice is image editing. In these type of cases, it can be useful to display the image to edit to the user already to give visual clues. The rest of the user interface containing the actual editing functionality will be loaded in a further step if loading the actual component is taking longer.

```
import React, { Suspense } from 'react';
import ReactDOM from 'react-dom';

const ImageCanvas = React.lazy(() =>  import('./ImageCanvas' ));
const ImageToolbar = React.lazy(() =>  import('./ImageToobar' ));

function App() {
  return (
    <Suspense fallback={<div>Application loading</div> }>
      <ImageCanvas url="https://via.placeholder.com/350x240"  />
      <Suspense fallback={<div>Image editing tools are being loaded</div>  }>
        <ImageToolbar />
      </Suspense>
    </Suspense>
  );
}
```

```
ReactDOM.render( <App />, document.getElementById('root'));
```

In this example we have defined two main components: `ImageCanvas` which displays an image and `ImageToolbar` which contains the editing tools for the images. Both of these elements are embraced by a Suspense element. The fallback `<div>Application loading</div>` will be shown until the `ImageCanvas` component has been loaded by the server.

If this happens **before** the `ImageToolbar` has loaded, the second inner `Suspense` element will take effect and show a message that *"Image editing tools are being loaded."* until it has been fully loaded.

If, however, the `ImageCanvas` component is only loaded **after** the `ImageToolbar` has completed loading, the outer `Suspense` will prevent the `ImageToolbar` from being displayed until the `ImageCanvas` has also loaded. It will display the outer fallback message and render the components to the screen as soon as the `ImageCanvas` has completed loading.

Thus, our user interface can take three different forms:

- `ImageCanvas` and `ImageToolbar` have loaded successfully and are both displayed
- `ImageCanvas` has not finished loading and the message "Application is loading" message is displayed (independent of the status of the `ImageToolbar`)
- `ImageCanvas` has loaded but `ImageToolbar` has not. In this case, `ImageCanvas` will be displayed but instead of the `ImageToolbar` , a message saying *"Image editing tools are being loaded."* will be shown.

This way we explicitly prevent the image editing tools from being displayed to the user without having a fully loaded image to display alongside it. Nesting `Suspense` fallbacks allow for a greater degree of flexibility and granular decision making of which components should be shown at any time.

Suspense and their associated fallbacks are only supported in conjunction with `React.lazy()` at the moment. However, in the future loading asynchronous data such as API calls should also be supported by **Suspense**.

 Be careful: Lazy and **Suspense** are only supported in **client-side** applications for now. Currently, there is no support for this feature for **server-side** rendering but it is in active development.

Typechecking with PropTypes, Flow and TypeScript

Typechecking is a simple method to avoid potential errors in an application. We have talked about basic principles to avoid potential errors, one of the most important being the existence of "Pure" components meaning that components do not have side effects. The non-existence of side effects describe the situation in which the **same input parameters** (in the case of React we are talking about **props** and **state**) should always render the **same output**.

We should be able to foresee and be clear about which props are passed into a component and how they are being processed. In order to achieve this, we can employ **typechecking** to make this process easier. JavaScript is slightly unusual in the sense that a variable which used to be **String** can easily be converted into a **Number** or even an **Object** without the JavaScript interpreter even complaining.

Even if this sounds useful for development, it opens doors for errors and also forces us to manually check for the correct types. When we want to access nested properties such as `user.settings.notifications.newMessages` we have to check user is actually an Object and not null, subsequently perform the same check for settings and so on. Otherwise, we might run into type errors:

 TypeError: Cannot read property 'settings' of undefined

Typechecking can help us to catch such errors before they actually happen. Apart from **Flow** and **TypeScript** which allow for their own static typing, React provides its own simple solution called **PropTypes**. While **Flow** and **TypeScript** can also be used in JavaScript applications, **PropTypes** are exclusively used in React components. If you are interested into static types, you might like exploring **Flow** or **TypeScript** in greater detail.

PropTypes

PropTypes have a long standing history in React and were part of React before it even gained popularity. In React version 15.5 **PropTypes** were removed from the core of React and converted into their own `prop-types` package. While you defined **PropTypes** via `React.PropTypes.string` in the past, you now access them via importing the `PropTypes` module and `PropTypes.string` .

This change also means that we now have to install the `PropTypes` module as a devDependency. We can execute the following step in the command line:

```
npm install --save-dev prop-types
```

```
yarn add --dev prop-types
```

PropTypes can be seen as some kind of interface and define which types the props can take and whether they are required or optional. If **PropTypes** encounter discrepancies, **React** will inform us of these as long as we find ourselves in **Development mode**. When applications have been built correctly and use either the production build of React or an environment variable `process.env.NODE_ENV=production`, this warning will not be shown anymore.

But how do **PropTypes** work? To answer this question, one needs to differentiate between **Class components** and **Function components**.

Class components implement **PropTypes** as a static property of the component in question:

```jsx
import React from 'react';
import ReactDOM from 'react-dom';
import PropTypes from 'prop-types';

class EventOverview extends React.Component {
  static propTypes = {
    date: PropTypes.instanceOf( Date).isRequired,
    description: PropTypes.string,
    ticketsUrl: PropTypes.string,
    title: PropTypes.string.isRequired
  };

  render() {
    const { date, description, ticketUrl, title } =   this.props;
    return (
      <div>
        <h1> {title} </h1>
        <h2> {date.toLocaleString()} </h2>
        {description && (
          <div className ="description"> {description}</div>
        )}
        {ticketsUrl &&   <a href={ticketsUrl} >Tickets!</a> }
      </div>
    );
  }
}
```

```
ReactDOM.render(
  <EventOverview date={new Date()} title="React Deep-Dive" />,
  document.getElementById('root')
);
```

In this example, we want to display an event overview. Thus, we have defined that the EventOverview component **has to** accept both, a date and a title prop. It **can** furthermore have a description prop as well as a ticketUrl prop. One can append .isRequired to the PropTypes to indicate that the prop is **required**. We can read from our list of **PropTypes** that the date prop has to be an instance of the native Date object and that title has to be of type string. If the optional props description and ticketsUrl have been passed, they also need to be of type string.

If any of these conditions have not been met, React will gracefully inform us with a warning in the console:

 Warning: Failed prop type: Invalid prop `title` of type `number` supplied to `EventOverview`, expected `string`.

Function Components do not have classes, thus we cannot define a static propTypes property. However, we can easily add a propTypes property to the function, which will result in the following:

```
const EventOverview = ({ date, description, ticketUrl, title }) => (
  <div>
    <h1>{title}</h1>
    <h2>{date.toLocaleString()} </h2>
    {description && <div className="description"> {description}</div> }
    {ticketsUrl && <a href={ticketsUrl} >Tickets!</a> }
  </div>
);

EventOverview.propTypes = {
  date: PropTypes.instanceOf( Date ).isRequired,
  description: PropTypes.string,
  ticketsUrl: PropTypes.string,
  title: PropTypes.string.isRequired,
};
```

And just like that, we have added propTypes to our **Function Component** .

In some cases, it can be useful to define sensible default values if no specific values have been passed. React allows us to define defaultProps which work similar to propTypes in that they can also be added as a static property. Here's a quick example:

```
const Greeting = ({ name }) => <h1>Hello {name}!  </h1>;

Greeting.propTypes = {
  name: PropTypes.string.isRequired,
};

Greeting.defaultProps = {
  name: 'Guest',
};
```

The name prop of the Greeting component is marked as required by string.isRequired which means that we usually expect that a value is passed in the form of a string. If however no value is passed for the prop, the default value will be used.

```
<Greeting name= "Manuel" />
```

will result in the following output: **Hello Manuel!**

```
<Greeting />;
// or:
const user = {};
<Greeting name={user.name} /> ;
```

This example however will fall back to the defaultValue which we have defined in the defaultProps as either no prop is passed at all or if the value is undefined. In this case, **Hello Guest!** will be displayed as we set **Guest** as our defaultValue. React will figure out if a defaultValue for a isRequired prop exists and only display a warning if the prop is actually missing and no defaultValue has been defined.

When **Deploying to production** it is worth installing **Babel-Plugin-Transform-React-Remove-Prop-Types**. This will save us a couple of bytes, as `propType` definitions are removed from the build and are only really taken into account in **Development Mode**.

You can find the plugin here:
https://github.com/oliviertassinari/babel-plugin-transform-react-remove-prop-types

You can install it via the command line with:

```
npm install --save-dev babel-plugin-transform-react-remove-prop-types
```

Or with yarn:

```
yarn add --dev babel-plugin-transform-react-remove-prop-types
```

Flow

In contrast to **React PropTypes**, **Flow** is a **static typechecker** for **JavaScript** not just for React components. **Flow** is also developed in-house at Facebook and thus integrates nicely with most React setups. Up to version **Babel 6**, it even came pre-installed as part of the `babel-preset-react` and could be used without any further setup.

Since **Babel version7**, **Flow** has been ported to its own **Babel preset**. In order to install it you can run `npm install @babel/preset-flow` or `yarn add @babel/preset-flow`. In addition to the installation step, you also have to manually set the `@babel/preset-flow` as a present in the Babel config. **Presets** allow us to remove non-JavaScript syntax — in this case **Flow syntax** — during the build process so that we will not run into errors in the browser.

Apart from the Babel Preset, the **Flow executable** needs to be installed via `npm install flow-bin` (or `yarn add flow-bin`) which takes care of the actual **typechecking**.

Once **Flow** has been installed and the Babel Preset has been set up, you have to create a **Flow config** by executing `./node_modules/flow init` in the terminal in your current project directory.

Hint: To avoid prepending `./node_modules` every time you are calling Flow, you can make an addition in the `script` section of the `package.json`:

```
{
  "scripts": {
    [...]
```

```
    "flow" : "flow"
  }
}
```

This allows us to call Flow via npm or yarn:

```
npm run flow init
```

```
yarn flow init
```

Once `flow init` has been executed, a new file called `.flowconfig` should have been created in the project directory. The file itself looks very empty for now but Flow needs it to function correctly. In the future, you can manage which files should be checked by Flow or which should not based on the options set in these files.

Did you update your Babel config, install `flow-bin` in your object and created the `.flowconfig`? Awesome. We can now start typechecking with Flow. In order to check that everything has been set up correctly, you can execute `flow`. If you added the entry to the `package.json` as shown above, running `yarn flow` will suffice. When everything has been set up correctly, a message such as this one is displayed to you:

```
No errors!
Done in 0.57s.
```

This means that Flow has checked all of our files and has not found any errors. But this is kind of self-explanatory as we have not created any files containing any typechecks - yet.

The standard settings of Flow mandate that only those files will be typechecked that have included a specific code comment at the top of the file:

```
// @flow
```

Let us look at our previous example, but this time using **Flow** instead of **PropTypes**:

```
// @flow
import * as React from 'react';
import * as ReactDOM from 'react-dom';

type PropsT = {
  date: Date ,
  description?: string,
  ticketsUrl?: string,
  title: string,
};
```

197

```
class EventOverview extends React.Component<PropsT> {
  render() {
    const { date, description, ticketUrl, title } =   this.props;
    return (
      <div>
        <h1> {title} </h1>
        <h2> {date.toLocaleString()} </h2>
        {description && <div  className ="description"> {description}</div> }
        {ticketsUrl &&   <a href ={ticketsUrl} >Tickets!</a> }
      </div>
    );
  }
}

ReactDOM.render(
  <EventOverview  date ={new Date()} title= "React Deep-Dive"  />,
  document.getElementById('root')
);
```

As opposed to **PropTypes**, we start off by defining a **Type definition** with the name of PropsT. You can choose freely which names to give to your Type definitions, but it has become some sort of Developer convention to use the suffix of T or Type. However, it is not enforced or technically necessary. This newly defined type can then be passed to the component using a so-called "generic type".

```
class EventOverview extends React.Component<PropsT>
```

Type definitions can be inlined as well, however the longer the list of the definitions, the harder it becomes to read them in this form.

```
class EventOverview extends React.Component<{
  date: Date ,
  description?: string,
  ticketsUrl?: string,
  title: string,
}> {
  [...]
}
```

But let's inspect the **Type definition** a little further: just as we already learned in the section on **PropTypes**, we define which **props** can be passed to the component and which **type** they have to be. In this case, we have defined a date prop which needs to be an instance of Date, the optional props description and ticketsUrl of type string which have been marked as optional due to their use of the ? after their name, and finally the `title` prop which also needs to be passed in the form of a `string`. In contrast to **PropTypes** where one needs to explicitly indicate which props are required by using `isRequired`, Flow syntax describes which fields are optional instead.

Function components can also be typed using Flow by passing the props and their Type as a function argument:

```
const EventOverview = (props: PropsT) => (/*…*/);
```

Or in even shorter, destructured form:

```
const EventOverview = ({ date, description, ticketUrl, title }: PropsT) => (/*…*/);
```

You can also use inline definitions in Function components:

```
const EventOverview = ({
  date,
  description,
  ticketUrl,
  title,
}: {
  date: Date ,
  description?: string,
  ticketsUrl?: string,
  title: string,
}) => {
  /*…*/
};
```

But that's not all! **Flow** can check any JavaScript and not only those bits that describe the props of React components. You can also type the State of your component by passing a second parameter in the so-called **Generics**.

```
// @flow
import * as React from 'react';
import * as ReactDOM from 'react-dom';

type PropsT = {
  date: Date ,
  description?: string,
  ticketsUrl?: string,
  title: string,
};
```

```
type StateT = {
  isBookmarked: boolean,
};

class EventOverview extends React.Component<PropsT, StateT> {
  state = {
    isBookmarked: false,
  };
  [...]
}
```

In contrast to previous examples in the book, the imports follow a slightly different structure. Instead of:

```
import React from 'react';
```

React has been imported like this:

```
import * as React from 'react';
```

This allows us to also import React's **type definitions** which is necessary if we want to return a React element from a function and type it, for example.

TypeScript

TypeScript has been created by Microsoft and is a so-called **typed superset** of JavaScript meaning that it cannot be directly executed in the browser but has to be compiled into "real" JavaScript first. Nevertheless, valid JavaScript is always valid **TypeScript**. **TypeScript** might look very similar to **Flow** at first glance, but differs in the sense that it offers a lot more functionality as it is a superset of JS. **Flow** is only a typechecker. Before **ES2015** was formally introduced, a lot of functionality such as classes and imports were already readily available in **TypeScript**.

TypeScript has been gaining momentum and lots of popularity lately and can now be found in many React projects. While I certainly find **TypeScript** worth mentioning in this chapter, **TypeScript** alone could easily fill up a whole book by itself which is why I would rather not go into more detail at this point.

TypeScript files are easy to spot as they usually have the file ending of .ts or, if **TypeScript** is used in a React project, .tsx.

With the release of **Babel 7**, the integration of **TypeScript** in projects has become much easier as one does not have to install the **TypeScript** compiler (tsc) anymore but can simply use a

200

Babel plugin. This plugin is installed once you install the Babel Preset `@babel/preset-typescript`. If you are looking for more information on how to use **TypeScript** in your React projects, the official **TypeScript** documentation is a great place to start: https://www.typescriptlang.org/docs.

IV – Hooks

Introduction to Hooks

Hooks are a completely new concept that has been introduced in React **16.8.0**. The concept of Hooks is so new and novel that I want to dedicate a full chapter to it. Many React Core Developers have already titled **Hooks** as one of the most exciting and fundamental shifts in React. Indeed, **Hooks** were making waves at **React Conf 2018** where they were first announced — before their introduction in the React 16.7 alpha release. Even other frameworks have followed suit and implemented their own version of **Hooks**. But what are Hooks exactly?

Hooks allow us to use certain mechanisms, that were only available to Class components in the past, in **Function components**. Features such as `setState` or lifecycle methods such as `componentDidMount()` or `componentDidUpdate()` that were reserved entirely for Class Components in the past, can now be used in **Function components** thanks to **Hooks**. Put simply, **Hooks** are nothing more than special functions that follow a pre-defined schema. One of them is the convention that the name of a **Hook** has to start with `use`.

React offers a number of internal **Hooks** that are ready to use out of the box such as `useState`, `useEffect` or `useContext`. It also allows for the creation of **custom Hooks**: functions in which we can use our own logic. To follow the convention mentioned already, they also have to start with the `use` keyword but apart from that the developer can freely choose to give the Hook any name they want as long as the name is also a valid JavaScript function name. Names such as `useAccountInfo` or `useDocumentInfo` are great examples.

> (i) A little personal anecdote: Since the introduction of **Hooks**, I have had to rewrite entire sections in the book and continually keep it up date to this day. In the past, the documentation has almost entirely focused on calling **Function components** - **Stateless Functional components** (SFC for short). This naming has disappeared immediately from the official React documentation since **Hooks** came to be, which is why I also removed this name from the book.

Hooks allow us to reuse component logic in a coherent manner. Before **Hooks**, many components often used identical `componentDidMount()` or `componentDidUpdate()` methods that followed the same implementation patterns with the difference of checking whether various parameters had changed during `componentDidUpdate()`. For example, whether a user ID (which was passed via props) had changed, which in turn initiated another API request.

Hooks were thus introduced with the aim to make it possible to easily share complex logic, without the need for writing a lot of unnecessary duplicated code. But I will be honest with you, if you are comfortable with Class components and how they work, Hooks might force you to completely re-think how components can and should interact. Processes as well as the composition of the components themselves have changed. Where complex classes with class properties, inheritance and a mutual `this` context have prevailed in the past, **Hooks** replace these with relatively simple and clean functions. How this is achieved in detail, is what we are going to look at through the course of this chapter.

Are class components still worth it?

Now we only have to answer the question: are class components still worth using?

This question came up again and again shortly after the announcement and introduction of **React Hooks**. The React Team has discouraged people from rewriting their existing applications which use classes at the moment into **Function components** using **Hooks**. Classes will remain part of React.

The community did not really take this advice to heart. Many developers started rewriting entire applications after **React 16.7.0-alpha** (the first version containing **Hooks**), announcing on Twitter how excited they were about the simplicity **Hooks** have introduced for their development and the reduced overhead from not having to use Class components.

Of course you can continue to use Class components for as long as they continue to be supported. There are no plans to remove them from React either. Once you have started getting used to writing components with React **Hooks** however, it will be tough to trade the simplicity and increased understanding of this new style for Class components.

Class Components vs Hooks - a comparison

In order to demonstrate just how much simpler a component definition can be by using Hooks, Sunil Pai (one of the React Core Team developers) created an example in which he compares a Class component with a **Function component** using **Hooks**. Logic that is shared between the two is colored in the same color in both examples, and logic from the class component that is no longer needed has been blacked out. The result below is rather interesting, and demonstrates clearly how the information is more concise in the version using Hooks, and not as dispersed as it is in the class component:

```jsx
import * as React from "react";
import { Card, Row, Input, Text } from "./components";
import ThemeContext from "./ThemeContext";

export default class Greeting extends React.Component {
  constructor(props) {
    super(props);
    this.state = {
      name: "Harry",
      surname: "Potter",
      width: window.innerWidth
    };
    this.handleNameChange = this.handleNameChange.bind(this);
    this.handleResize = this.handleResize.bind(this);
    this.handleSurnameChange = this.handleSurnameChange.bind(this);
  }

  componentDidMount() {
    window.addEventListener("resize", this.handleResize);
    document.title = this.state.name + ' ' + this.state.surname
  }

  componentDidUpdate() {
    document.title = this.state.name + ' ' + this.state.surname
  }

  componentWillUnmount() {
    window.removeEventListener("resize", this.handleResize);
  }

  handleNameChange(name) {
    this.setState({ name });
  };

  handleSurnameChange(surname) {
    this.setState({ surname });
  };

  handleResize() {
    this.setState({ width: window.innerWidth });
  };

  render() {
    let { name, surname, width } = this.state;
    return (
      <ThemeContext.Consumer>
        {theme => (
          <Card theme={theme}>
            <Row label="Name">
              <Input value={name} onChange={this.handleNameChange} />
            </Row>
            <Row label="Surname">
              <Input value={surname} onChange={this.handleSurnameChange} />
            </Row>
            <Row label="Width">
              <Text>{width}</Text>
            </Row>
          </Card>
        )}
      </ThemeContext.Consumer>
    );
  }
}
```

Class component

```
import React, { useState, useContext, useEffect } from "react";
import { Card, Row, Input, Text } from "./components";
import ThemeContext from "./ThemeContext";

export default function Greeting(props) {
  let theme = useContext(ThemeContext);

  let [name, setName] = useState("Harry");
  let [surname, setSurname] = useState("Potter");
  useEffect(() => {
    document.title = name + " " + surname;
  });

  let [width, setWidth] = useState(window.innerWidth);
  useEffect(() => {
    let handleResize = () => setWidth(window.innerWidth);
    window.addEventListener("resize", handleResize);
    return () => {
      window.removeEventListener("resize", handleResize);
    };
  });

  return (
    <Card theme={theme}>
      <Row label="Name">
        <Input value={name} onChange={setName} />
      </Row>
      <Row label="Surname">
        <Input value={surname} onChange={setSurname} />
      </Row>
      <Row label="Width">
        <Text>{width}</Text>
      </Row>
    </Card>
  );
}
```

The same functionality with React Hooks

Source: Sunil Pai on Twitter

Use of Hooks

React currently offers **10** Hooks for us to use. Of these 10, **3** of these are fundamental or **basic**, the remaining 7 are **additional** — according to the official React documentation. It is a useful distinction though, as the **3 basic Hooks** useState(), useEffect() and useContext() will be sufficient in most cases.

The remaining **additional Hooks** will help us to cover edge cases or to deal with certain optimizations at a later date. In this chapter however, we will focus on "simple" Hooks and how we can now implement functionality in **Function components** that was previously reserved for **Class components**.

State with useState()

Let us have a look at how we previously accessed and modified state:

```
import React from 'react';
import ReactDOM from 'react-dom';

class Counter extends React.Component {
  state = {
    value: 0 ,
  };
  render() {
    return (
      <div>
        <p> Counter: {this.state.value}</p>
        <button
          onClick ={() => this.setState((state) => ({ value: state.value + 1 }))}
        >
          +1
        </button>
      </div>
    );
  }
}

ReactDOM.render(<Counter /> , document.getElementById('root'));
```

Here we have implemented a simple counter which keeps track of how many times we press the **+1** button. While it is not the most creative of examples, it demonstrates quite nicely how we can use Hooks to simplify code. In this example, we read the current value with

207

`this.state.value` and increment the counter by a button that is placed below. Once the button is clicked, `this.setState()` is called and we set the new `value` to the previous value which we increment by 1.

But let's have a look how the same functionality can be implemented using `useState()` in a **Function component**:

```
import React from 'react';
import ReactDOM from 'react-dom';

const Counter = () => {
  const [value, setValue] = React.useState(0 );
  return (
    <div>
      <p>Counter: {value}</p>
      <button onClick ={() => setValue(value + 1)}>+1</button>
    </div>
  );
};

ReactDOM.render(<Counter /> , document.getElementById('root'));
```

Watch out: we do not use a state object anymore and have also not used the `this` keyword to access our state. Instead, a simple `useState()` Hook is called. It works by taking in an **initial value** (0 in this case) and returning a tuple — an array with a set number of values. In the case of the `useState()` Hook, this tuple consists of the value of state, and a setter function which we can use to modify this value.

In order to directly access this state value and the associated setter function, we are making use of **ES2015 Array destructuring**, meaning the first value in the array will give us access to `value` while the second will be written into `setValue`. While you can certainly use your own names for these values, conventions have emerged to give short and precise names to state values and using verbs such as set, change or update in conjunction with the name of the state value to indicate what it is doing. The syntax itself is a much shorter equivalent of the following ES5 code:

```
var state = React.useState(0 );
var value = state[ 0];
var setValue = state[ 1];
```

We now directly access `value` instead of `this.state.value` inside of the `Counter` component. Moreover, we can set a new value with `setValue(value + 1)` instead of the slightly wordier `this.setState((state) => ({ value: state + 1}))` .

208

It's time to celebrate: We've just created our first **stateful Function Component!**

> (i) We just used our very first **Hook**: useState() by calling `React.useState()`. We can also import **Hooks** directly from the `react` package.
>
> ```
> import React, { useEffect, useState } from 'react';
> ```
>
> This way, we can easily use useState() instead of having to write out `React.useState()` every single time.

Components are not limited to use each type of Hook only once. Thus, we can easily implement two counters which we can increment and manage independently by creating their own states:

```
import React from 'react';
import ReactDOM from 'react-dom';

const Counter = () => {
  const [firstValue, setFirstValue] = React.useState( 0);
  const [secondValue, setSecondValue] = React.useState( 0);
  return (
    <div>
      <p>Count 1: {firstValue} </p>
      <p>Count 2: {secondValue}</p>
      <button onClick ={() => setFirstValue(firstValue + 1)}>+1 </button>
      <button onClick ={() => setSecondValue(secondValue + 1)}>+1</button>
    </div>
  );
};

ReactDOM.render(<Counter /> , document.getElementById('root'));
```

If, at this point, you are wondering how you would manage very complex state, I would urge you to "hold that thought" as we will learn about the useReducer() Hook in a later chapter. For now, we will focus on the three **basic** Hooks.

Side effects with useEffect()

The name of the useEffect() **Hook** derives from its intended usage: for **Side Effects**. In this case, we mean loading data via an API, registering global events or manipulating DOM elements. The useEffect() Hook includes functionality that was previously found in the `componentDidMount()`, `componentDidUpdate()` and `componentWillUnmount()` lifecycle methods.

If you are wondering whether all these lifecycle methods have now been replaced and been combined in to a single Hook, I can assure you: you have read correctly. Instead of using *three* methods, you only need to use *a single* **Hook** which takes effect in similar places where the class component methods were previously used. The trick is to use particular function parameters and return values which are intended for the `useEffect()` Hook.

In order to use the `useEffect()` Hook, you pass the `useEffect()` function another function as its first parameter. This function, which we will call the **Effect function** for now, is invoked **after** each rendering of the component and "replaces" the `componentDidMount()` part of class components.

As this **Effect function** is called after **each** render of the component, it is also called after the **first** render. This equates to what has been typically covered in the `componentDidMount()` lifecycle method.

Moreover, the *Effect function* can optionally return another function. Let's call this function a **Cleanup function**. This function is invoked during the **unmounting** of the component, which roughly equates to the `componentWillUnmount()` class component method.

But be careful: while this sounds similar, the `useEffect()` Hook works a little differently compared to class components' lifecycle methods. Our *cleanup function* is not only called during the **Unmounting** of the component but also **before each new execution** of the *Effect function*.

The second parameter of the `useEffect()` Hook is the **dependency array**. The values of this array indicate the values upon which the execution of the **Effect function** depends on. If a **dependency array** is passed, the Hook is only invoked initially and then only when at least one of the values in the **dependency array** has changed.

If you explicitly try to replicate behavior previously covered by `componentDidMount()`, you can pass an empty array as your second parameter. React then only executes the **Effect function** on initial render and only calls a cleanup function again during **unmount**.

This probably sounds all very complex and theoretical now, especially if you are new to Hooks and do not quite understand how they work. Let us look at an example to clear things up a little bit:

```
import React, { useEffect, useState } from 'react';
import ReactDOM from 'react-dom';


const defaultTitle = 'React with Hooks' ;
```

```
const Counter = () => {
  const [value, setValue] = useState(0 );

  useEffect(() => {
    // `document.title` is set with each change (didMount/didUpdate).
    // Given the `value` has changed
    document.title =  `The button has been clicked ${value} times.`  ;

    // Here we're returning our "Cleanup function" which resets the title to the
default
    // before each update
    return () => {
      document.title = defaultTitle;
    };

    // Lastly, our dependency array. This way the Effect function is only invoked
    // when the `value` has actually changed.
  }, [value]);

  return (
    <div>
      <p>Counter: {value}</p>
      <button onClick ={() => setValue(value + 1)}>+1</button>
    </div>
  );
};

ReactDOM.render(<Counter /> , document.getElementById('root'));
```

As the Hook is always found *inside* of the function, it has complete access to **props** and **state** (as has been the case already in the lifecycle methods of class components). In this case, the state of the Function component is another **Hook** that is implemented using the useState() Hook.

By using the useEffect() **Hook**, we can dramatically reduce the complexity of this component, as it does not have to execute many similar pieces of code through different functions. Instead it can deal with all the associated lifecycle methods with just a single function, the **Hook**.

To compare this with class component code, I have prepared a little example which implements the same functionality as the useEffect() Hook:

```
import React from 'react';
import ReactDOM from 'react-dom';
```

```
const defaultTitle = 'React with Hooks' ;

class Counter extends React.Component {
  state = {
    value: 0,
  };

  componentDidMount() {
    document.title = `The button has been clicked ${ this.state.value} times`;
  }

  componentDidUpdate(prevProps, prevState) {
    if (prevState.value !== this.state.value) {
      document.title = `The button has been clicked ${ this.state.value} times`;
    }
  }

  componentWillUnmount() {
    document.title = defaultTitle;
  }

  render() {
    return (
      <div>
        <p> Counter: {this.state.value}</p>
        <button
          onClick ={() => {
            this.setState((state) => ({ value: state.value + 1 }));
          }}
        >
          +1
        </button>
      </div>
    );
  }
}

ReactDOM.render(<Counter /> , document.getElementById('root'));
```

Of course you can debate whether it would be useful to extract the call to change document.title into its own class method such as setDocumentTitle() however this is not really adding much to our discussion as they do not change anything about the complexity at hand.

Even then, we would still need to call the same (and now abstracted) function in two places: `componentDidMount()` and `componentDidUpdate()`. Additionally, we would have to add another class method which further bloats our class component and only reduces duplication by adding more abstraction layers.

Accessing Context with useContext()

The third and final basic Hook is useContext(). It allows us to consume data from a Context Provider without having to define a Provider component with a function as a child.

useContext() is passed a context object, which you can create by using React.createContext(). It will then return the value of the next higher up provider in the component hierarchy. If the value in the context is changed within the provider, the useContext() Hook will trigger a re-render with the updated data from the provider. And that just about sums up the functionality of the useContext() Hook.

In practice, this translates to something like the following example:

```
import React, { useContext } from 'react';
import ReactDOM from 'react-dom';

const AccountContext = React.createContext({});

const ContextExample = () => {
  const accountData = useContext(AccountContext);

  return (
    <div>
      <p>Name: {accountData.name}</p>
      <p>Role: {accountData.role}</p>
    </div>
  );
};

const App = () => (
  <AccountContext.Provider value={{ name: 'Manuel ', role: 'admin' }}>
    <ContextExample />
  </AccountContext.Provider>
);

ReactDOM.render(<App /> , document.getElementById('root'));
```

The ContextExample component is receiving its data from the pseudo-account data provider: theAccountContext provider. This works without having to wrap an AccountContext.Consumer component around ContextExample. It does not only save us

213

multiple lines of code in the component itself, but also leads to a much better debugging experience as the component tree is not as deeply nested as it would be otherwise.

However, this simplification is entirely optional. If you prefer to keep using the well-known Consumer component to access data from a provider, that is completely fine.

Principles and Rules of Hooks

If we want to use **Hooks** and implement them in our applications, we need to follow a few rules that prevent us from running into unexpected errors or behavior. **ESLint** and the `eslint-plugin-react-hooks` package, which has been developed by the React Team itself, help us to follow these rules and indicate when you might be breaching one. I have advocated for the use of **ESLint** in the chapter on **Tools and Setup** already and recommend that you use it if you have not done so already.

To install the plugin, you can execute the following command on the command line:

```
npm install --save-dev eslint-plugin-react-hooks
```

or using Yarn:

```
yarn add --dev eslint-plugin-react-hooks
```

In addition, you need to amend the `.eslintrc` as shown:

```
{
  "plugins" : [
    // ...
    "react-hooks"
  ],
  "rules" : {
    // ...
    "react-hooks/rules-of-hooks" : "error",
    "react-hooks/exhaustive-deps" : "warn"
  }
}
```

I've got good news for those of you who are using **Create React App**: you do not need to do any of these previous steps as those two specific rules ship with **Create React App** out of the box!

The rules of Hooks

We talked about the formalities and how to check that we are not violating these pre-defined Hooks rules. But what are those rules exactly?

Hooks can only be used in React function components

Hooks can only be called in React function components, not in **class components** or anywhere else. This means that a function that uses Hooks always has to be a React component, meaning it always has a return value (either JSX, Arrays, Strings or *null*).

 This is now allowed as it uses a Class component:

```
class MyComponent extends React.Component {
  render() {
    const [value, setValue] = useState();
    return <input type="text" onChange={(e) => setValue(e.target.value)} />;
  }
}
```

However:

 The following snippet is allowed as it uses a function component:

```
const MyComponent = () => {
  const [value, setValue] = useState();
  return <input type="text" onChange={(e) => setValue(e.target.value)} />;
};
```

Hooks are only allowed to be used on the highest layer inside of the function component

It is **not possible** to use **Hooks** inside of **loops, conditions or nested functions**. Why you might wonder? This is due to how React treats **Hooks** internally. The order in which **Hooks** are executed has to be identical for each re-render of the component and explains why it is not possible to call a **Hook** conditionally. If we did in fact executed a **Hook** based on a condition, we would change the order in which the **Hooks** are being executed. We can use conditions *inside* of **Hooks** though!

 Not allowed: Hook is used inside of a condition

```
if (title) {
  useEffect(() => {
    document.title = title;
```

216

```
  }, [title]);
}
```

✅ **Allowed: condition is used inside of Hook**

```
useEffect(() => {
  if (title) {
    document.title = title;
  }
}, [title]);
```

If you installed the ESLint plugin as outlined above and configured the .eslintrc to use the rules as described, you don't have to fear accidentally run into any of those errors. ESLint will prompt you with a warning as to how you violated one of the rules.

Implement your own Hooks

Apart from the **internal Hooks** such as useState or useEffect, it is also possible to create our own **custom Hooks**. These in turn can use **internal Hooks** or other **custom Hooks**, and encapsulate logic in a reusable form. Creating **custom Hooks** can be really useful if you want to use the same logic in multiple components. Even if the complexity of the component's logic grows, it can be useful to **divide** it and break it up into **custom Hooks** with meaningful names in order to keep the current **Function component** more manageable and readable.

Your first custom Hook

Let's start with a relatively simple example and assume that we want to create a **custom Hook** with which we can invoke Side Effects and change the background-color of a component whenever it is mounted. A typical name for such a **custom Hook** would be useBackgroundColor() — remember that Hooks always need to start with use. This Hook expects a valid CSS color and then applies the color as the current background color. It is applied as soon as a component using it is mounted or passes a new value to the **custom Hook**.

As we might want to use this logic in other components and do not want to repeat ourselves every time and implement the same functionality with useEffect again and again, it is worth extracting our **first custom Hook**:

```
// useBackgroundColor.js
import { useEffect } from 'react';

const useBackgroundColor = (color) => {
  useEffect(() => {
    document.body.style.backgroundColor = color;
    return () => {
      document.body.style.backgroundColor = '';
    };
  }, [color]);
};

export default useBackgroundColor;
```

To use this component, we are creating a little Tabs component which allows us to select content based on three buttons. Depending on which component is currently shown to us, we would like to change the background color of our application. Thus, we can use our useBackgroundColor() Hook:

```
// Tabs.js
import React, { useState } from 'react';
import ReactDOM from 'react-dom';
import useBackgroundColor from './useBackgroundColor';

const DefaultContent = () => {
  return <p>Default Content </p>;
};

const SpecialContent = () => {
  useBackgroundColor( 'red');
  return <p>Special Content </p>;
};

const OtherSpecialContent = () => {
  useBackgroundColor( 'orange');
  return <p>Other Special Content </p>;
};

const Tabs = () => {
  const [tab, setTab] = useState( 'home');

  return (
    <div className="tabs">
      <div className="tabBar">
        <button onClick={() => setTab('home')}>Home </button>
        <button onClick={() => setTab('special')}>Special</button>
        <button onClick={() => setTab('other')}>Other Special </button>
      </div>
      <div className="tabContent">
        {tab === 'home' && <DefaultContent /> }
        {tab === 'special' && <SpecialContent /> }
        {tab === 'other' && <OtherSpecialContent /> }
      </div>
    </div>
  );
};

ReactDOM.render(<Tabs /> , document.getElementById('root'));
```

We've implemented three basic components in this example which help us to display our content: DefaultContent, SpecialContent and OtherSpecialContent. Two of these components already use our **custom Hook** useBackgroundColor() to change the global background color in a useEffect() once the component has mounted.

Alternatively, we could have implemented the useEffect() Hook manually in each component that needs to change its background color. However, this would have led to a lot of code duplication. Instead, we are much better off extracting this logic into its own custom Hook and making it configurable by passing the required color as an argument. This can then be used in as many **Function components** as we like.

While JSX allows us to create reusable components for the user interface, Hooks offer us the opportunity to reuse logic across components without having to make any compromises.

Working with data in Hooks

Passing data via **Custom Hooks** is no one-way street. In our first custom Hook example we've seen that we can pass data into a **custom Hook** as a function parameter. The Hook can also *return* data that can then be used in the component. The form in which this data is returned from the **Hook** is entirely at the discretion of the developer. You can easily return strings, tuples but also entire React components or elements or even a combination of all of them. You're free to choose so to say.

Let's assume that we want to access data from an API. We should parameterize the data that we want to access to make it easier to work with. Hooks can help us to access this data in this case (it does not matter in which component it ends up being used) and then return it to the component that needs it. In our next example, we will deal with user data from GitHub. Thus, a good name for our next **Custom Hook** would be useGitHubUserData .

We pass a GitHub username to this Hook and obtain an object with all the relevant information from the user. The Hook itself deals with requesting the data from the GitHub API and will pass it to the component:

```
// useGitHubAccountData.js
import { useEffect, useState } from 'react';
import axios from 'axios';

const useGitHubAccountData = (account) => {
  const [accountData, setAccountData] = useState({});

  useEffect(() => {
    if (!account) {
      return;
    }

    axios.get( `https://api.github.com/users/ ${account}`).then((response) => {
      setAccountData(response.data);
    });
  }, [account]);
```

```
      return accountData;
};


export default useGitHubAccountData;
```

Once again, we've made use of the Hooks that we have already encountered: useEffect() and useState(). We're using the state, accountData, to manage the GitHub user data inside of it. The effect is only ever executed if the username changes. Afterwards, we request the user data for this account from the GitHub API, wait for the response and then write the data of this response using setAccountData() into state. Finally, we pass the state accountData back to the component which has called the Hook in the first place.

We can now safely access the data from this component and use it as we see fit:

```
// RepoInfo.js
import React from 'react';
import ReactDOM from 'react-dom';
import useGitHubAccountData from './useGitHubAccountData';

const RepoInfo = () => {
  const accountData = useGitHubAccountData('manuelbieh'  );

  return (
    <p>
      GitHub user {accountData.name} has {accountData.public_repos} public
      repositories.
    </p>
  );
};


ReactDOM.render(<RepoInfo /> , document.getElementById('root'));
```

At this point, we could implement further info based on RepoInfo. For example, we could implement a search for a particular GitHub Account instead of setting this beforehand. To achieve this, we can use useState() to create a new **state** in which we write the account that the user has provided and then pass this **state** to our **Custom Hook**.

As our useEffect() Hook contains the account name in the dependency array, it will be executed once a new user account has been passed in. This means that a new API request will be fired each time we make a change to the search field and will then request the data for the provided account:

```
// RepoLookup.js
import React, { useState } from 'react';
import ReactDOM from 'react-dom';
import useGitHubAccountData from './useGitHubAccountData';

const RepoLookup = () => {
  const [account, setAccount] = useState( '' );
  const accountData = useGitHubAccountData(account);

  return (
    <div>
      <input value={account} onChange={(e) => setAccount(e.target.value)} />
      {!account ? (
        <p> Please provide a GitHub username </p>
      ) : (
        <p>
          GitHub user {accountData.name} ({accountData.login}) has{' '}
          {accountData.public_repos} public repositories.
        </p>
      )}
    </div>
  );
};

ReactDOM.render(<RepoLookup /> , document.getElementById('root'));
```

Side note: GitHub's public API only allows about 60 API requests per hour. If you feel that you want to access more and play around with these examples a bit more, you should create a GitHub API token and append it to the URL with access_token=xyz . The token can be generated here: https://github.com/settings/tokens.

222

Hooks API

In this chapter I want to summarize all the Hooks which are available to us internally and describe how and when they can be used. The official React documentation differentiates between three basic Hooks and seven additional Hooks. These additional Hooks are often used for very specific use cases (such as performance optimizations) or they are extensions of the basic Hooks.

The three **basic Hooks** which I mentioned briefly beforehand are:

- useState
- useEffect
- useContext

The **seven additional Hooks** are:

- useReducer
- useCallback
- useMemo
- useRef
- useImperativeHandle
- useLayoutEffect
- useDebugValue

useState

```
const [state, setState] = useState(initialState);
```

This Hook returns a **value** as well as a **function** to us, which we can use to update the **value**. During the first rendering of a component that uses this Hook, this value is equal to the initialState which you pass to the state. If the parameter that has been passed in is a function, it will use the return value of the function as its initial value.

When the update function is called, React ensures that the function always has the same **identity** and does not create a new function whenever the Hook is called. This is important as it reduces the number of renders and also means that we do not need to pass any other **dependencies** (as is the case in useEffect() or useCallback()).

useState() will return an **array** to us of which the first **value** always denotes the state and the second value is always a **function** which we use to update said **value**. Due to array destructuring, we are not limited in naming this value and function. However, conventions have developed that follow the pattern of `value` / `setValue`. For example, `user` and `setUser`. But of course you could also go for something along the lines of this: `changeUser` and `updateUserState`.

The mechanism of actually updating the state is very similar to that of `this.setState()` which we already encountered in the chapter on Class components. The function can either receive a **new value** which then replaces the current old value or we can pass an **updater function** to the function. The updater function receives the previous value and uses the **return value** from the function as its new state.

But be careful: in contrast to `this.setState()`, objects are **not merged** with their previous state but the old state is completely **replaced** by the new state.

To illustrate this, let's have a look at the following example:

```
import React, { useState, useEffect }  from 'react';
import ReactDOM from 'react-dom';

class StateClass extends React.Component {
  state = { a: 1 , b: 2 };

  componentDidMount() {
    this.setState({ c: 3 });
    this.setState(() => {
      return { d: 4 };
    });
  }

  render() {
    // { a: 1, b: 2, c: 3, d: 4 }
    return <pre>{JSON.stringify(this.state, null, 2)} </pre>;
  }
}

const StateHook = () => {
  const [example, setExample] = useState({ a: 1 , b: 2 });

  useEffect(() => {
    setExample({ c: 3 });
    setExample(() => {
      return { d: 4 };
    });
  }, []);
```

```
  // { d: 4 }
  return <pre>{JSON.stringify(example, null, 2)} </pre>;
};

const App = () => {
  return (
    <>
      <StateClass />
      <StateHook />
    </>
  );
};

ReactDOM.render(<App /> , document.getElementById('root'));
```

While `StateClass` collects and merges the data of all calls of `this.setState()`, the `setState()` function in the `StateHook` completely replaces the old value with the new one. In the **Class component,** the output returned to us will be {a: 1, b: 2, c: 3, d: 4} whereas the **Function component** containing the Hook will only return {d: 4} as this has been written into state last.

If the updater function returns the **exact same value** as the value currently in state, the state update is cancelled and no re-render or side-effects are triggered.

useEffect

```
useEffect(effectFunction, dependenciesArray);
```

This **Hook** is intended for **imperative side effects** such as API requests, timers or global event listeners. Normally, these **side effects** should be avoided in **Function components** as they can lead to unexpected behaviour or bugs that might be hard to solve for.

The useEffect() **Hook** combats this problem and allows for a *safe* mechanism to use side effects within **Function components**.

The **Hook** expects a **function** as its first parameter and a **dependency array** as its second. The function is called **after** the component has rendered. If we have passed an **optional dependency array** to this Hook, the function we pass will only be executed if at least one of the values in the **dependency array** has changed. If an **empty dependency array** is passed, the function will only be run on the **first render** of the component - similar to the `componentDidMount()` lifecycle method which we learned about with Class components.

Cleaning up side effects

Sometimes side effects leave "traces" that have to be cleaned up once a component is no longer in use. If for example you had intervals which you had started with `setInterval()`, these should be stopped with `clearTimeOut()` once the component has been removed. If left untreated, these side effects can lead to actual problems or even memory leaks.

Globally registered event listeners such as `resize` or `orientationchange` which have been added to the `window` object with `addEventListener()` should also be removed once the component unmounts by using `removeEventListener()` so they will not be executed anymore if the component itself is not even part of the component tree anymore.

In order to make this cleanup a bit more systematic and easier, we can return a **cleanup function** from the **effect function**. If an **effect function** returns a **cleanup function**, it is called before each call of the **effect function** with the exception of the very first call:

```
import React, { useState, useEffect } from "react";
import ReactDOM from "react-dom";

const Clock = () => {
  const [time, setTime] = useState( new Date());

  useEffect(() => {
    const intervalId = setInterval(() => {
      setTime( new Date());
    }, 1000);
    return () => {
      clearInterval(intervalId);
    };
  }, []);

  return `${time.getHours()} : ${time.getMinutes()} : ${time.getSeconds()} `;
);

ReactDOM.render(<Clock /> , document.getElementById("root"));
```

In the above example we have set up an interval that starts once the component **mounts**. Once the component **unmounts** we stop the timer as we would otherwise change the state of the component which is not part of the component tree anymore. If we tried to do this, React would inform us with a warning and suggest to **clean up** asynchronous tasks and subscriptions in a **cleanup function**:

Warning: We can't perform a React state update on an unmounted component. This is a no-op, but it indicates a memory leak in your application. To fix, cancel all subscriptions and asynchronous tasks in a useEffect cleanup function.

By returning a cleanup function from the **effect function** we can stop the interval with a call of `clearInterval()`. This happens before each call of the effect function, but at the very latest it would happen during unmounting.

Conditional calls of the effect function

Normally the `useEffect()` Hook or its associated effect function is executed after each render of a component. This way, we ensure that the effect is executed each time once of its dependencies have changed. If we access state or props of a component within the effect function, the side effect should also be executed if one of the dependencies change. If we wanted to display profile data of a particular user and requested this data from an API, the API request should also be initiated if the user's profile that we want to look at changes while the component is already mounted.

However, this might lead to a lot of unnecessary calls of this function and it might even be executed if no data has actually changed since the last render (which are relevant for the side effect). This is why the React allows us to define a **dependency array** as a second parameter in the **effect function**. Only if one or more values in the **dependency array** have changed, the function will be called again. Let's put our previous example into a little code snippet:

```
useEffect(() => {
  const user = api.getUser(props.username);
  setUser(user);
}, [props.username]);
```

In this example, we have put the username into the dependency array which we use to request data from the API.

While creating such a **dependency array**, we should take the utmost care to include all values that are present in the function and could change within the lifetime of the component. If the effect function should only be run once and perform a similar task such as `componentDidMount()` , we leave the **dependency array** empty.

In order to facilitate or automate the creation of **dependency arrays**, the eslint-plugin-react-hooks offers an exhaustive-deps rule which will automatically write dependencies used in the effect function into the **dependency array** or at least warn that they should be included. These could be run on *Format on Save* or another similar editor configuration.

You can active it by setting "exhaustive-deps": "warn" in the rules block of the ESLint configuration.

Sequence of operations

The **effect function** is called **asynchronously** with a little bit of delay after the **layout and paint phase** of the browser. For most side effects this should be sufficient. You might run into situations though in which it is necessary to to **synchronously** run side effects. For example, you might need to perform DOM mutations and a delay in execution would lead to an inconsistent user interface or jarring content on the screen.

To deal with these problems, React introduced the useLayoutEffect() Hook. It works almost identical to the useEffect() Hook: it expects an **effect function** which can also return a **cleanup function** and also contains a dependency array. This dependency array is identical to that of the regular useEffect() Hook. The difference in the two Hooks is that the useLayoutEffect() Hook is executed synchronously and run just after all DOM mutations have finished, as opposed to asynchronously as is the case in the regular useEffect() Hook.

useLayoutEffect() can read from the DOM and can also synchronously modify it **before** the browser will display these changes in its **paint phase**.

Asynchronous effect functions

Even if **effect functions** can be run with delay, they are not allowed to be asynchronous by definition, and are not allowed to return a promise. If we tried to perform such an operation, React would give us the following warning:

In the above example, an **incorrect** useEffect() Hook could have looked like the following (please don't do this):

```
useEffect( async () => {
  const response =  await fetch( 'https://api.github.com/users/manuelbieh');
  const accountData =  await response.json();
  setGitHubAccount(accountData);

  fetchGitHubAccount( 'manuelbieh' );
}, []);
```

This is **not allowed** as the effect function is declared with the async keyword. So how would we go about solving this problem? There's a relatively simple solution to this problem. We move the asynchronous part of this function into its own asynchronous function **within the effect function** and then only call this function:

```
import React, { useEffect, useState }  from 'react';
import ReactDOM from 'react-dom';

const App = (props) => {
  const [gitHubAccount, setGitHubAccount] = useState();

  useEffect(() => {
    const fetchGitHubAccount =  async () => {
      const response =  await fetch(
        `https://api.github.com/users/ ${props.username}`
      );
      const accountData =  await response.json();
      setGitHubAccount(accountData);
    };

    fetchGitHubAccount();
  }, [props.username]);
```

```
  if (!gitHubAccount) {
    return null;
  }

  return (
    <p>
      {gitHubAccount.name} has {gitHubAccount.public_repos} public repos
    </p>
  );
};

ReactDOM.render(<App username="manuelbieh" />, document.getElementById('root'));
```

In this case, the effect function itself is not asynchronous. The asynchronous functionality has been extracted into its own asynchronous function `fetchGitHubAccount()` which is defined **inside** of the `useEffect()` Hook.

The asynchronous function does not necessarily need to be defined **inside** of the effect function. But the effect function itself is not allowed to be asynchronous.

useContext

```
const myContextValue = useContext(MyContext);
```

This Hook only expects one parameter: a context type which we create by calling `React.createContext()` . It will then return the value of the next highest context provider in the component hierarchy.

The `useContext()` Hook acts like a context consumer component and causes a re-render of the **Function component** as soon as the value of the context in the provider element changes.

Using this Hook is optional and it is still possible to create Context consumers in **JSX** using **Function components**. However, the Hook is much more convenient and easier to read as no new hierarchical layer is created in the component tree.

useReducer

```
const [state, dispatch] = useReducer(reducerFunc, initialState, initFunc);
```

The `useReducer()` Hook is an alternative solution for `useState()` and allows us to manage more complex states. It is based on flux architecture in which a **reducer function** creates a new state by being passed the **last state** and a so-called **action**.

The **reducer function** is called by executing a **dispatch function** which in turn receives an **action**. The **action** is an object which always has a `type` property and often a `payload` property attached. From this **action** and the **previous state**, the **reducer function** can then create the **new state**. One could summarize this in the following form: `(oldState, action) => newState`.

Let us have a look at a simple example. We have developed a `Counter` component which can increment or decrement a counter by pressing a + and - button:

```
import React, { useReducer } from 'react';
import ReactDOM from 'react-dom';

const initialState = {
  count: 0,
};

const reducerFunction = (state, action) => {
  switch (action.type) {
    case 'INCREMENT':
      return { count: state.count + 1 };
    case 'DECREMENT':
      return { count: state.count - 1 };
    default:
      throw new Error('Unknown action');
  }
};

const Counter = () => {
  const [state, dispatch] = useReducer(reducerFunction, initialState);

  return (
    <div>
      <h1>{state.count}</h1>
      <button onClick={() => dispatch({ type: 'INCREMENT' })}>+</button>
      <button onClick={() => dispatch({ type: 'DECREMENT' })}>-</button>
    </div>
  );
};

ReactDOM.render(<Counter /> , document.getElementById('root'));
```

We have defined the initial State `initialState` and the reducer function `reducerFunction`. The initial state only consists of an object which holds a count property which is initially 0. The reducer function on the other hand expects a `state` and an `action` which are later passed to the reducer function by calling the `dispatch` function. These two parameters will then create

231

the **new** state. **But beware**: instead of mutating an existing state, we always have to create a new state! Otherwise mutations of the existing state will lead to side effects which are not intended and cause incorrect display of components. A **reducer** function should always be a **pure** function.

The **reducer function**, as well as the initial state, are then passed to the useReducer() Hook which will return a tuple. The tuple consists of two values: the first element will portray the **current state** in this particular rendering phase and the second value will be the so-called **dispatch** function.

If we want to change our current state, we call the dispatch function and pass this function an **action**. In our current example, we achieve this by clicking one of the two buttons which will either dispatch the { type: "INCREMENT" } (to increase the counter) action or { type: "DECREMENT" } (to decrease the counter) action/

If an action has been *"dispatched"*, a new state is created and React will trigger a re-render. The new state will now be accessible in the new state variable which was returned by the reducer function. If however the same state was returned from the **reducer**, no re-render will be triggered.

The third parameter

Apart from the reducer function and initialState which we always need to specify, we can also pass a third optional parameter to the useReducer() Hook. This third parameter is called an init function which can be used to calculate the initial state. The function could be used to extract the value of a **reducer** in an external function which is outside of the reducer itself.

If such an init function has been passed to the Hook, it will be called during the **first** call. The initialState will be passed to it as its **initial argument**. This can be really useful if the **initial state** of your component is based on props for example. These props can be passed as the second parameter inside of the init function which can then create the initial state of the **reducer** based on these:

```
import React, { useReducer } from 'react';
import ReactDOM from 'react-dom';

const reducerFunction = (state, action) => {
  switch (action.type) {
    case 'INCREMENT':
      return { count: state.count + 1 };
    case 'DECREMENT':
      return { count: state.count - 1 };
    default:
      throw new Error('Unknown action');
```

```
    }
  };

  const initFunction = (initValue) => {
    return { count: initValue };
  };

  const Counter = (props) => {
    const [state, dispatch] = useReducer(
      reducerFunction,
      props.startValue,
      initFunction
    );

    return (
      <div>
        <h1>{state.count}</h1>
        <button onClick={() => dispatch({ type: 'INCREMENT' })}>+</button>
        <button onClick={() => dispatch({ type: 'DECREMENT' })}>-</button>
      </div>
    );
  };

  ReactDOM.render(<Counter  startValue={3} />, document.getElementById('root'));
```

In this example, the useReducer() Hook has been extended to include a third and optional
parameter: the **init** function. The initialState is now an argument for the **init** function. The
value for this argument is passed to the component via **props** — startValue in our case.

Reducers in practice

The guiding principle of **reducers** should be known to those in the React community who have
had exposure to **Redux**. **Redux** is a library that allows us to manage complex state in a
comfortable manner and was the first point of call whenever handling local state became hard
to read and cumbersome. It also created a solution for the so-called "prop drilling" which meant
that previous props needed to be passed through multiple hierarchical layers.

Redux manages reducer functions and makes state and their dispatch functions available to
those components which should read or modify the global state. The useReducer() Hook is
React's custom solution to realize complex state management using reducer functions.

A common use case for reducers forms the management of API requests. Common
conventions dictate that three actions for each API request should be defined:

- an action which informs the application that the data is loading when the request has started
- an action which resets the loading state and (if the request has failed) can inform the state of an error
- an action which writes the data received by the API request into state if it was successful

Let's have a look at an example using our previous account data example using the GitHub API:

```
import React, { useEffect, useReducer }  from 'react';
import ReactDOM from 'react-dom';

const initialState = {
  data: null,
  isLoading: false,
  isError: false,
  lastUpdated: null ,
};

const accountReducer = (state, action) => {
  switch (action.type) {
    case 'REQUEST_START' :
      return {
        ...state,
        isLoading: true ,
      };
    case 'REQUEST_SUCCESS' :
      return {
        ...state,
        data: action.payload,
        isLoading: false,
        isError: false,
        lastUpdated: action.meta.lastUpdated,
      };
    case 'REQUEST_ERROR' :
      return {
        ...state,
        isLoading: false,
        isError: true ,
      };
  }
};

const RepoInfo = (props) => {
  const [state, dispatch] = useReducer(accountReducer, initialState);

  useEffect(() => {
```

```
const fetchGitHubAccount =  async (username) => {
  try {
    dispatch({
      type: 'REQUEST_START' ,
    });
    const response = await fetch(
      `https://api.github.com/users/ ${username}`
    );

    const accountData = await response.json();
    dispatch({
      type: 'REQUEST_SUCCESS' ,
      payload: accountData,
      meta: {
        lastUpdated:  new Date(),
      },
    });
  } catch (err) {
    dispatch({
      type: 'REQUEST_ERROR' ,
      error: true ,
    });
  }
};

fetchGitHubAccount(props.username);
}, [props.username]);

if (state.isError) {
  return <p>An error occurred. </p>;
}

if (state.isLoading) {
  return <p>Loading...</p> ;
}

if (!state.data) {
  return <p>No GitHub account has been loaded. </p>;
}

return (
  <p>
    {state.data.name} has {state.data.public_repos} public repositories.
  </p>
);
};
```

```
ReactDOM.render(
  <RepoInfo username= "manuelbieh" />,
  document.getElementById('root')
);
```

The useReducer() Hook is used and passed to the accountReducer function. In this function, we deal with the three **actions** of **type** REQUEST_START, REQUEST_SUCCESS, and REQUEST_ERROR.

The initialState consists of an object with an empty data property, an isLoading and isError flag and a lastUpdated property. The flags inform us whether the data has actually loaded or whether an error occurred whilst the lastUpdated property will store a timestamp of the last successful request. We can use these later to only use one request per minute or to signal to the user that they might be seeing data but that the interface has not changed for a while.

In addition, we use a useEffect() Hook to initiate loading the data once the GitHub username in the **props** changes. Once this has happened, we dispatch the REQUEST_START **action**. The reducer will then create the new state:

```
{
  data: null,
- isLoading: false,
+ isLoading: true,
  isError: false,
  lastUpdated: null,
}
```

As we have defined a condition a bit lower down in our component, we will now display the following:

```
if (state.isLoading) {
  return <p>Loading...</p> ;
}
```

This is a clear signal for the user that data is currently being loaded.

After this state, we can be left with one of the following cases: the request either fails, or data is successfully obtained from the API.

If the requests failed, the REQUEST_ERROR **action** would be dispatched. The state would be reflected as such:

```
{
  data: null,
- isLoading: true,
+ isLoading: false,
- isError: false,
+ isError: true,
  lastUpdated: null,
};
```

As no further request will be fired, the isLoading flag will be reset from true to false so as to not signal to the user that data might still be loading. When an error has occurred, the state of isError is set from false to true. The code snippet above also contains a condition to handle the state of an error, so we can display a message to the user:

```
if (state.isError) {
  return <p>An error occurred. </p>;
}
```

It might be a good idea to tell the user which operation has failed and how they might be able to recover from the error. Maybe the provided username did not exist and we could offer an opportunity to the user to re-enter their username and correct their mistake. Another possibility could be that the API might not be available at the moment which could inform the user to try again at a later point of time.

If however the request was dealt with successfully and we could obtain data from the API, we dispatch the REQUEST_SUCCESS **action**. This not only contains a payload but also a meta property which includes the timestamp of the request.

The **new state** which is created by the **reducer** differs from the previous state in the following way:

```
{
- data: null,
+ data: {
+   "login": "manuelbieh",
+   "name": "Manuel Bieh",
+   "public_repos": 59,
+   [...]
+ },
- isLoading: true,
+ isLoading: false,
  isError: false,
- lastUpdated: null,
```

```
+ lastUpdated: "2019-03-19T02:29:10.756Z",
}
```

The data property contains the data which we have received from the API. The state of isLoading is set back to `false` andlastUpdated is updated to reflect the point in time when the data was successfully written to state. Based on this information, we can now display to the user:

```
return (
  <p>
    {state.data.name} has {state.data.public_repos} public repositories.
  </p>
);
```

Apart from writing our first more complex reducer, we have also successfully learned about how useEffect() and useReducer() can be used together.

As an aside: Similar to the useState() Hook, the useReducer() Hook will not trigger another re-render if the reducer function returns the exact same state as before.

useCallback

```
const memoizedFunction = useCallback(callbackFunction, dependencyArray);
```

The useCallback() Hook can be used to optimize the performance of an application. It receives a function and then creates a **unique identity** of that function, which will remain active until the **dependencies** of the Hook itself change.

This is important as we need to provide the same reference to a function, when dealing with PureComponents, when functions implement their own shouldComponentUpdate() method or if they are wrapped by React.memo().

useCallback() expects two parameters. The first being a function and the second being a dependency array (similar to that in useEffect()). It will return a **stable** reference to the function that we passed in, meaning that the reference only changes if one of its **dependencies** changed. Up to this point, references to PureComponents or components with React.memo() are the same.

But this sounds a little complicated in theory, let's look at an example:

```
import React, { useState, useCallback } from 'react';
import ReactDOM from 'react-dom';

const FancyInput = React.memo(({ name, onChange }) => {
```

```
  console.log('Rendering FancyInput');
  return <input type="text" name={name} onChange={onChange} />;
});

const Form = () => {
  const [values, setValues] = useState({});

  const changeHandler = (e) => {
    const { name, value } = e.target;

    setValues((state) => {
      return {
        ...state,
        [name]: value,
      };
    });
  };

  return (
    <>
      <pre>{JSON.stringify(values, null, 2)}</pre>
      <FancyInput name="example" onChange={changeHandler} />
    </>
  );
};

ReactDOM.render(<Form />, document.getElementById('root'));
```

We have defined two components here: `FancyInput` and `Form`. The `Form` component renders a `FancyInput` component and not only passes it a name attribute but also a function. It will change the state of the `Form` component whenever changes are made to the input field and subsequently trigger a re-render.

The `changeHandler` function is created in the **form component** and is thus generated fresh with every render, meaning **the reference to the function changes**. We are passing the same function but not an identical one.

Thus, we cannot make use of the `React.memo()` optimization mechanism in `FancyInput`. `React.memo()` checks **before** each re-render of a component if its **props** changed compared to the previous render and will trigger a re-render if this is the case. As the `changeHandler` function is generated from scratch every time the `Form` component renders, this condition will always be true and the `FancyInput` will always re-render too.

We can use `useCallback()` to combat this. By wrapping our `changeHandler()` function in this Hook, React can create a **unique** and **stable** reference and can safely return it so it can be used in the `FancyInput` component without triggering unnecessary re-renders:

```
const changeHandler = useCallback((e) => {
  const { name, value } = e.target;

  setValues((state) => {
    return {
      ...state,
      [name]: value,
    };
  });
}, []);
```

We can now use the optimization techniques of `React.memo()` (or in Class components: `PureComponent`) without triggering unnecessary renders.

If the function depends on values which can change in the lifespan of the component, we can put these in the **dependency array** (as was the case in `useEffect()`) as the second parameter. React will then create a new function with a new reference, if one of the dependencies changes.

 As was the case in the `useEffect()` Hook, the exhaustive-deps rule of `theeslint-plugin-react-hooks` can help us to configure **Dependency Arrays**.

useMemo

```
const memoizedValue = useMemo(valueGetterFunction, dependencyArray);
```

The other Hook that's useful for hardcore **performance optimization** is the `useMemo()` Hook. It works similarly to the `useCallback()` Hook, however it does not provide a unique identity for the function going in, but for the return value from the function which has been passed into the `useMemo()` Hook.

So this snippet of code:

```
useCallback(fn, deps);
```

corresponds to this:

```
useMemo(() => fn, deps);
```

While useCallback() returns a *memoized* (a "remembered") version of the **function that has been passed in**, useMemo() provides a *memoized* version of the **return value** of the function that has been passed in. useMemo() can be really useful in situations where functions perform complex computational tasks that do not need to be executed in each render.

Let us have a look at a non-optimized component:

```jsx
import React, { useState, useMemo }  from 'react';
import ReactDOM from 'react-dom';

const fibonacci = (num) =>
  num <= 1 ? 1 : fibonacci(num - 1 ) + fibonacci(num -  2);

const FibonacciNumber = ({ value }) => {
  const result = fibonacci(value);
  return (
    <p>
      {value}: {result}
    </p>
  );
};

const App = () => {
  const [values, setValues] = useState([]);

  const handleKeyUp = (e) => {
    const { key, target } = e;
    const { value } = target;
    if (key === 'Enter' ) {
      if (value > 40 || value <  1) {
        alert( 'Invalid value' );
        return;
      }
      setValues((values) => values.concat(target.value));
    }
  };

  return (
    <>
      <input type="number" min={1} max={40} onKeyUp={handleKeyUp} />
      {values.map((value, i) => (
        <FibonacciNumber value={value} key={`${i}:${value}`} />
      ))}
    </>
  );
};
```

```
ReactDOM.render(<App />, document.getElementById('root'));
```

This app consists of an input field for numbers. If a number is entered and submitted with the **enter** key, the number is written into state within the `values` field. In this case, this state corresponds to an array which will hold all the numbers we have entered. The component will then iterate through all of the numbers entered and then renders a `FibonacciNumber` component which will receive each of these values.

The `FibonacciNumber` component will then calculate the corresponding Fibonacci number for the entered number and display it to the user. Depending on the number and computational power, it might take some time to calculate this number (on my PC it took about 2-3 seconds for the 40th Fibonacci number).

Currently, the calculation will happen **each** time **even if the number is already present** in the array. If I entered 40, I would have to wait 3 seconds to get a result. If I entered 40 again, I would need to wait 3 seconds again (on top of the previous 3 seconds) as the value is calculated in both components again.

We can use useMemo() to deal with such situations more efficiently. By changing the following line from

```
const result = fibonacci(value);
```

to:

```
const result = useMemo(() => fibonacci(value), [value]);
```

... we have created a *memoized* value.

React will calculate this value during the **first render**, **remember** the value and will only re-calculate if the value of the value prop changes for this component. If the value or the **dependencies** do not change between the two renders, React will use the value of the previous calculation without actually performing the computation.

But be careful: This is all happening due to a **single** call of the useMemo() Hook. If I called the same function twice in two different useMemo() Hooks, the calculation would still be performed twice even if both functions use the same parameters. The second Hook will **not** use the result of the previous calculation.

useRef

```
const ref = useRef(initialValue);
```

useRef() is used to create **Refs** by using a dedicated Hook.

```
import React, { useEffect, useRef } from 'react';
import ReactDOM from 'react-dom';

function App() {
  const inputRef = useRef();
  useEffect(() => {
    inputRef.current.focus();
  }, []);

  return <input ref={inputRef} />;
}

ReactDOM.render(<App /> , document.getElementById('root'));
```

We are not usually doing this Hook enough justice: **refs** in **function components** also serve a different purpose: they allow us to create a **mutable reference** which will persist for the entire lifespan of the component (meaning until it unmounts). It can be compared to performing similar tasks as instance variables in class components.

useRef() takes in an optional initial value and returns an object with a current property which can then be accessed within the **function component**. This access is not limited to read access but also allows write access. If we wanted to provide data whose changes would not trigger a re-render but whose reference would stay the same between two rendering cycles, we can use the useRef() Hook.

useLayoutEffect

I have briefly mentioned useLayoutEffect() when I presented useEffect(). It follows a similar pattern as the useEffect() Hook but differs in the timing of its execution and its synchronous nature.

While useEffect() is executed with a little bit of delay **after** the **layout and paint** phase of the browser, useLayoutEffect() is executed **after layout** but **before paint**. This difference in timing allows useLayoutEffect() to read the current layout from the DOM and change it **before** it is being displayed in the browser.

This kind of behavior is similar to what was previously achieved by componentDidMount() or componentDidUpdate() in class components. Due to performance reasons however, it is advisable to use useEffect() in most cases and only use useLayoutEffect() if we know exactly what we are doing. useLayoutEffect() can also help if we are struggling to migrate **class components** to **function components** due to the different timings of the effects.

But be careful: neither useEffect() nor useLayoutEffect() will be executed server-side. While this does not pose a problem for useEffect() as it is only executed after the layout and painting phase of the browser, useLayoutEffect() might lead to differences in the server-side rendered markup compared to the initial client-side render. React will usually inform us of these differences and create a warning in the console. In these cases, useEffect() should be used instead or components using useLayoutEffect() should be mounted after the browser's paint phase.

```
import React, { useState, useEffect }  from 'react';
import ReactDOM from 'react-dom';

const App = () => {
  const [mountLayoutComp, setMountLayoutComp] = useState(  false);

  useEffect(() => {
    setMountLayoutComp( true);
  }, []);

  return mountLayoutComp ? <ComponentWithLayoutEffect />   : null;
};

ReactDOM.render(<App /> , document.getElementById('root'));
```

In this example, the component using useLayoutEffect() is only registered after the component is mounted. We achieve this by checking for the mountLayoutComp state after the first paint phase.

useDebugValue

```
useDebugValue(value);
```

This Hook (useDebugValue()) is purely for optimizing the developer's debugging experience. It does not create any real value in an application for the **end user**. useDebugValue() allows us to give custom Hooks a label which we can then inspect in the **React Dev tools**:

```
import React, { useDebugValue, useEffect }  from 'react';

const usePageTitle = (title) => {
  useDebugValue(title);
  useEffect(() => {
    document.title = title;
  }, [title]);
};
```

```
export default usePageTitle;
```

In this example, we have implemented a **Hook** to change the page title in the browser. In the Dev tools, we can see the following:

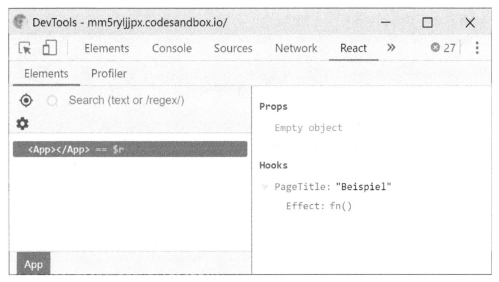

The debugValue appearing next to the name of the Hook

Delayed formatting of the debug value

If you recall, I have just mentioned that useDebugValue() does not have any real positive implication for the end user. However, this does not mean that it does not influence the user experience of the user interface. Slow calculations to display the value of the debug value can indeed decrease the rendering performance of an application.

As this is not really desirable, it is possible to pass a second parameter to the useDebugValue() Hook: a formatting function. The formatting of the value is only executed, once the value is actually inspected in the Dev tools. Declaring the Hook could look like this:

```
useDebugValue(value, (value) => formattedValue);
```

The Hook is passed a **debug value** as its first argument just as we have provided before. However, as the second argument it will not receive a function that will executed the formatting of the debug value. This function will receive the **value** from the **Hook** and will return the formatted value.

If you are looking for a clear if unrealistic example, I can provide another example using the Fibonacci function we have already seen in the useMemo() example. We are going to display the debug value once with, and once without the formatting function and inspect how the time to display the app changes:

```
import React, { useDebugValue, useEffect }  from 'react';
import ReactDOM from 'react-dom';

const fibonacci = (num) =>
  num <= 1 ? 1 : fibonacci(num - 1 ) + fibonacci(num -  2);

const useNumber = (number) => {
  useDebugValue(number, (number) => fibonacci(number));
  // without formatting function:
  // useDebugValue(fibonacci(number));
  useEffect(() => {});
  return number;
};

function App() {
  useNumber( 41);
  return <p>Debug Value Formatting Function example </p>;
}

ReactDOM.render(<App /> , document.getElementById('root'));
```

Using useDebugValue() without the formatting function does significantly increase the loading time of the app which affects the user experience for the end user.

useImperativeHandle

```
useImperativeHandle(ref, createHandle, [deps]);
```

I will be entirely honest with you all: I found it extremely difficult to construct a use case in which useImperativeHandle() will pose a useful solution to an encountered problem. Frustrated, I took to Twitter and crafted a post to ask for help. I was lucky enough to get an answer by Dan Abramov, core developer in the React team at Facebook, who informed me that I must be doing something right. This Hook should not be used and has a long name to dissuade people from using it. For matters of completion and for understanding why this Hook exists, I want to present it to you anyway.

Manuel Bieh @ManuelBieh · Mar 19, 2019
Has anyone here ever used the useImperativeHandle Hook in React in a real world application and can tell me how and why and for what? I'm really struggling to find a valid use case for this hook 😖

 Dan Abramov
@dan_abramov

That's a sign you're doing it right. It intentionally has a long name to discourage use. It exists mostly as a way to simulate class methods for refs.

♡ 8   12:53 AM - Mar 20, 2019

 See Dan Abramov's other Tweets   >

Dan Abramov advising me that useImperativeHandle should not really be used in the wild

I have spent a lot of time thinking about use cases worth of using the useImperativeHandle() . In most cases you should indeed explore other ways to express logic without the use of this Hook. The official React documentation also discourages anyone from using this Hook. As the name might suggest, it caters to imperative code and does not work well with the mostly declarative style that React openly advocates. However, there are situations in which one might need to work with classes and objects, especially when working with external libraries.

But be careful, examine the following example which illustrates the use of this **Hook**. We have created a FancyForm component which displays its **children** and offers a couple of methods which can be called in the parent component consuming them. In this example, we have implemented a method called focusFirstInput to be able to focus onto the first input in our FancyForm form. We furthermore extend the form with another method called getFormValues which allows us to return our data that we entered in JSON format. The form can be sent off programmatically and reset by passing the forwarded **forwardRef** the imperative methods reset() and submit() from the HTML <form> element.

```
import React, { useImperativeHandle, useEffect, useRef }   from 'react';
import ReactDOM from 'react-dom';

const FancyForm = React.forwardRef((props, forwardedRef) => {
  const formRef = useRef();
```

```
useImperativeHandle(
  forwardedRef,
  () => ({
    focusFirstInput: () => {
      (formRef.current.querySelector( 'input') || {}).focus();
    },
    getFormValues: () => {
      return Array.from( new FormData(formRef.current)).reduce(
        (acc, [value, name]) => {
          acc[name] = value;
          return acc;
        },
        {}
      );
    },
    reset: () => formRef.current.reset(),
    submit: () => formRef.current.submit(),
  }),
  []
);

  return <form ref={formRef} >{props.children}</form> ;
});

const App = () => {
  const formRef = useRef();

  useEffect(() => {
    formRef.current.focusFirstInput();
  }, []);

  const submit = (e) => {
    e.preventDefault();
    console.log(formRef.current.getFormValues());
  };

  return (
    <FancyForm ref={formRef}>
      <p>
        <input type="text" name="name" placeholder="name" />
      </p>
      <p>
        <input type="email" name="email" placeholder="email" />
      </p>
      <input type="submit" onClick={submit} />
    </FancyForm>
```

```
    );
  };

ReactDOM.render(<App />, document.getElementById('root'));
```

V – The Ecosystem

For one it's a curse, for another it's a blessing: the **freedom** that **React** offers.

While fully-fledged frameworks like Angular provide very clear guidelines about how an application should be structured and also provide their own methods for data management, services and business logic, React follows more of a "bring your own" pattern - meaning as much as that you can use whichever tools you might already be using.

As already mentioned at the beginning of this book, React is just a **library for the development of user interfaces** (Small anecdote on the side: This sentence is one of the few lines of documentation I quoted in this book that hasn't changed in the course of working on this book ;)). In the world of classical MVC (*Model View Controller*) architecture, so to speak, React only touches on the view layer. If you look for extended state management, if you want to develop a multilingual application or if you need client-side routing out-of-the-box, React alone will often not make you happy.

But there is a very valuable and active ecosystem that has evolved around React, with tools that integrate well with a React setup and give developers the choice of choosing from multiple tools to find the one that best suits their personal needs. If none fits at all, this is usually not a problem. React offers a variety of functions and APIs that allow for the possibility to develop a robust, own solution.

With such a great and vast ecosystem around a single library, you might lose track as to which additional tools are actually useful. I want to dedicate some time and effort in this chapter to outline the most common tools and libraries which have proven to be effective in the daily work with React. Most of these have thousands of starts on GitHub and are installed ten thousand times or more via npm.

Routing

Most **Single Page Applications** will need some form of **routing** at some point of time, meaning that we want to map certain functions or behavior to a URL. For example, if I visited the URL of /users/manuel, I would like to present the profile of the user `manuel`.

React Router has established itself as the standard for **routing** in React Single Page Applications. Developed by Michael Jackson (yes, that's his name!) and Ryan Florence (who has built over 10 different routers throughout the years), it boasts with over 35,000 stars on GitHub showing its great popularity. It's well maintained, has over 500 different contributors listed on GitHub and integrates well with React principles due to its declarative nature. Moreover, it can be used on the web (client- and server-side) and in React Native. It's a very universal, well-tested and popular choice for routing.

The interface of React Router is relatively simple. In 95% of situations, you will only really encounter five core components: `BrowserRouter`, `Link`, `Route`, `Redirect` and `Switch`. It also offers an imperative History API, which can be extended via the `history` package which forms a thin layer over the native browser implementation making it cross-browser compatible. It also provides a Higher-Order-Component called `withRouter` which allows us to pass in routing relevant data from the router to another component.

You can install **React Router** via:

```
npm install --save react-router-dom
```

or:

```
yarn add react-router-dom
```

React Router's usage is *declarative* and can be achieved via the components mentioned above. Routers can be used anywhere in the application as long as the page tree itself is nested in a **Router Context.** In most cases, this context will wrap the entire application and exist only once:

```
import React from 'react';
import ReactDOM from 'react-dom';
import { BrowserRouter as Router } from 'react-router-dom' ;

const App = () => {
  return <Router>[...]</Router> ;
};
```

```
ReactDOM render( <App />, document.getElementById('root'));
```

Defining routes

Each component placed inside of the `<Router></Router>` element, can access the **Router Context**, react to it or manage it. We create routes, by using the Route component and providing a `path` prop as well as an optional `render` or `component` prop (the exception being the 404 route). The value of a `render` prop has to be a **function** that returns a valid **React element** whereas the `component` prop expects a **component** (not an *element*).

The correct implementation of both props can be summarized as the following:

```
import React from 'react';
import ReactDOM from 'react-dom';
import { BrowserRouter as Router } from 'react-router-dom';

const Example = () => <p>Example Component</p>;

const App = () => {
  return (
    <Router>
      <Route path="/example" component={Example} />
      <Route path="/example" render={() => <Example />} />
    </Router>
  );
};

ReactDOM.render(<App />, document.getElementById('root'));
```

This example would render the `Example` component twice once the `/example` route is hit, as the Route component merely checks whether the path of the current URL is the same as the one provided in the `path` prop. This might sound a little odd at first, but there's a logical explanation.

As mentioned previously, React Router works declaratively which means that if we ask for two different routes we will also receive two components if the URL matches. This can be useful if we want to render different parts of the page independently, based on a URL. Assume that we define an App with a sidebar and a content area. Both of these should react to a URL:

```
import React from "react";
import ReactDOM from "react-dom";
import { BrowserRouter as Router, Route } from 'react-router-dom';
```

```
const Home = () => <p>Home Content</p>;
const Account = () => <p>AccountContent</p>;
import HomeSidebar = () => <p>Home Sidebar</p>
import AccountSidebar = () => <p>AccountSidebar</p>

const App = () => {
  return (
    <Router>
      <main>
        <Route path="/account" component={Account} />
        <Route path="/" component={Home} />
      </main>
      <aside>
        <Route path="/account" component={AccountSidebar} />
        <Route path="/" component={HomeSidebar} />
      </aside>
    </Router>
  );
}

ReactDOM.render(<App />, document.getElementById("root"));
```

In this example, we can see that two different components are rendered in different parts of our application, depending on the URL which is currently active.

However, while the above is completely valid code, one could argue that we are creating unnecessary duplication in this example. Thus, many try to avoid this structure and would rewrite the above example as the following:

```
import React from 'react';
import ReactDOM from 'react-dom';
import { BrowserRouter as Router, Route } from 'react-router-dom';

const Home = () => (
  <>
    <main>Home Content</main>
    <aside>Home Sidebar</aside>
  </>
);

const Account = () => (
  <>
    <main>Account Content</main>
    <aside>Account Sidebar</aside>
  </>
);
```

253

```
const App = () => {
  return (
    <Router>
      <Route path="/account" component={Account} />
      <Route path="/" component={Home} />
    </Router>
  );
};


ReactDOM.render(<App />, document.getElementById('root'));
```

While we avoided duplication of routing in this case, we have created duplication of the layout code. We should probably abstract this structure in its own layout component.

```
import React from 'react';

const Layout = (props) => (
  <>
    <main>{props.content}</main>
    <aside>{props.sidebar}</aside>
  </>
);

const Home = () => <Layout content="Home Content" sidebar="Home Sidebar" />;
const Account = () => (
  <Layout content="Account Content" sidebar="Account Sidebar" />
);

const App = () => {
  return (
    <Router>
      <Route path="/account" component={Account} />
      <Route path="/" component={Home} />
    </Router>
  );
};


ReactDOM.render(<App />, document.getElementById('root'));
```

If you have tried these code examples on your own, you might have noticed something that strikes you as a little odd. **React Router** intentionally has a rather relaxed approach to path matching. When we hit the /account URL, we do not only render the Account component, but also the Home component as the /account URL **also includes** the path of / which then

254

renders both components. This is intentional as it allows us to group certain areas of the page under a certain URL prefix and have all components render on these types of routes.

Imagine a user account and a sidebar within this user account. Let's assume that we are building a community which has a user area which is divided into different subcategories: `/account/edit` to edit your profile, `/account/images` to view your own pictures or `/account/settings` to change your account settings. We can use a generic route in this application:

```
<Route path= "/account"  component={AccountSidebar} />
```

This `AccountSidebar` component would now be rendered on every subpage that is part of the `/account` area, as all their URLs would also include `/account`.

Limit matching with props

In order to limit the matching between `path` and the URL, React Router provides an `exact` prop on the `Route` component. If this Boolean prop is provided, the route is only rendered if the path prop exactly matches the current URL.

```
<Route exact path= "/"  component={Home} />
```

Where exactly you place this prop in **JSX** is not important. I like to place it just before the path prop to let it speak for itself: "Here's a route that matches an **exact path.**" If we included the exact prop in the Account Sidebar, the sidebar would only be rendered if the URL with `/account` was hit, and would not register the components for `/account/edit`, `/account/images` or `/account/settings`.

Limiting matching to a single route via Switch component

The `exact` prop only ever covers a **single route** and does not affect other routes at all. If we have a number of URLs which could all match multiple routes, it would be very cumbersome to add an exact prop to all of these routes. **React Router** offers a solution to this problem though by offering the `Switch` component.

The `Switch` component that can wrap a number of `<Route />` elements, helps us to only ever render the **first** route whose `path` matches with the one currently present in the URL. It is not a bad idea to wrap Routes with a `Switch` element by default unless you want more than one route rendered. In the above example, we could have used a `Switch` component instead of the exact prop too:

```
<Router>
  <Switch>
    <Route path="/account" component={Account} />
    <Route path="/" component={Home} />
  </Switch>
</Router>
```

Once the `/account` URL is hit, the first route would match and all other routes that follow would be ignored. In this case, only the `Account` component would get rendered. `Switch` components only match the URL of their **direct** children. If the `Account` component contained its own routes, the Switch component would not take care of these. These routes would get rendered if the `path` matched the current URL.

Using Switch, we can implement a 404 page as a fallback route. If we remove the `path` prop from the route, the route now matches **every** URL. However, if it is used within a `Switch` element as the very last component, we inform **React Router** to only ever render this component if no other component matches:

```
const Error404 = () => <h1>404  - Page not found</h1>;

const App = () => (
  <Router>
    <Switch>
      <Route path="/account" component={Account} />
      <Route path="/contacts" component={Contacts} />
      <Route path="/inbox" component={Inbox} />
      <Route exact path="/" component={Home} />
      <Route component={Error404} />
    </Switch>
  </Router>
);
```

In this particular `Switch` element example, we also need to provide an `exact` prop for the `/` route. Why? If we did not provide the exact prop, this route would always match. Even an error route like `/does-not-exist` would be found under the `/` route. By providing the `exact` prop on the `/` route, we avoid this particular problem and an error component at the end of the `Switch` component can be safely rendered (if no other route matches). It fulfills a similar job to the `default` case of a `switch` statement in JavaScript.

Parameters in URLs

Most applications require some sort of usage of parameters in URLs. React Router also supports parameters by using colons (:) which some of you might be already familiar with.

```
<Route path= "/users/:userid" component={UserProfile} />
```

We can easily restrict which parameters should be detected and can even provide further customization. For example, React Router allows the limitation of matching of routes by providing an asc (ascending) or desc (descending) keyword in regular expressions just after the parameter:

```
<Route path= "/products/:order(asc|dec)" />
```

The above route would only match, if the URL provided was either /products/asc or /products/desc.

If we were to only allow numerical values in the :userid, we would define routes such as /users/:userid(\d*) or /users/:userid([0-9]*) to limit these. A URL of /users/123 would lead to a render of the UserProfile component, while /users/abc would not.

If **React Router** finds such a URL, the value of the parameter is extracted and passed in to the rendered component via the match prop.

Controlling redirects of particular routes

Apart from the usual Route component to react to particular Routes, **React Router** also offers a Redirect component. The Redirect component is initialized with a to prop in which we can provide a destination URL that the component should redirect to. It allows us to declaratively decide in **JSX** where to send a particular user in certain situations. Whenever a Redirect component is equipped with only a to prop, a redirect to the URL provided will take place.

Redirect components are a great solution to the common use case of having to redirect users to a login page if they are not logged in. Logged in users will continue to be directed to a Dashboard:

```
<Route
  exact
  path= "/"
  render={() => {
    return isLoggedIn ? <Dashboard /> : <Redirect to="/login" />;
  }}
/>
```

The render prop of the Route component can be used to check whether a user is logged in. If they are, a Dashboard component will be shown on the / Route, otherwise the user will be redirected to the /login Route via the Redirect component.

Redirect components can also be used inside `Switch` elements. They behave just like a `Route` component and only match if no other `Route` or `Redirect` has matched with the current URL.

If the `Redirect` is used inside of a `Switch` element, it can also receive a `from` prop. This is the equivalent to the path prop of the `Route` component, but ensures that the `Redirect` is taking place whenever the URL matches the value provided in the from prop:

```
<Switch>
    <Redirect from="/old" to="/new" />
    <Route path="/new" component={NewComponent} />
</Switch>
```

The `Redirect` component behaves just as the `Route` component concerning URL matching. It also supports the exact prop and also supports redirects to other routes with parameters:

```
<Switch>
    <Redirect from="/users/:userid" to="/users/profile/:userid" />
    <Route path="/users/profile/:userid" component={UserProfile} />
</Switch>
```

If the URL /old is hit (first example) or /users/123 (second example), the user will be redirected to the URL specified in the to prop.

Using Router Props

Each component that was rendered by React Router and has been added as a component prop to a `Route` component, automatically receives three other props:

- `match`
- `location`
- `history`

Each of these props can be accessed just like any other props. **Class components** can access these via `this.props` whereas **function components** can access these with props:

```
import React from 'react';
import ReactDOM from 'react-dom';
import { BrowserRouter as Router, Route } from 'react-router-dom';

const Example = (props) => {
  console.log(props);
  return <p>Example</p>;
};
```

```
const App = () => (
  <Router>
    <Route path="/users/:userid" component={Example} />
  </Router>
);
```

```
ReactDOM.render(<App /> , document.getElementById('root'));
```

Let's have a look at the console output of this component when the route /users/123 is hit:

```
{
  history: { /* ... */ },
  location: { /* ... */ },
  match: {
    path: "/:userid",
    url: "/users/123" ,
    isExact: true ,
    params: {
      userid: "123"
    }
  }
}
```

Without getting into too much detail for each property, we get a feel for which properties of the router we are able to access. For now, we only care about the match property which will contain the paths we have defined in the match.params once a matching URL is called. In this case, we can access match.params.userid which will yield the value of 123.

A possible extension of this use case could be the start of an API request in a user profile component. The user id could be used to fetch the particular data for the user 123 and then display their user profile.

React Router ensures that each component connected to the Router will have a match property which always has its own params property. This will either contain the actual parameters or an empty object. props.match.params is therefore safe to access without having to fear that the property might be undefined and throwing an error.

The render prop on the Route component also receives the props of the router:

```
<Route
  path= "/users/:userid"
  render={(props) => {
    return <p>Profile of ID {props.match.params.userid}</p>  ;
```

```
    }}
/>
```

Navigating different routes

Once we've divided the application into different routes, we would also like to be able to link between these URLs. While we could easily use regular HTML anchors <a href="...">... </a>, this is not recommended. Each time such an anchor is used, we would trigger a "hard" page refresh in the browser. The page would be left **completely** and then be loaded again.

In practice, we would ask for an HTML document which would in turn load CSS and the JavaScript containing our React application from the server again (unless it is in the browser cache). Doing this would mean that everything is re-initialized based on each new URL. Any state that might have been set globally previously would be reset.

Single Page Applications should not follow this pattern and any HTML, CSS and JavaScript should only be loaded from the server once. Global state should be persisted once we navigate through the routes and only those parts of the page which actually change, should re-render.

To facilitate said behavior, **React Router** supports a Link component. It can be imported from the react-router-dom package and also comes with a to prop, which roughly equates to the regular href attribute on a HTML anchor element.

```
<Link to= "/account" >Account< /Link>
```

React Router also uses an <a href /> under the hood. However, any clicks to this page are being intercepted and sent to an internal function which then deals with displaying new page content based on the new URL - without triggering a complete refresh of the page.

Apart from the to prop, Links can also be equipped with an innerRef. These will be filled by createRef() or useRef() which both create a ref that can be used by the component. Moreover, Link also supports a replace prop which allows us to replace the current URL in the browser history instead of creating a new history entry. Be careful though, you cannot access the previous route when pressing the back button in the browser anymore if you chose to make use of the replace prop.

Any other props that are passed to the <Link /> element, will be passed down to the generated anchor element. <Link to="/" title="Homepage">Home</Link> would generate the following markup: <a href="/" title="Homepage">Home</a> .

Special case: NavLink

A special form of the Link element is the NavLink element. Apart from the usual props that can also be received by the Link component, NavLinks can change based on their state. NavLinks can access information relating to which page they are currently linking to and whether that page is the same as the current page. If this is the case, we can alter its display using activeClassName and activeStyle.

A classic example for this type of behavior is the overall page navigation. The currently active route in the menu is highlighted in a different color:

```
<NavLink to="/" activeClassName="active">Home</NavLink>
<NavLink to="/account" activeClassName="active">Account</NavLink>
<NavLink to="/contacts" activeClassName="active">Contacts</NavLink>
```

Only the Link of the current page receives the activeClassName active. If we had navigated to the /account URL, the markup would resemble the following:

```
<a href="/">Home</a>
<a href="/account" class="active">Account</a>
<a href="/contacts">Kontakte</a>
```

NavLinks can also receive an exact and strict prop (similar to the same **props** for the Route component) as well as an isActive prop. The latter expects a function which either returns true (if the current page is the same as the one provided in NavLink) or false (active page is not the same as NavLink). The function takes the aforementioned match object as its first argument and a location object as its second which are passed in from the router. The function can then decide whether to mark the NavLink as active or not - based on the information available.

Navigating programmatically using the History API

We now know how we can use Route elements on different URLs and how to react with different components. We have also learned how to avoid a full page reload by using the <Link /> element. In some cases however, it can be useful to programmatically force the change of a URL. For example, we might want to send the user to another site after successful completion of an asynchronous request.

The history property which can be accessed via each Route's props can help with this endeavor:

```
{
  history: {
    action: "POP"
    block: Function(prompt),
    go: Function(number),
    goBack: Function(),
    goForward: Function(),
    length: 1
    push: Function(path, state)
    replace: Function(path, state)
  },
  location: { /* ... */ },
  match: { /* ... */ }
}
```

Let's look at the push() and replace() functions in particular. Using props.history.push('/destination'), we can change the URL to /destination as well as triggering a re-render. This will create a new entry in the browser's history just as using a Link component did. If no entry in the browser's history is desired, the props.history.replace('/destination') function can be used instead.

We also have access to a so-called props.history.go() function which allows us to programmatically switch between entries in the browser's history. The function expects a parameter which indicates how many pages ahead or back should be turned. A negative value informs the function to go back in the entries whereas a positive value informs the function to go forward in the collection of entries. goBack() and goForward() are shortcuts for going back a step in the browser's history and forward. They are equivalent to calling go(-1) and go(1).

The action property in history confirms how the user has ended up on the current page. Possible values include POP, PUSH or REPLACE. POP can either signify that the user has pressed the back button in the browser or that they have loaded the page for the first time. PUSH informs us that the history.push() method has been called which is also the case once a <Link /> has been clicked. If the action properties value is REPLACE, history.replace() has been called or a <Link /> element has been clicked that contained a replace property.

Connecting components with a router using HOC

Each component which is used as a component prop in a Router element, is automatically passed the router props history, location, and match. Sometimes however, it would prove useful to not only be able to access Router functionality in components which are not using a direct Route. For example: to redirect to another page using history.push().

262

In order to allow for such use cases, **React Router** provides a `withRouter` Higher Order Component. Each component wrapped by this HOC will automatically receive the router's props even though they are not used as a Route component:

```
withRouter(MyComponent);
```

This component is sometimes used in another situation: it can prevent **"Update blocking"**. This used to be a necessary workaround before **React Router 5.0.0**. Since then however, this problem has been solved and is no longer necessary. I will still outline the reasons and rationale as to why this was necessary though should you ever find yourself working with older versions of **React Router**.

If components have been implemented as `PureComponent`s or have been wrapped by a `React.memo()` call for optimization reasons, re-renders are suppressed if no **props** or **state** have changed. As most Router components, for example `NavLink`, access data in the router via **React context**, a `PureComponent` or component wrapped by `React.memo()` might not receive any information that its children need re-rendered.

In those types of situations, it is recommend to wrap these components with a `withRouter()` HOC. Whenever a change in the Routing occurs and new props with a new location are passed to the respective component, a re-render will be triggered. This principle also applies to the state management library **Redux**. If a component is connected to the **Redux** store via the `connect()` function, the component would prohibit the re-rendering of router-specific logic, unless something has also changed in the store.

To avoid such cases, these components should be wrapped by a `withRouter()` HOC:

```
withRouter(connect()(MyComponent));
```

Since **React 16.3.0** however and **React Router 5.0.0**, this issue has been solved and you will only come across it while working with previous versions of these two libraries.

React Router and Hooks

Since React Router **5.1.0**, the library has been enhanced by a number of own Hooks that are available to the developer. It is now possible to access Router information in **function components** without using the `withRouter()` HOC provided that these components are not directly used as argument for the `<Route />` element prop component (`<Route component={MyComponent} />`).

As is the case with most Hooks, using React Router's own Hooks is a very pleasant and straightforward experience. Four Hooks allow us to access the `location` object, the `history` instance, the Route parameter or the `match` object. Conveniently, these Hooks are aptly called `useLocation`, `useHistory`, `useParams` and `useRouteMatch`. In order to use these Hooks, the component intended for the Hooks implementation needs to be be nested within a `<Router>` tree. However, it is not necessary for the component to follow directly after the Router element or be placed on the most upper layer. These Hooks can access the Router context and can thus be used anywhere in your application.

useLocation()

First, let's have a closer look at the arguably simplest Hook in our list. We can import it via the `react-router-dom` package. Once installed, we can access location data by using the return value of the Hook:

```
import React from 'react';
import { useLocation } from 'react-router-dom';

const ShowLocationInfo = () => {
  const location = useLocation();
  return <pre>{JSON.stringify(location, null, 2)}</pre> ;
};
```

In this example, we would obtain the following output for the `showLocationInfo` component:

```
{
  "pathname": "/" ,
  "search": "",
  "hash" : ""
}
```

useHistory()

This Hook allows us to use the `history` instance of React Router. It can access and change the URL via the `push()` and `replace()` methods and thus trigger a re-render of the application. `goBack()`, `goForward()` as well as the more general `go()` can be used to navigate the browser's history.

```
import React from 'react';
import { useHistory } from 'react-router-dom';

const NavigateHomeButton = () => {
  const history = useHistory();

  const goHome = () => {
    history.push( '/' );
```

```
    };

    return <button onClick={goHome}> Take me home </button>;
};
```

This example demonstrates how we can implement a button which will direct us to the home page once it's clicked using the useHistory() Hook.

useParams()

This Hook is basically a shortcut for accessing parameters which were hidden in match.params. If a route has been implemented using placeholders, such as /users/:userid , and then a URL such as /users/123 has been called, the params object will contain a key/value pair in the form of { "userid": "123" }.

The useParams() Hook allows us to *directly* access this object:

```
import React from 'react';
import { useParams, useLocation }  from 'react-router-dom';

const ShowParams = () => {
  const params = useParams();
  const location = useLocation();
  return <pre>{JSON.stringify({ location, params }, null, 2)}</pre>  ;
};
```

If a route such as /users/:userid had been created and a URL such as /users/123 has been called, the output would look like this:

```
{
  "location": {
    "pathname": "/users/123" ,
    "search": "",
    "hash" : ""
  },
  "params": {
    "userid": "123"
  }
}
```

useRouteMatch()

The last Hook introduced by React Router **5.1.0** forms the useRouteMatch() Hook. It allows us to access the whole match object of a Route, meaning we can now obtain information on `params`, `url`, `path` and `isExact`. We can now safely check whether the URL matches the `path` of a route.

The function can take in a path which will in turn return a `match` object for the route. If no particular path is provided to the function, the path of the current route will be used. Using our previous example with the path of `/users/:userid`, the Route `<Route path="/users/:userid">` will return the following `match` object if the URL `/users/123` is provided as an argument:

```
{
  "path": "/users/:userid",
  "url": "/users/123",
  "isExact": true,
  "params": {
    "userid": "123"
  }
}
```

If the Hook is called with a path that does not match with the current route, `null` will be returned from the function:

```
useRouteMatch( '/orders/:orderid' );
```

Calling this function with `/users/:userid` will return a value of `null`.

State Management

The more an application grows in size, the more its complexity and data grows. Managing **application state** becomes increasingly difficult and cumbersome to do. When do I pass props to which component and how? How do the props influence the state of my components and what happens if I change the state of a component?

React has introduced great tooling in the last few years to deal with this increase of complexity in application state. The **Context API** as well as the **useReducer Hook** have been great additions to the React developer's toolbox and allow us to work more comfortably with complex data. However, in some cases it is still very difficult to keep track of all the different pieces of data and how they transform. To deal with this type of problem, external tools for **global state management** can be a great choice. The React ecosystem has seen a number of players enter this space giving us lots of libraries to choose from.

One of the more commonly known tools is **MobX** which describes itself as a *"Simple, scalable state management"* solution. The other well-known tool in the industry is **Redux**. Redux was in part developed by Dan Abramov and Andrew Clark who are now part of the official React Core Team. It positions itself as *"A predictable state container for JavaScript apps"*. Redux is arguably the more dominating tool boasting with higher usage stats and downloads.

This chapter will dive deeper into **Redux**. This is due to a number of reasons: first of all, I have experience with **Redux** myself and have used in it a number of different projects. Additionally, my experience with Redux has been very pleasant. But those are not the only reasons. Redux still has around **4 million weekly installations**. Compared to **MobX** which still has a very respectable number of **200.000 installations** per week, Redux is the dominant force in the React ecosystem though.

Despite a number of voices which keep proclaiming Redux's death, the interest in **Redux** has remained steady over the years and the number of downloads is still growing. When the **Context API** was introduced with **React 16.3.0**, **Redux** was said to be obsolete. Once **React 16.8.0** introduced Hooks, more specifically the **useReducer Hook**, the critics' voices were raised again. Despite all this criticism, the number of installations of Redux keeps growing.

In fact, **Redux** makes use of **Context** and **Hooks** under the hood and uses these principles to optimize its own performance and simplify its API. Moreover, **Redux** has seen a great increase of custom add-ons and tools for their own ecosystem which is enhanced, rather than replaced, by the new functionality offered by React.

Introduction to Redux

As mentioned earlier, **Redux** is a predictable state container. But what exactly does this mean? I want to add some back story here to answer this question properly. It's important to really understand the principles of Redux to avoid common errors and set yourself up for success.

Redux as a tool is based on the principles of **Flux Architecture**. This type of architecture has been developed at **Facebook** with the aim to simplify development in client-side web applications. As is the case in **React**, **Flux** dictates a **unidirectional data flow**, meaning data is only ever flowing one way: an **action** (could be triggered by a button click) alters the **state**, and this **state change** will cause a re-render and thus allow further actions.

Redux works almost the same. However, state is managed only within one component - **globally**. In practice, this translates to all components gaining access to this state no matter where they are placed.

In order to use **Redux** in a particular project, we have to install it via the command line:

```
npm install redux react-redux
```

Or using Yarn:

```
yarn add redux react-redux
```

We have to install **two** packages: `redux` and `react-redux`. The `redux` package will install the main state management library whereas `react-redux` will install the so-called **bindings**. While the name might sound a little obscure, there is no actual magic involved. **Bindings** refer to **React components** which have been specifically optimized for usage with **Redux**, allowing us to use these out of the box.

While in theory **Redux** could be used as a stand-alone solution, we would then need to manage components rendering and data flow from the state container ourselves. While possible, it introduces a great deal of complexity which most of us do not want to deal with. `react-redux` is thus a sensible choice for most of us.

Store, Actions and Reducers

I've just introduced another set of new terminology to you. Don't be scared if any of these sound unfamiliar to you now. We will look at all of them in turn and hopefully clear up any confusion you might have.

All data in **Redux** is managed in so-called **stores** which manage the **global state**. Theoretically, applications could have a number of different stores. In fact, **Flux architecture** even

268

encourages the use of multiple stores. However, in most React applications using **Redux** we will only find a single store. This reduces complexity dramatically and also declares this *single store* as the **single source of truth** for all of our data. The store also provides a number of methods which can be used to change (dispatch) the data currently stored in the store, read (getState) the data from the store and react to changes (subscribe).

The only way to change data in a store is to "*dispatch*" an **action**. Once again, **Redux** has taken its inspiration from **Flux Architecture** and prescribes for these **actions** to be in **Flux Standard Action** (FSA) format. **FSAs** consist of a simple JavaScript object which always **has to have** a type property and *can* contain a payload, meta and error properties. We are going to focus mostly on the payload. In 9 out of 10 cases, we are going to deal with a payload when we are *dispatching* an **action**.

The **payload** describes the actual *content* of an **action** and can take the form of data which is serializable in JSON format. This could include strings, booleans, numerical values or even complex arrays or objects.

Let's have a look at a typical **action** in **Redux**:

```
{
  type: "SET_USER",
  payload: {
    id: "d929e553-7079-4309-8c7d-2d2db39922c6",
    name: "Manuel"
  }
}
```

Once an **action** has been *dispatched* (the **store** provides this dispatch method for us), the current **state** as well as the **action** dispatched are passed to the **reducer**. The **reducer** is a **pure function** which we also already encountered in React. Its primary aim is to create a **new state** based on the **current state** and the action's type and payload properties. A little reminder: a **pure function** always creates the **same output**, given the **same input parameters** - no matter how many times it is being called. This behavior makes **Reducers** predictable and also easy to to test.

Example of a **reducer**:

```
const reducer = (state, action) => {
  switch (action.type) {
    case 'PLUS': {
      return state + action.payload;
    }
    case 'MINUS' : {
      return state - action.payload;
```

```
    }
    default: {
      return 0;
    }
  }
};
```

A **store** generally expects only a **single reducer**. **Redux** allows us to split the **reducer** function into many small little parts, making them more digestible and easy to read. A `combineReducers()` function then takes care of merging all these parts into one main **reducer** - the **root reducer**. When an action is *dispatched*, each **reducer** is called with the same parameters: **state** and the **action**.

Each **reducer** reacts to the type property of an **action**. Due to this, a convention has emerged to extract all used types into variables with the same name which allow us to avoid typos. Why is that? Typos might be hard to spot (e.g. USER_ADDDED) without. On top of that, the JavaScript interpreter will throw an error if we tried to access a variable which is not defined, eliminating yet another source of error that's hard to track down. Thus, you often find the following code-blocks at the beginning of a file in **Redux** applications:

```
const PLUS = 'PLUS' ;
const MINUS = 'MINUS' ;
```

This allow us to create some sort of coherence among the different **action types**.

Creating a store

To create a store which will manage the global state, we have to import the `createStore` function from the `redux` package. We can call it by passing it a **reducer** function. This function will return a store object to us which will contain all the methods necessary to interact with the store, namely `dispatch`, `getState` and `subscribe`. The latter two are not of the same importance when working with React, but I have mentioned them for the sake of completion. In React and Redux applications, the `react-redux` binding components take care of the re-rendering of components if they are affected by a change of the **state**.

```
import { createStore } from 'redux';

const initialState = 0 ;

const counterReducer = (state = initialState, action) => {
  switch (action.type) {
    case 'PLUS': {
      return state + (action.payload || 0);
    }
```

```
      case 'MINUS': {
        return state - (action.payload || 0);
      }
      default: {
        return state;
      }
    }
};

const store = createStore(counterReducer);
```

We've just created our first simple store with a counter reducer. The createStore function only takes a single parameter in this example (the counterReducer) indicating that the initial state will be set to undefined. Thus, we have set the initialState as the standard parameter which equates to 0 in this example.

If we pass another parameter to the createStore function, this parameter would be passed as first state to our reducer function:

```
const store = createStore(counterReducer, 3);
```

Instead of undefined, the initial value for our state parameter that is passed to the counterReducer would equate to 3. The initialState would not be set and our counter would start counting at 3 instead of 0.

The first initial **action** being *dispatched* takes the form of {type: '@@redux/INIT5.3.p.j.1.8'} . Looking at our example, this means that the default case will get activated and that only the state passed will be returned (which also equates to the initialState).

This default case is important. If no other case of the switch statement can be fulfilled, the current state needs to be returned from the function to avoid unwanted side-effects. The reducer function is executed after **each** dispatch call and dictates the value of the **next state** by returning it from the function.

Calling store.getState() after initialization, we obtain an initialState of 0:

```
console.log(store.getState()); // 0
```

Let's try things out a bit and try **dispatch a few actions** to see how **state** reacts to these **actions**:

```
store.dispatch({ type: 'PLUS', payload: 2 });
console.log(store.getState()); // 2
```

271

```
store.dispatch({ type: 'PLUS' , payload: 1 });
console.log(store.getState()); // 3

store.dispatch({ type: 'MINUS' , payload: 2 });
console.log(store.getState()); // 1
```

We've *dispatched* an **action** of type PLUS twice and of type MINUS once. A payload is also passed that indicates by how many numbers our last state is supposed to be incremented or decremented by. These operations result in the following **state mutations**:

```
0 (initialized state) +  2 (payload) = 2 (new state)
2 (old state)         +  1 (payload) = 3 (new state)
3 (old State)         -  2 (payload) = 1 (new State)
```

This state remains relatively simple and only consists of a single value. We will look at more complex **state** consisting of different objects soon and create a number of different **reducers**.

Action Creators vs Actions

Those who read articles or the official documentation of **Redux** will have encountered the two terms **action** and **action creators**. The difference is not completely clear in the beginning. I struggled to really understand the differences myself and know many others who have felt the same. The situation is further complicated by the fact that some use the terms interchangeably, although they mean different things. Let's quickly dive into how **action creators** and **actions** differ.

Actions, which were already introduced earlier, are simple, *serializable* **objects** that can be used to describe how exactly **state** should change. They always contain a type property and often a payload.

An **action creator** however describes a **function** that returns an **action**. One could also say that it is a **factory** which creates **actions** (thus the name *Creator*). In most situations, **action creators** are used to **encapsulate logic** that is necessary to create to an **action**. Sometimes they are also used to abstract away complex logic from the **actions** themselves. In those cases, the **action creator** function is called instead of the **action** and passed to the dispatch method.

Typical **action creators** might take the following form using the previous example:

```
const add = (number) => {
  return { type: 'PLUS' , payload: number };
};
```

```
const subtract = (number) => {
  return { type: 'MINUS' , payload: number };
};
```

Or using **ES2015+ shorthand notation**:

```
const add = (payload) => ({ type: 'PLUS'  , payload });
const subtract = (payload) => ({ type: 'MINUS'  , payload });
```

Consequently, the **action creators** will be called as parameters of the dispatch method instead of passing an **action** directly:

```
store.dispatch(add(2 ));
store.dispatch(add(1 ));
store.dispatch(subtract(2 ));
```

By following sensible naming conventions, the readability of the overall code is greatly improved. **Action creators** are a powerful piece of functionality in Redux and can allow us to eliminate repetition. Using **action creators** can also help to avoid common mistakes such as typos in a type of an action - for example PLSU instead of PLUS.

Complex reducers

The previous examples were intended for us to form an understanding of **actions** and **reducers**. Moreover, they allowed us to understand how **actions** are used in practice and how the **reducer** mutates the **store**. Typically, most React applications will deal with much more **complex state** than what we have seen in the examples. To understand **Redux** in the context of much larger state, we will look at a more realistic example.

The example will describe a simple **To-Do** app and we will have a look at how the **state management** for this app can be implemented. The to-do app will manage lists of todos and also contain a logged-in user area. The state will consist of two top level properties: todos (of type array) and user (of type object). This is reflected in our current state:

```
const initialState = Object .freeze({
  user: {},
  todos: [],
});
```

To ensure that a new state object is being created instead of mutating the previous object, the initial state object is wrapped by Object.freeze(). If there was an attempt to directly mutate the **state object** a TypeError would be thrown.

Let's have a look at how a **reducer function** could be implemented that manages the todos (adding, removing and changing the status of todos) and sets the login area of a user:

```
const rootReducer = (state = initialState, action) => {
  switch (action.type) {
    case 'SET_USER': {
      return {
        user: {
          name: action.payload.name,
          accessToken: action.payload.accessToken,
        },
        todos: state.todos,
      };
    }
    case 'ADD_TODO': {
      return {
        user: state.user,
        todos: state.todos.concat({
          id: action.payload.id,
          text: action.payload.text,
          done: Boolean (action.payload.done),
        }),
      };
    }
    case 'REMOVE_TODO': {
      return {
        user: state.user,
        todos: state.todos.filter((todo) => todo.id !== action.payload),
      };
    }
    case 'CHANGE_TODO_STATUS' : {
      return {
        user: state.user,
        todos: state.todos.map((todo) => {
          if (todo.id !== action.payload.id) {
            return todo;
          }
          return {
            ...todo,
            done: action.payload.done,
          };
        }),
      };
    }
    default: {
      return state;
```

```
        }
    }
};
```

```
const store = createStore(rootReducer);
```

I do not want to go into too much detail, however a few things should be explained properly. Let's look at each `switch` block in turn in which each `case` block returns a new state object.

Let's start with SET_USER: the **state object** being created here changes the `user` object and sets its name property to `action.payload.name` as well as the `accessToken` property to `action.payload.accessToken`. One could also set `user` to `action.payload` but this would mean that the complete **payload** of the **action** would be transferred to the `user` object. Moreover, one has to ensure that the `action.payload` is an object as to not change the initial form of the `user` object. This could become problematic if other parts of the **reducer** also access this object and its type had suddenly changed. We have ignored all other properties in our example by explicitly accessing name and `accessToken` from the **payload** of the action.

Apart from the modified `user`, we also return a `todos` property which we set to `state.todos`. This indicates that we do not change this value and leave it as is (initial value). **This is important** - as the `todos` would have otherwise disappeared from the state. We would have set the user but removed all their todos from state.

Let's continue with ADD_TODO: this works differently from SET_USER as the `user` is returned unchanged from the state tree. A new todo is added to the array of todos via the `.concat()` method. It's important to make the distinction between push() and concat(): push() is a *mutating* method which means that it would change our current state instead of creating a new one. By using `state.todos.concat`, we use the current todos array as the basis and create a new array which contains the previous array as well as the newest todo item.

The case of REMOVE_TODO works in a similar fashion. The `user` is returned just as was the case in ADD_TODO. The `todos` array on the other hand is filtered by the entry to remove. We pass an id to the filter which has been provided in terms of an action as part of the `action.payload`. The filtered array forms the new todos state. Again, the choice of `Array.filter()` has been made as it is non *mutating* and creates a new array as opposed to comparable methods such as `Array.splice()` which mutate the original array.

The last case illustrated in our example is CHANGE_TODO_STATUS . It allows us to set the status of our todo element from to do - `false` - to done - `true` or vice-versa. The `user` object remains unchanged and the previous state is returned. To change the status of a todo, we use a map function to iterate over the array of todos. In this map, we check whether the id of the current todo object is equal to the id of the `action.payload`. If this is not the case, we just return the unchanged todo element.

If the id of the payload is equal to the id of the current todo element, a new object is created and all properties with their respective values are copied over into the new object while overriding the done property with the new value from the action payload. This is achieved via the ES2015+ spread syntax ({...todo}). Creating new objects instead of mutating the existing ones helps to ensure that our **reducers** remain **pure functions**, creating a new state every single time. Using `Array.map()` ensures that a new array is created each time.

We've only dealt with two parts of the state tree: user and todos but the **reducer function's** complexity has already become apparent. If the complexity of the state grew, the function would become increasingly longer and more prone to **mistakes**. As we not only return the changed parts of the state but also the parts that have not changed, the function becomes even harder to read and manage. To combat this we can use ES2015+ **Object Spread Syntax** to create a new state from the previous state and override the changing branch of the state tree. In terms of the ADD_TODO case, one could refactor to the following snippet:

```
case "ADD_TODO": {
  return {
    ...state,
    todos: state.todos.concat(action.payload),
  };
}
```

This only minimizes the risk to an extent. We might still forget to return the unchanged part of the state along with the newly created state. `combineReducer()` function to the rescue! This method allows to separate the **reducer** (or to say the **state** which they create) into many smaller parts which only deal with a particular task. They can even be placed into their own files.

Applying this logic to our current example, user and todos can be extracted into their own **reducer functions**. Both can be placed in their own respective files while the **reducer** functions have to be exported with default:

```
// user/reducer.js
const initialState = Object.freeze({});

export default (state = initialState, action) => {
  switch (action.type) {
    case 'SET_USER': {
      return {
        name: action.payload.name,
        accessToken: action.payload.accessToken,
      };
    }
    default: {
```

```
        return state;
      }
    }
};


// todos/reducer.js
const initialState = Object .freeze([]);

export default (state = initialState, action) => {
  switch (action.type) {
    case 'ADD_TODO': {
      return state.concat(action.payload);
    }
    case 'REMOVE_TODO': {
      return state.filter((todo) => todo.id !== action.payload);
    }
    case 'CHANGE_TODO_STATUS' : {
      return state.map((todo) => {
        if (todo.id !== action.payload.id) {
          return todo;
        }
        return {
          ...todo,
          done: action.payload.done,
        };
      });
    }
    default: {
      return state;
    }
  }
};
```

This way, we have not only achieved readability by creating two **reducer** functions but the functions themselves could also be simplified. Instead of returning the *unchanged* parts of the **state tree** as well, we only return those parts of the **reducer** *which are relevant to this reducer.* For the **user reducer** we only return the **user** while in the **todos reducer** we only return **todos**.

In order to combine the *smaller* **reducers** into a ****big* **reducer**, we can use the aforementioned combineReducers() method which will create a root reducer which can then be passed to the createStore() method. The combineReducers() function expects an object whose property name matches that of the newly created state tree. The values also have to be *valid* **reducers**.

```
import { combineReducers, createStore } from 'redux';
import userReducer from './store/user/reducer';
import todosReducer from './store/todos/reducer' ;

const rootReducer = combineReducers({
  todos: todosReducer,
  user: userReducer,
});

const store = createStore(rootReducer);
```

The `combineReducers()` function is used to put together all the reducers from the passed object into a new function, the so-called **root reducer**. This **root reducer** can now be passed to the `createStore()` function. The created function calls *each* reducer passed when executed and creates a new state object based on all the return values. It matches the form of the initial state object to achieve this task:

```
{
  "todos" : [],
  "user" : {}
}
```

Another piece of advice: by using ES2015+ object shorthand notation in a clever way, we can save even more lines of code by calling the imports by the same name as the properties which they will represent in state:

```
import user from './store/user/reducer';
import todos from './store/todos/reducer' ;
```

The object which we have to then pass to `combineReducer()` reduces to the following:

```
const rootReducer = combineReducers({ todos, user });
```

To use `combineReducers()` , a few formal rules have to be followed. They do not hinder us from developing code effectively but have to be followed. Each reducer function that is passed to `combineReducers()` has to fulfill the following criteria

- For each unknown **action** (so each **action** whose type argument we do not react to) that the **reducer** receives, the first `state` that the **reducer** receives needs to be returned.
- Reducer functions used in the `combineReducer()` function can never return `undefined`. This is different to the **root reducer** which is allowed to do this. In the case of the former, the `combineReducers()` function will throw an **error** to inform us of this error. We deal

with this effectively in our example by including a `default` case in the `switch` block which will simply return the `state`

- If the `state` passed in the first argument is of type `undefined`, the **initial state** has to be returned. It's probably easiest to use the initial state as a default value as we have done in the above example (`state = initialState`).

An aside: `combineReducer()` can be nested as many times as you like. The **reducer** functions that have been passed to `combineReducer()` can be created by other `combineReducer()` calls. While this might help to an extent, you should be cautious to not provide unnecessary granularity which will make your code harder to read when your state branches are hard to find. In my own experience, nesting is only really useful up to a *single* layer (meaning two `combineReducer()` calls).

Asynchronous actions

All **actions** in the previous examples were executed **synchronously**. This means that each **action creator** was executed whenever we wanted to modify state without having to wait for the result of an asynchronous process to finish. In many dynamic web applications, this situation is highly unlikely though. Many **React applications** have to deal with **asynchronous data flows**, network requests in particular. *Synchronous* **action creators** do not really offer a great solution to this problem as the `dispatch` method of a **store** expects an **action** which contains a simple object containing a `type` property.

Redux middleware concepts, **Redux Thunk middleware** in particular, can help to deal with this problem.

The `createStore()` function from the `redux` package can deal with up to three parameters:

- The **reducer** function: this is the only **mandatory** parameter and deals with the executed **actions** of our **state** by returning a **state** for each **action** dispatched
- **Initial state**: One can pre-populate the store with data by providing a value in the initial state. This initial state is also passed to the **reducer function**.
- An **enhancer function**: This function can be used to enhance the store's capability with our own functionality: in this case we enhance it with the **middleware** mentioned above.

If the `createStore` function receives a **function** as a second parameter, the second parameter will be treated as an **enhancer function**. If the second parameter takes the form of anything different, the second parameter will be treated as **initial state** and passed to the **reducer function** as such.

Redux middleware is wrapped around the `dispatch` method and interrupts the usual call before it is executed. It can modify the **action** *before* it is sent to the **reducer** and returns a new `dispatch` function. If we wanted to pass asynchronous functions (for examples Promises) to the `dispatch()` method, we can use the **store enhancer** to register the **middleware** that allows us to do just that. The most common piece of middleware is the so called **thunk middleware.**

Install it via:

```
npm install redux-thunk
```

or using Yarn:

```
yarn add redux-thunk
```

Once the **thunk middleware** has been installed, it has to be *registered* via the **Redux** `applyMiddleware()` function in the **enhancer**. We import the **middleware** and import the `applyMiddleware()` function from the `redux` package. The **middleware** we want to use has to be passed to the `applyMiddleware()` function as a parameter. In this case, we are passing thunk:

```
import { applyMiddleware, createStore } from 'redux';
import thunk from 'redux-thunk';

// ...

const store = createStore(reducer, applyMiddleware(thunk));
```

By implementing this piece of **thunk middleware**, we can now easily compose **action creators** that execute *asynchronous* code and only *dispatch* the **actions** once we have obtained a result. The **thunk function** is an **action creator** which returns a function whose parameters are also a `dispatch()` and a `getState()` function. We can decide ourselves when we should *dispatch* an action in the **thunk action creator** function.

```
const delayedAdd = (newTodo) => {
  return (dispatch, getState) => {
    setTimeout(() => {
      return dispatch({
        type: 'ADD_TODO',
        payload: newTodo,
      });
    }, 500);
  };
};

store.dispatch(
  delayedAdd({
    id: 1,
```

```
      text: 'Explaining thunk actions' ,
      done: false,
   })
 );
```

In this example we have created a delayedAdd **action creator**. It receives a new todo element and then returns a new function in the form of (dispatch, getState) => {}) . The **thunk middleware** ensures that that this function always receives the dispatch() and getState() functions. After a delay of 500ms, we call the dispatch() function with the ADD_TODO **action** and add the new object.

To be able to *dispatch* said action, we can use the *asynchronous* **action creator** in the same fashion as the *synchronous* **action creator** - by passing the called function to the dispatch() function to the **store**: store.dispatch(ActionCreator) . The thunk middleware will recognize if a **thunk** function is being used, execute it and pass it dispatch and getState as an argument.

If you are familiar with **arrow function syntax** of ES2015, you can simplify things further:

```
const delayedAdd = (newTodo) => (dispatch, getState) => {
   setTimeout(() => {
      return dispatch({
         type: 'ADD_TODO',
         payload: newTodo,
      });
   }, 500);
};
```

In this example, we have used a shorter **arrow function** with an **implicit return** which can then be directly returned by the function called by the **thunk middleware**. By not having to write another return, we have eliminated another two lines of code. Beware however, that you do not trade readability and understanding for shorter code.

Typical asynchronous action example

Many applications working with APIs inform the user that data is loading while it is being fetched from the API. Loading Spinners or text such as *"Loading data ..."* are common ways of conveying this information. **Thunk actions** are a great way to cover this case using a **reducer**.

Let's set up three cases in the **reducer** which react to the following three **actions**:

- FETCH_REPOS_REQUEST : will reset any previously failed network requests and initiate a loading status

- `FETCH_REPOS_SUCCESS` : will be called upon once a successful request has taken place. It will receive the result of the request as well the date of the last update of the data
- `FETCH_REPOS_FAILURE` : will react to any errors and potentially set an `error` flag to inform the user that the request has failed

A possible implementation could look like this:

```js
import { applyMiddleware, createStore }  from 'redux';
import thunk from 'redux-thunk';
import axios from 'axios';

const initialState = Object .freeze({
  error: null ,
  items: [],
  isFetching: false,
  lastUpdated: null ,
  selectedAccount: 'manuelbieh' ,
});

const rootReducer = (state = initialState, action) => {
  switch (action.type) {
    case 'FETCH_REPOS_REQUEST' : {
      return {
        ...state,
        isFetching: true ,
        error: null ,
      };
    }
    case 'FETCH_REPOS_SUCCESS' : {
      return {
        ...state,
        isFetching: false,
        items: action.payload.items,
        lastUpdated: action.payload.lastUpdated,
      };
    }
    case 'FETCH_REPOS_FAILED' : {
      return {
        ...state,
        isFetching: false,
        error: action.payload,
      };
    }
    default: {
      return state;
    }
```

```
    }
  };

  const fetchGithubRepos = () => (dispatch, getState) => {
    dispatch({ type: 'FETCH_REPOS_REQUEST'  });
    const state = getState();
    axios
      .get( `https://api.github.com/users/ ${state.selectedAccount}/repos`)
      .then((response) => {
        dispatch({
          type: 'FETCH_REPOS_SUCCESS' ,
          payload: {
            lastUpdated:  new Date(),
            items: response.data,
          },
        });
      })
      .catch((error) => {
        dispatch({
          type: 'FETCH_REPOS_FAILURE' ,
          error: true ,
          payload: error.response.data,
        });
      });
  };


  const store = createStore(rootReducer, applyMiddleware(thunk));


  store.dispatch(fetchGithubRepos());
```

Once the fetchGitHubRepos() **action creator** has been *dispatched*, a few things will happen:

First of all, the **thunk middleware** will register that we do not deal with a simple **action** (an object) but a function, meaning that it will execute it it in the form of Action()(dispatch, getState). The **action creator** receives the dispatch function to be able to *dispatch* **actions** from the **action creator** function.

Inside of the **action creator**, the FETCH_REPOS_REQUEST is *dispatched*. The **reducer** will react to the **action**, create a new **state object** by copying the *existing* **state** into a new object using the **ES2015+ spread operator** and potentially reset any existing error to null. The state is informed that a request will follow via isFetching at the same time. But this is personal taste and I am aware that some people prefer to set the error property to null only if the subsequent request has been successful.

The request will access the *current* **state** via `getState()` from which it will access the `selectedAccount`. Once obtained, we can use this to perform the API request for the `selectedAccount`'s GitHub repositories. The request is performed using Axios (mainly for simplicity). We can then react to the following two cases:

- The request was successful: This means that we obtain data from the GitHub API and can *dispatch* the `FETCH_REPOS_SUCCESS` **action**. The current time (which can later be used for caching or automated reloads) as well as the array containing the repos hidden in `response.data` are both passed to the action. We also set `isFetching` to `false` as the request is no longer active.
- The request fails: Should this occur, the `FETCH_REPOS_FAILURE` **action** is *dispatched*. The error messages provided by Axios in `error.response.data` will be provided to the **action** as a payload. `isFetching` is set to `false` as the request has been performed already (even if it was not necessarily the desired result).

The state now either contains a number of GitHub repositories if the request was successful (for user in `state.selectedAccount`) or an error if it failed. Both cases have now been dealt with effectively and their results can be used to take appropriate action in the user interface.

Debugging using the Redux Dev Tools

We have a number of tools available to inspect what's currently in the **store**. For example, **Logger middleware** such as redux-logger from LogRocket allows us to log each dispatched **action**, its previous state and the new state into the browser console (https://github.com/LogRocket/redux-logger).

We can also manually log these to the console using `console.log(store.getState())`. However, this can become cumbersome quickly and difficult especially when dealing with asynchronous actions.

The **Redux Devtools** are another great alternative for debugging purposes. Implemented as a browser extension for Chrome, Firefox and soon Edge as well, the **Redux Devtools** integrate seamlessly with the existing developer tools. You can find them in the stores here:

- Chrome: https://chrome.google.com/webstore/detail/redux-devtools/lmhkpmbekcpmknklioeibfkpmmfibljd
- Firefox: https://addons.mozilla.org/en-US/firefox/addon/reduxdevtools/

Once installed, the browser developer tools are extended by an extra tab called **"Redux"** now easily accessible for any debugging purposes. In order to use it fully, we have to make a few modifications to our codebase though: another **enhancer** has to be ****added to the **store**.

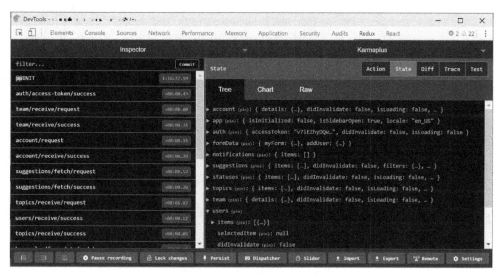

Browser Devtools including the Redux addon

The **Redux Devtools** can be registered on the `window` object with two global variables: `window.REDUX_DEVTOOLS_EXTENSION` and `WINDOW.REDUX_DEVTOOLS_EXTENSION_COMPOSE`. If no own store enhancer is used (for example not using `applyMiddleware()` to register middleware such as Thunk), then things can be solved pretty simply: We check whether the **Redux Devtools** are installed and if they are, we pass a call of `WINDOW.REDUX_DEVTOOLS_EXTENSION` to the `createStore()` function:

```
createStore(
  rootReducer,
  window.__REDUX_DEVTOOLS_EXTENSION__ && window.__REDUX_DEVTOOLS_EXTENSION__()
);
```

This allows us to automatically supervise any dispatched **action** in the **devtools**, see which **action** was *dispatched* with which **payload**, or even manually *dispatch* **actions**. Another cool feature that can be used with the **devtools** is **Time Traveling** - the ability to "travel back" and inspect previous states of the store. This can be a very powerful debugging technique.

Reducers need to be **pure functions** so that they will always create the same **state**, even if we "travel back" through states in the **store**. Otherwise, we might not be able to reproduce bugs as every call would create a different **state**.

If we are using an enhancer function, the `window.REDUX_DEVTOOLS_EXTENSION_COMPOSE` function will be used instead. This function of type `compose` allows the bundling of *multiple* **enhancer** functions into a *single* one, allowing us to call each of them in turn. The principle is similar to that we have talked about in the `combineReducers()` section for **reducers**.

Redux offers a compose function too, which allows us to bundle multiple enhancers into a single one. It can be imported to be used to create a custom composeEnhancer() function. If the Redux Devtools are installed, we will use the REDUX_DEVTOOLS_EXTENSION_COMPOSE function to add the **devtools** of the **store enhancer**. If they are not installed however, Redux' own compose() function can be used instead to create the same signature:

```
import { applyMiddleware, compose, createStore }  from 'redux';
import thunk from 'thunk-middleware' ;


const composeEnhancers =
  typeof window === 'object' && window.__REDUX_DEVTOOLS_EXTENSION_COMPOSE__
    ? window.__REDUX_DEVTOOLS_EXTENSION_COMPOSE__({})
    : compose;

// ...


const store = createStore(
  rootReducer,
  composeEnhancers(applyMiddleware(thunk))
);
```

If you feel a little overwhelmed by the number of different functions and the terminology introduced, I can provide a little reassurance: in most applications, it is not necessary to understand all these moving parts in great detail. I use the **Redux Devtools** in almost all of my projects but still have to check each and every time how I can set them up properly. This text should serve as an introduction as to how **redux stores** can be debugged and provide an opportunity to learn for those that want to learn more.

Using Redux with React

We've now covered how to create a **store**, how to *dispatch* **actions**, what exactly **reducers** do and how we can use **middleware**. So far, we haven't looked at how Redux interacts with React though, so let's do that now.

I've briefly mentioned the react-redux package at the beginning of the chapter. This package includes the *"official React bindings for Redux"* and was developed originally by Dan Abramov (now part of the Core React Team) and is maintained by the Redux community.

The package consists of two components: one component and a function which will create a **Higher Order Component** (there's also another function that is used by React Redux internally but developers typically never come into contact with it). The Provider component forms the entry point for Redux. We can wrap the component tree with a Provider component and then access a common **store** via the `connect()` function. This function returns a **Higher Order Component** and allows us to connect components to the store.

The Provider Component

As most applications tend to only consist of a single **store**, it is useful to place the `Provider` component up high in the component tree. In many situations, it might even make sense to use the `Provider` component as the very first component of the component tree. The `Provider` component receives a **Redux store** as a `store` prop and also contains a number of children. All children have access to the `store` prop value (the **store** provided) and can also read it or change it via the *dispatching* of **actions**.

```
import React from 'react';
import ReactDOM from 'react-dom';
import { createStore } from 'redux';
import { Provider } from 'react-redux';

const dummyReducer = (state = {}, action) => {
  return state;
};

const store = createStore(dummyReducer);

const App = () => <p>We can have access to the Redux store here.</p>;

ReactDOM.render(
  <Provider store={store}>
    <App />
  </Provider>,
  document.getElementById('root')
);
```

In most previous examples, only the `<App />` component was passed to `ReactDOM.render()`. Here however, we place a `<Provider />` component around the App and also pass a dummy store to it.

In theory, `Provider` components can be nested inside each other. Components connected to a store, will always the **store** of the next `Provider` component up. However, this is not common practice and leads to more confusion than necessary. When two stores exist in parallel, reducers of both stores should be combined via `combineReducer()` into one big store. This will allow the `Provider` to wrap around the rest of the elements using only a single store.

Connecting components to a store using the connect function

Now onto the harder part of React with Redux: **connecting** a React component to a **Redux store** using a connect() function. This function can take up to 4 parameters of which the first 3 are functions which can also take 3 parameters. That sounds like a lot. But be rest assured: in most cases, we only really need 2 out of these 4 parameters and the functions will only take a single argument. But let's go through everything step by step increasing the complexity with each step.

The function takes the following form:

```
connect(
  mapStateToProps,
  mapDispatchToProps,
  mergeProps,
  options
);
```

Calling the connect() function will create a **Higher Order Component**. It can be used to transfer parts of the state of the store to this component. In order to decide which parts of the state should be passed as props, we use the first parameter: mapStateToProps.

Accessing parts of the global state with mapStateToProps

mapStateToProps receives the complete **state** as a first parameter and the so-called ownProps of the component as a second parameter. These props might be passed to the HOC. Depending on whether only the first or both parameters are passed, the function is either called if something changes within the **Redux state** *or* if the **props** change which are passed to the component.

```
const mapStateToProps = (state, ownProps) => {
  // ...
};
```

The function will always expect an **object** return value. The properties of this object will then be passed to the component as stateProps. Let's remember our previous Todo Store example. We would now like to pass pre-filtered todos based on their status as well as the overall number of todos to the component.

This would result in a mapStateProps function which looks like this:

```
const mapStateToProps = (state) => {
  return {
    openTodos: state.todos.filter((todo) => todo.completed !==   true),
```

```
    completedTodos: state.todos.filter((todo) => todo.completed ===    true),
    totalCount: state.todos.length,
  };
};
```

The properties of this object, openTodos, completedTodos and totalCount will be passed to the wrapping component as **props**. How? By passing mapStateToProps to the connect() function. This will in turn return an HOC which we can then pass our component to (in which we access the props from state):

```
const ConnectedTodoList = connect(mapStateToProps)(TodoList);
```

We've defined a ConnectedTodoList which can now be used in **JSX** and be wrapped by a Provider component. It will render the TodoList with the given props from the global **Redux store:**

```
import React from 'react';
import ReactDOM from 'react-dom';
import { combineReducers, createStore }  from 'redux';
import { Provider, connect }  from 'react-redux';
import user from './store/user/reducer';
import todos from './store/todos/reducer' ;


const rootReducer = combineReducers({ todos, user });


const store = createStore(rootReducer);


const TodoList = (props) => (
  <div>
    <p>
      {props.totalCount} Todos. {props.completedTodos.length} completed and{' '}
      {props.openTodos.length} open.
    </p>
  </div>
);


const mapStateToProps = (state) => {
  return {
    openTodos: state.todos.filter((todo) => todo.completed !==    true),
    completedTodos: state.todos.filter((todo) => todo.completed ===    true),
    totalCount: state.todos.length,
  };
};


const ConnectedTodoList = connect(mapStateToProps)(TodoList);
```

```
ReactDOM.render(
  <Provider store={store}>
    <ConnectedTodoList />
  </Provider>,
  document.getElementById('root' )
);
```

This will render a very small and spartan TodoList component showing us the number of all todos as well as the number of completed and open todos.

If we only wanted to display open *or* closed todos meaning only parts of the state, we can make use of the second parameter in the mapStateToProps function (ownProps) which will allow us to access the **props** of the component and decide which parts of the state we want to pass to the connected component.

```
const mapStateToProps = (state, ownProps) => {
  const filteredTodos =
    ownProps.type === 'completed'
      ? state.todos.filter((todo) => todo.completed ===    true)
      : state.todos.filter((todo) => todo.completed !==    true);

  return {
    totalCount: state.todos.length,
    todos: filteredTodos,
  };
};

const ConnectedTodoList = connect(mapStateToProps)(TodoList);

ReactDOM.render(
  <Provider store={store}>
    <ConnectedTodoList type="completed" />
  </Provider>,
  document.getElementById('root')
);
```

Let's step through this snippet: Initially, we check whether we want to show completed or open todos by passing the ownProps.type. We can then filter state.todos and only return those todos which we are actually interested in. As we do not have to filter these todos according to type anymore (we're defining a pre-selection in mapStateToProps), we only return a regular todos property which we can then access with props.todos in the component.

Let's recap: with mapStateToProps() , we can get read-access to the whole **state** from the **Redux store**. All the data that we might like to use in a component will be returned to us in object form. The relevant React component will only re-render if data in the store has actually changed. Only then a re-render will be triggered.

Dispatching actions via mapDispatchToProps

Let's look at the second parameter for the `connect()` function: `mapDispatchToProps` :

```
const mapDispatchToProps = (dispatch, ownProps) => {
  // ...
};
```

or alternatively:

```
const mapDispatchToProps = {
  // ...
};
```

While `mapStateToProps` grants us access to the store to **read** data, `mapDispatchToProps` allows us to change the store's data with **write** access. `mapDispatchToProps` 's function signature looks similar to that of `mapStateToProps`. However, instead of receiving the whole state as a first parameter, we receive the `dispatch` method of the store that we connect to. The second parameter of `mapDispatchToProps` form `ownProps` - the **props** of the component itself - that are passed to component. It is also possible to pass a `mapDispatchToProps` **object** instead of a function to the `connect()` call. But let's look at that later. First, let's investigate how to use `mapDispatchToProps` .

We want to add the possibility of adding new todos to our `TodoList`, mark them as resolved and remove them from the list completely. We've already defined these **actions** a bit further up in the chapter already: `ADD_TODO`, `REMOVE_TODO` and `CHANGE_TODO_STATUS` . We now want to add the option for a user to *dispatch* these **actions** by interacting with our application:

```
// Helper function to create a (hopefully ;)) unique ID
const getPseudoRandomId = () =>
  Math.random()
    .toString(36)
    .slice(-6);

const mapDispatchToProps = (dispatch) => {
  return {
    addTodo: (text) =>
      dispatch({
        type: 'ADD_TODO',
        payload: {
          id: getPseudoRandomId(),
```

```
        text,
      },
    }),
  removeTodo: (id) =>
    dispatch({
      type: 'REMOVE_TODO',
      payload: id,
    }),
  changeStatus: (id, done) =>
    dispatch({
      type: 'CHANGE_TODO_STATUS' ,
      payload: {
        id,
        done,
      },
    }),
  };
};
```

A new object with the object properties addTodo, removeTodo and changeStatus is returned. Each of these is passed as **props** to a connected component with the same name. We pass mapStateToProps() to the connect() function as a second parameter to achieve this:

```
const ConnectedTodoList = connect(
  mapStateToProps,
  mapDispatchToProps
)(TodoList);
```

The **actions** which have been passed to mapDispatchToProps inline are normally extracted into respective **action creators**. These lead to better readability, are easier to test and often easier to read:

```
const addTodo = (text) => ({
  type: 'ADD_TODO',
  payload: {
    id: getPseudoRandomId(),
    text,
  },
});

const removeTodo = (id) => ({
  type: 'REMOVE_TODO',
  payload: id,
});
```

```
const changeStatus = (id, done) => ({
  type: 'CHANGE_TODO_STATUS' ,
  payload: {
    id,
    done,
  },
});
```

This reduces `mapStateToProps` drastically and makes it much easier to read:

```
const mapDispatchToProps = (dispatch) => {
  return {
    addTodo: (text) => dispatch(addTodo(text)),
    removeTodo: (id) => dispatch(removeTodo(id)),
    changeStatus: (id, done) => dispatch(changeStatus(id, done)),
  };
};
```

But there's another advantage here: in order to avoid repetition as much as possible, Redux offers a shorthand. If the function signature of the **action creators** match those of the function which we return from `mapDispatchToProps` , we can return the **action creators** as **ES2015+ shorthand objects**. **Redux** will automatically wrap the `dispatch()` call around all of the functions.

The following snippet achieves the exact same functionality as that from the previous example but does so in a much more concise fashion:

```
const mapDispatchToProps = {
  addTodo,
  removeTodo,
  changeStatus,
};
```

Be careful though: This only works when *all* **action creators** functions are called with the same functions from their connected React component counterparts and when `mapDispatchToProps` is passed in this exact form.

By combining `mapStateToProps` and `mapDispatchToProps` , we obtain a call which resembles this:

```
<TodoList todos={...} addTodo={...} removeTodo={...} changeStatus={...} />
```

All the properties returned by `mapStateToProps` as well as `mapDispatchToProps` are passed to the component which is connected to the **store** via the `connect()` function. We can then access these via **props**, *dispatch* **actions** via `mapDispatchToProps` or read state from the store using the properties from `mapStateToProps`.

If we wanted to only pass `mapDispatchToProps()` to the `connect()` call to be able to dispatch **actions** from a component, we can pass `null` as a first parameter. This means that we do not have read access to the component.

```
const ConnectedTodoList = connect(
  null,
  mapDispatchToProps
)(TodoList);
```

Merging StateProps and DispatchProps using MergeProps

The third parameter, `mergeProps()`, deals with a more special use case that is not really encountered out in the wild. For the sake of completion though, I want to explain it briefly.

```
const mergeProps = (stateProps, dispatchProps, ownProps) => {
  // ...
};
```

The function receives the result of `mapStateToProps` as its first parameter, that of `mapDispatchToProps` as a second and `ownProps` as a third. The return value is a new object whose properties are also passed via props to the component connected to the store.

`mergeProps()` can be powerful if you want to dispatch certain **actions** which are dependent on data from the state but do not use **thunk middleware**. It's also possible to filter the **actions** based on the state so that a component would not receive an `updateProfile()` **action** if `state.profile` does not exist (meaning if a user is not logged in). However, such scenarios are usually solved more elegantly on the component level.

Lastly: the fourth parameter for connect()

If you actually want to use the fourth parameter of the `connect()` method, you should really know what you're doing. Redux is optimized to only ever really need these options in very rare edge cases. For example, you can define your own context for Redux to use or define functions that compare whether a component needs re-rendered or not. This list is a complete summary of the options available:

```
{
  context: Object ,
  pure: boolean,
  areStatesEqual: Function,
```

```
  areOwnPropsEqual: Function,
  areStatePropsEqual: Function,
  areMergedPropsEqual: Function,
  forwardRef: boolean,
}
```

If you feel like you might need these options (Spoiler alert: in most cases the answer is "No, you don't need these"), you should check out the official documentation: https://react-redux.js.org/api/connect#options-object

Combining the puzzle pieces

We now know how to use the `connect()` method and why we need a `Provider`. Let's have a look at a more detailed but very complete example that outlines a totally functional TodoList App. It allows us to add new todos, mark them as complete or not and allows us to remove them if we want:

```
// store/todos/reducer.js
const initialState = Object.freeze([]);

export default (state = initialState, action) => {
  switch (action.type) {
    case 'ADD_TODO': {
      return state.concat(action.payload);
    }
    case 'REMOVE_TODO': {
      return state.filter((todo) => todo.id !== action.payload);
    }
    case 'CHANGE_TODO_STATUS' : {
      return state.map((todo) => {
        if (todo.id !== action.payload.id) {
          return todo;
        }
        return {
          ...todo,
          done: action.payload.done,
        };
      });
    }
    default: {
      return state;
    }
  }
};
```

```js
// store/todos/actions.js
const getPseudoRandomId = () =>
  Math.random()
    .toString(36)
    .slice(-6);

export const addTodo = (text) => ({
  type: 'ADD_TODO',
  payload: {
    id: getPseudoRandomId(),
    text,
  },
});

export const removeTodo = (id) => ({
  type: 'REMOVE_TODO',
  payload: id,
});

export const changeStatus = (id, done) => ({
  type: 'CHANGE_TODO_STATUS' ,
  payload: {
    id,
    done,
  },
});
```

```js
// TodoList.js
import React, { useState } from 'react';
import { connect } from 'react-redux';
import { addTodo, removeTodo, changeStatus } from './store/todos/actions' ;

const TodoList = (props) => {
  const [todoText, setTodoText] = useState('');

  return (
    <div>
      <p>{props.todos.length} Todos.</p>
      <ul>
        {props.todos.map((todo) => (
          <li key={todo.id}>
            <button
              type="button"
              onClick={() => {
                props.removeTodo(todo.id);
              }}
```

296

```
            >
              remove
            </button>
            <label
              style={{ textDecoration: todo.done ? 'line-through' : 'none' }}
            >
              <input
                type="checkbox"
                name={todo.id}
                checked={Boolean(todo.done)}
                onChange={(e) => {
                  const { name, checked } = e.target;
                  props.changeStatus(name, checked);
                }}
              />
              {todo.text}
            </label>
          </li>
        ))}
      </ul>
      <input onChange={(e) => setTodoText(e.target.value)} value={todoText} />
      <button
        type="button"
        onClick={() => {
          props.addTodo(todoText);
          setTodoText('');
        }}
      >
        add
      </button>
    </div>
  );
};

const mapStateToProps = (state) => ({
  todos: state.todos,
});

const mapDispatchToProps = {
  addTodo,
  removeTodo,
  changeStatus,
};

export default connect(
  mapStateToProps,
```

```
  mapDispatchToProps
)(TodoList);

// index.js
import React from 'react';
import ReactDOM from 'react-dom';
import { combineReducers, createStore } from 'redux';
import { Provider } from 'react-redux';
import todosReducer from './store/todos/reducer' ;
import TodoList from './TodoList' ;

const rootReducer = combineReducers({
  todos: todosReducer,
});

const store = createStore(rootReducer);

const App = () => (
  <Provider store={store}>
    <TodoList />
  </Provider>
);

ReactDOM.render(<App /> , document.getElementById('root'));
```

We've defined the todosReducer as well as addTodo, removeTodo and changeStatus **actions**
- all of which should sound familiar from previous examples. To aid readability, both **reducers**
and **actions** have been extracted into their own files within the ./store/todos directory.

 There's always heated debate about how folders and files should be structured
within an application. I have worked with a number of different structures but have
found a separation by domain (i.e. todos, user, repositories ...) and according to
type (actions, reducer) to be most effective. However, others prefer to place all of
the actions in a single actions directory and all the reducers in a reducer
directory. Some even avoid the separation of actions and reducers entirely.

There's no *Right* or *Wrong* here. While some of this decision will be influenced by
personal taste, it will also depend on the size, setup, complexity and users of the
application.

Let's now define a file which will contain the TodoList component: ./TodoList.js. This file
will display the todos, create todos or remove them as well as enable the user to mark them as

298

complete. In order to to do this, we connect the component to the store via connect(). The component also needs to import the **actions** which are passed to the connect() function in mapDispatchToProps . **Object shorthand syntax** allows us to keep things concise:

```
const mapDispatchToProps = {
  addTodo,
  removeTodo,
  changeStatus,
};
```

React Redux will automatically wrap these with a dispatch call.

in mapStateToProps, we define that the want to pass the todos branch of our store to our components. Then, mapStateToProps as well as mapDispatchToProps will be passed to the connect() function:

```
connect(
  mapStateToProps,
  mapDispatchToProps
);
```

But that's not at all: connect() creates a new **HOC** which we pass to our TodoList component.

```
connect(...)(TodoList);
```

We've now connected the TodoList component with the **Redux store**. As long as we use this component within a <Provider> element, we are good to go! Moreover, export default should be used before calling connect() so that the component will be exported using connect.

Lastly, we will have a look at index.js which marks the entry-point of our app. ReactDOM.render() is placed here in which we render our application to its respective DOM element. A few steps happen just before that:

combineReducers and createStore are imported from Redux and used to create the store object. We also import the todosReducer which we defined previously and pass it to combineReducers() to create a new **root reducer**. While this is not strictly necessary at this point as we only use a single **reducer**, it is worth doing so anyway as we expect our application to grow in size and complexity.

Moreover, the Provider component is imported from react-redux which will receive the created **store**. We also import the connected component from TodoList.js. This component can then be used within App inside of the Provider component.

Once we are set up, we can create new todos, mark them as complete or remove them completely - all by interacting with the `TodoList` component.

Go and try changing some actions and interactions and see how the changes affect the store. To see this in action, it would be best to have the Redux Devtools all setup. We change the following line in `index.js`:

```
const store = createStore(rootReducer);
```

into this:

```
const store = createStore(rootReducer, __REDUX_DEVTOOLS_EXTENSIONS__());
```

Please ensure that you have the Redux Devtools installed in your browser.

Redux with React Hooks

With React-Redux v7.1.0, Hooks have officially landed in the official React bindings for Redux. Hooks increase the usability of Redux in React manyfold. While creating a store is much the same, the `connect()` HOC can be avoided completely. Each method of access - reading or writing by dispatching actions - can be achieved by Hooks.

The most important Hooks to remember are `useSelector` and `useDispatch` which can be loosely compared to `mapStateToProps` and `mapDispatchToProps`. Following this analogy, the `useSelector` Hook is used to *read* data from the store while `useDispatch` is used to *dispatch* actions to write data to the store. React Redux offers a third Hook, `useStore`, which is not really used in the wild. Its usage should be more of a last resort should you really need access to the store object.

These Hooks can be imported as named imports from react-redux:

```
import { useSelector, useDispatch, useStore } from 'react-redux';
```

As is the case with other Hooks, Redux Hooks can only be used in function components. If you prefer using Class components, you can keep using the `connect()` HOC.

useSelector(selectorFn, equalityFn)

The `useSelector` Hook enables us to read values from the store. It expects a so-called selector function as its first parameter. This function receives the complete Redux store and then returns a simple or calculated value (or even a whole tree) of data:

```
import React from 'react';
import { useSelector } from 'react-redux';
```

```
const TodoList = () => {
  const openTodos = useSelector((state) =>
    state.todos.filter((todo) => todo.completed !==    true)
  );
  const completedTodos = useSelector((state) =>
    state.todos.filter((todo) => todo.completed ===    true)
  );
  const allTodos = useSelector((state) => state.todos);

  return (
    <div>
      <p>
        {allTodos.length} Todos. {completedTodos.length} complete and{' '}
        {openTodos.length} open.
      </p>
    </div>
  );
};
```

The selector function can be extracted if you wish to increase reuse and structure:

```
import { useSelector }  from 'react-redux';

const selectOpenTodos = (state) =>
  state.todos.filter((todo) => todo.completed !==    true);

const selectCompletedTodos = (state) =>
  state.todos.filter((todo) => todo.completed ===    true);

const selectAllTodos = (state) => state.todos;

const TodoList = () => {
  const openTodos = useSelector(selectOpenTodos);
  const completedTodos = useSelector(selectCompletedTodos);
  const allTodos = useSelector(selectAllTodos);

  return (
    <div>
      <p>
        {allTodos.length} Todos. {completedTodos.length} complete and{' '}
        {openTodos.length} open.
      </p>
    </div>
  );
};
```

Whenever a component is rendered, the selector function is called. It may return a temporary value if the selector function has already been called and the value has not changed since. To determine whether this is the case, Redux uses a *Strict Reference Equality Check* (===) to check whether the current render has the same reference as the one before.

If an action has been *dispatched*, useSelector will trigger a re-render of the component if the value is not strictly the same as before. Compared to the connect() HOC, we might encounter more re-renders. For example, selector functions will also be called if the component has re-rendered without actually receiving new props. If you encounter this issue while using the useSelector Hook, you have a number of options:

- The component can be wrapped by React.memo. This will avoid unnecessary re-renders of components in which the props did not change.
- The useSelector Hook can be configured to use a shallowEqual comparison (==) instead and avoids testing for referential equality (===). shallowEqual can be imported from react-redux and be passed to the Hook as a second parameter
  useSelector(selectorFn, shallowEqual)
- Reselect[29] can be useful to use instead as Reselect will always return the same values for as long as nothing has changed in state.

useDispatch()

The useDispatch() Hook will return a reference to the dispatch function of the store. It can be used to *dispatch* actions in a similar fashion to the connect() HOC using mapDispatchToProps :

```
import React from 'react';
import { useDispatch } from 'react-redux';

const addTodoAction = (text) => ({
  type: 'ADD_TODO',
  payload: { text },
});

const TodoApp = () => {
  const dispatch = useDispatch();
  const addTodo = () => dispatch(addTodoAction('A new todo element'  ));

  return <button onClick={addTodo}>Add todo</button> ;
};
```

The action is triggered by the call of dispatch(). However, it does not need to be passed via mapDispatchToProps to arrive in the component, as was the case in the connect() HOC.

Summary

Confession time: I underestimated the complexity of this chapter - by a lot. **Redux** has become one of the go-to tools for me in the last few years and using it now feels *natural* to me. In my opinion, **Redux** is a great tool that effectively manages very complex state and does so in a predictable and reasonable fashion.

However, while writing this chapter I noticed how overwhelming and daunting **Redux** can seem to a beginner. It might be possible that some of the explanations in this chapter do not make sense right away for a beginner. If you feel this might be the case for you, I suggest you open the Redux Devtools to play around with **actions** and **reducers** in the browser. This way, it might become more intuitive how one influences the other and how components, store, state, props and `connect()` as well as **actions** and **reducers** interact with each other.

Should there be any remaining questions after reading this chapter, please feel free to contact me.

Internationalization

Apart from **Routing** and **State Management, internationalization** is the last important topic left to discuss. Internationalization aims to solve the problem of effectively displaying different interfaces to users who speak another language. A German user will be prompted to interact with a German interface whereas an English user will be given an English interface to interact with.

I do not want to dive deeply into the general topic of **internationalization** (or **i18n** for short) but rather focus on **internationalization** in **React**. I assume that you have a very rough understanding of internationalization in user interfaces and thus focus on how internationalization can be implemented in **React**.

I provided a very simple example on how internationalization can be achieved using the **Context API** in the respective chapter for the **Context API** already. As the complexity of our applications grows though, the complexity of issues regarding internationalization grow as well. Using the plural in different languages or meaningful placeholders suddenly become important parts of the applications we're building. In order to be prepared well to deal with such cases, it is recommended to use one of the well-known internationalization packages which have been developed to cater specifically to these use cases.

The **React ecosystem** boasts with a number of options to choose from. The most notable options form **Lingui, Polyglot, i18next** or **react-intl**. Facebook has developed its own framework for internationalization called **FBT**. In this chapter we will mainly look at i18next and its react bindings: `react-i18next` .

You might wonder why we are focusing on i18next; I have worked with both `react-intl` and `react-i18next` extensively in the past and have also evaluated the alternatives I mentioned above. Through these evaluations and my extensive use of `react-intl` and `react-i18next` , I have found **i18next** to be the best package for a number of reasons. It supports a number of different frameworks, libraries and platforms (apart from **React**), and offers a very big and active community. Moreover, it works seamlessly client-side as well as server-side in Node.js. Most of the bigger translation services offer **i18next** as one of their export formats.

i18next was also one of the first packages to implement support and even implement optimizations for React Hooks, without comprising backwards compatibility. The API has remained simple and easy to use in that process and still offers the greatest amount of flexibility. The package is complete and caters to most use cases a developer could possibly imagine making it a very solid choice for us.

Setup of i18next

In order to install this package, we enter the following lines into the terminal window:

```
npm install i18next react-i18next
```

Or if you are using yarn:

```
yarn add i18next react-i18next
```

We install i18next, the **internationalization framework**, as well as react-i18next, the associated **React bindings**. These offer a number of components and functions which will simplify the work with i18next in React. Similar to the principle which we have already seen in the chapter on state management with redux and react-redux.

Let's start by creating two objects containing our translations. One will hold German translations while the other will hold English translations:

```
const de = {
  greeting: 'Hallo Welt!',
  headline: 'Heute lernen wir Internationalisierung mit React' ,
  messageCount: '{{count}} neue Nachricht' ,
  messageCount_plural: '{{count}} neue Nachrichten' ,
};

const en = {
  greeting: 'Hello world!' ,
  headline: 'Today we learn Internationalization with React' ,
  messageCount: '{{count}} new message' ,
  messageCount_plural: '{{count}} new messages',
};
```

To use **i18next** in our application, we have to import it, initialize it and pass the React plugin. Ideally, all these steps should happen somewhere in the beginning of our application meaning before our app component is given over to ReactDOM.render() .

We start by importing the i18next package as well as the named export initReactI18next from the react-i18next package:

```
import i18next from 'i18next';
import { initReactI18next } from 'react-i18next';
```

Consequently, we can make use of the .use() method to pass the React plugin to **i18next** as well as using the .init() method to initialize **i18next**.

```
i18next
  .use(initReactI18next)
  .init({ ... });
```

The `init()` function expects a config object which should at least contain a `lng` property as well as a `resources` property. `lng` indicates the chosen language whilst `resources` will contain the actual translations. It is also useful to define a `fallbackLng` which can be used if one of the translations chosen is not available in the chosen language. **i18next** offers up to 30 different configuration options, however the three I have mentioned should be enough for the moment:

```
i18next.use(initReactI18next).init({
  lng: 'en',
  fallbackLng: 'en',
  resources: {
    en: {
      translation: en,
    },
    de: {
      translation: de,
    },
  },
});
```

The main language of the application as well as the fallback language is initially set to English. The `resources` object which follows needs a little more explanation. It follows the following pattern:

```
[Language].[Namespace].[Translation Key] = Translation
```

It should be clear enough what exactly we are referring to with language. This can either be `en` for English, `de` for German or even `de-AT` for German with a focus on the Austrian dialect. The language property has an object which contains from one to an infinite number of **namespaces**.

The **namespace** is a central feature of **i18next**. It allows for splitting large translation files into different parts which can be dynamically lazy loaded. While this feature is not necessary for smaller applications, it can be a game-changer for larger and more complex applications. It will help us to contain the size of the translations and to aid the readability of the translations, for example by using a **namespace** for each page. Translation files for these different pages can then be cared for independently and will only be loaded if they are actually needed.

We always have to use at least **one namespace** in **i18next**. By default, it will be `translation`, but it can be changed in the `defaultNS` option in the configuration object of the `.init()` method. The **namespace** itself is also an object which contains the translations in the form of `translationKey: value` — or `greeting: 'Hello world!'` to be precise.

The value *could* also be an object:

```
{
  greeting: {
    morning: 'Good morning!' ,
    evening: 'Good evening!' ,
  }
}
```

Or for short:

```
{
  'greeting.morning' : 'Good morning!' ,
  'greeting.evening' : 'Good evening!' ,
}
```

It is entirely up to you which form you like best.

Using translations in React components

Once **i18next** is set up correctly and the translations have been set up as well, we can start to translate our components. **i18next** offers full flexibility: we can work with a `withTranslation` HOC in **class components** or a `useTranslation` Hook in **function components**. In the rare case of having to use components inside of translations, `react-i18next` boasts with a so-called `Trans` component.

Using the withTranslation() HOC in class components

The `withTranslation()` function will create a **HOC** which we can pass to the component that is supposed to be translated. The `t` and `i18n` props will be passed to this component. To do this, we import the function as a named export from the `react-i18next` package:

```
import { withTranslation } from 'react-i18next' ;
```

Once imported, we call the function and obtain a HOC which we pass the component to that we want to access the translated values with. If we are using **namespaces**, we can also pass the **namespace** we want to use to the `withTranslation()` function:

307

```
// Without namespaces (using the default value):
const TranslatedComponent = withTranslation()(TranslatedComponent);

// Using a single namespace:
const TranslatedComponent = withTranslation( 'namespace')(Component);

// Using multiple namespaces:
const TranslatedComponent = withTranslation([ 'namespace1' , 'namespace2' ])(
  TranslatedComponent
);
```

For myself, it has proven useful to extract components into their own files and wrap them with the withTranslation() HOC when they are exported:

```
// Greeting.js
class Greeting extends React.Component {
  render() {
    const { t } = this.props;
    return <h1>{t('greeting')} </h1>;
  }
}

export default withTranslation()(Greeting);
```

We can then immediately import the translated component:

```
import Greeting from './Greeting.js' ;
```

Not only have we imported the actual component, but we have also gained access to the extended props t, i18n and tReady via i18next.

The t function forms the central function for everything related to translations. It is passed a **translation key** and will return the translated value to us, based on the chosen language.

```
<h1>{t('greeting')}</h1>
// -> <h1>Hello world!</h1>
```

If plurals or placeholders are used in the translations, they can be defined in the second parameter:

```
<p>{t('messageCount', { count: 3 })}</p>
// -> <p>3 new messages</p>
```

The i18n prop contains the initialized **i18next** instance. It offers a number of properties and methods that can be relevant for our translations. The most notable are:

- i18n.language to read the currently selected language
- i18n.changeLanguage() to switch the currently selected language

In order to switch the language from en to de, we can call i18n.changeLanguage('de') .

Using the useTranslation() Hook in function components

The use of the withTranslation() HOC is not constrained to **class components** but can also be used in **function components**. However, the use of the useTranslation() Hook often simplifies the component and makes it much more readable. The Hook can be imported similarly to the HOC:

```
import { useTranslation } from 'react-i18next';
```

This **Hook** allows us to extract the t and i18n properties by using **destructuring assignment** from ES2015+.

```
const Greeting = () => {
  const { t, i18n } = useTranslation();
  return (
    <div>
      <h1>{t('greeting')} </h1>
      <button onClick={() => i18n.changeLanguage('de')}>de</button>
      <button onClick={() => i18n.changeLanguage('en')}>en</button>
    </div>
  );
};
```

As was already the case in the withTranslation() HOC, t refers to the function which allows us to display translations based on their **translation key**. i18n refers to the respective **i18next** instance. The useTranslation() Hook offers the same set of functionality as the withTranslation() HOC, however it is much more explicit and thus more readable. In order to use different **namespaces**, we can pass a string or an array of strings containing the namespaces to the Hook:

```
const { t } = useTranslation('namespace');
const { t } = useTranslation([ 'namespace1' , 'namespace2' ]);
```

If no namespace has been provided, the default settings will be used.

Complex translations using the Trans component

In a few select cases, it might be necessary to use a React component in the translations. For example, one might want to use the `Link` component from **React Router** to link to a different URL within a translation. The `t()` function does not support this out of the box. The solution to this problem comes in the form of the `Trans` component from `react-18next`. It is not always easy to understand how it should be used but it can be powerful tool.

Let's assume that we want to use a `Link` component inside of our translations. The code might resemble something like this:

```
<p>
  <label>
    <input type="checkbox" name="terms" />
    Ich akzeptiere die  <Link to="/terms"> AGB</Link>
  </label>
</p>
```

Using the Link component in such a translation would not work as translations are strings and would thus not be able to define that the `<Link>` component refers to the Link component from the React Router package.

The `Trans` component offers the solution to our problem. Translations using this component can include numbered placeholders. These placeholders will later be replaced with components which will appear in the same place as they are used as in the `Trans` component.

Let's look at the above example using the `Trans` component:

```
// Translations:
const de = {
  terms: 'Ich akzeptiere die <1>AGB</1>.'  ,
};

const en = {
  terms: 'I accept the <1>Terms and Conditions</1>.'  ,
};

// JSX:
<p>
  <label>
    <input type="checkbox" />
    <Trans i18nKey="terms">
      I accept the <Link  to="/terms"> Terms and Conditions </Link>.
    </Trans>
```

310

```
    </label>
  </p> ;
```

Our text is wrapped by a `Trans` element. The text itself is only a placeholder that is used if the `i18nKey` prop does not contain a value which corresponds to a translation. Let's look at the numbering now. Where the text is placed and which text in particular is decided by the index value of the child element, similarly to `React.createElement()`.

Using the above example, we have the following counting result:

```
0: I accept the
1: <Link to="/terms">Terms and Conditions</Link>
2: .
```

The `<1>Terms and Conditions</1>` will be replaced by the `<Link>` element as it corresponds to the index value of 1 in the array of children.

In complex structures where we might even deal with a number of links, this procedure can become a little bit cumbersome. Luckily, `react-i18next` offers the ability to automatically generate placeholders. These can be set as an option when **i18next** is initialized.

The first option to change is `saveMissing` which should now be set to `true`. Additionally, a `missingKeyHandler` function should be set. In the following example, a simple `console.log()` is used to log missing translations to the browser console:

```
i18next.use(initReactI18next).init({
  saveMissing: true ,
  missingKeyHandler: (language, namespace, key, fallbackValue) => {
    console.log('Missing translation:', fallbackValue);
  },
  // other options
});
```

If an `i18nKey` not currently in existence is used, the fallback value, meaning the value in the Trans element, will be written to the console instead:

> ⓘ Missing translation: I accept the <1>Terms and Conditions</1>.

We can now set up a translation for this case. **React Router's** `Link` has already been replaced by the corresponding placeholder **(1)** in the output.

As a second option, we could also replace the `missingKeyHandler` function with a `debug` option set to `true`.

```
i18next.use(initReactI18next).init({
  debug: true,
  // other options
});
```

We now get detailed debugging information, including a hint concerning our missing translations. The output would resemble the following:

 i18next::translator: missingKey de translation terms I accept the <1>Terms and Conditions</1>.

The output generated by the `debug` option is a little more extensive than the one provided by the `missingKeyHandler` variant. However, it is possible to set this option by only setting its value to `true`.

By the way: You can still use the `t()` function as you are used to if you find yourself in a `<Trans>` element. This means, the following example is completely valid:

```
<Trans i18nKey="terms">
  I accept the{' '}
  <Link to="/terms" title={t('termsTitle')}>
    Terms and Conditions
  </Link>
  .
</Trans>
```

Summary

Using the examples provided in this chapter, it is relatively simple to provide internationalization in our applications. For my personal and professional use, i18next has proven to be a universal and complete tool to build international applications. Integrating with different libraries and frameworks has been a breeze. It offers all sorts of functionality that should be supported by a i18n framework and is easy to understand and learn with only a small set of functions: `i18n.changeLanguage()`, `t()`, `<Trans>`.

Once set up correctly (I would advise you to check out the complete options of i18next[30]), internationalization in React applications is easy to achieve without having to deal with a great deal of effort. One could even integrate with online services such as Locize.com[31] or Lokalise.co[32] (to name a few) which help to create and manage translations or even outsource them automatically.

312

Keeping up to Date

Twitter

Twitter is a great source of information for current trends in the tech community. The React Team even announces their changes publicly on Twitter very shortly after releasing them. If you do not have an account yet, but like to stay up to date, you should think about creating an account for yourself and checking in every now and then to make sure you are getting the most relevant content.

I will try and name a few accounts that I have found invaluable when it comes to working with React and who generally tweet on the topic. This list is not exhaustive by any means though and I know that there are a great number of other people who also do great work in the React space. I do however follow these people myself and can therefore wholeheartedly recommend them:

@reactjs @dan_abramov @sophiebits @sebmarkbage @acdlite @brian_d_vaughn @trueadm @threepointone @aweary @necolas @tomocchino @yuzhiz @rachelnabors @lunaruan (all react core members or alumni) @ryanflorence @mjackson @ken_wheeler @kentcdodds @kyleshevlin @mweststrate @jaredpalmer @sebmck @thekitze @philippspiess @monicalent @nikkitaftw @rwieruch @jlongster @eveporcello @vincentriemer @kylemathews @rauchg @erinfoox @jevakallio @okonetchnikov @manuelbieh @manjula_dube @acemarke @wisecobbler @mxstbr @cpojer @taeluralexis @gurlcode @lithinn @dabit3 @saifadin @rickhanlonii @tylermcginnis @wesbos @_developit @provablyflarnie @emmabostian @grabbou @cassidoo @s_ibylle

Newsletters

Don't worry, I'm not referring to those kind of newsletters that constantly try to sell stuff to us. Luckily, the React community has a number of very interesting, cared for and nicely designed newsletters which are well worth subscribing to. Most of these newsletters are sent out on a weekly basis and contain a great overview of what has happened in the React World in the previous week. A great choice for all those who find Twitter a little bit too fast-paced or stressful:

- React Status[33] (Peter Cooper / Cooperpress)
- This Week in React[34] (Philipp Spiess)
- React.js Newsletter[35] (Tyler McGinnis)
- Fullstack React[36] (Sophia Shoemaker)
- React Digest[37] (Jakub Chodounsky / Bonobopress)

- Tiny React[38] (Siddharth Kshetrapal)

Communities

- https://spectrum.chat/react
- https://www.reactiflux.com/
- https://www.reddit.com/r/reactjs

Podcasts

There are a few very good podcasts which mainly cover React topics:

- The Undefined[39] (Ken Wheeler and Jared Palmer)
- React Podcast[40] (Michael Chan aka @chantastic[41])
- Syntax.fm[42] (Wes Bos and Scott Tolinski)

Tools and Frameworks

As React has been around for a while, an ecosystem has grown around it that boasts an abundance of tools. Ranging from static site generators (in order to realize simple to medium-sized and complex static website on the basis of React) to prototyping tools to tools which allow us to display our components in some sort of styleguide, the React ecosystem has much to offer. In this small sub-chapter I want to provide a *short* overview of the most commonly used tools and frameworks.

Storybook

> Storybook is a development environment for UI components. It allows us to browse through a component library, view the different states of each component, and interactively develop and test components.

Storybook is a tool that allows us to create isolated UI components for React, Vue.js and Angular. **Storybook** bundles our components in some form of Sandbox environment in which components can be independently developed in so-called **stories** and can then be displayed and viewed in a tidy and easy-to-use interface. By isolating these components, we allow for a great degree of abstraction and can also easily test and display for edge cases.

License: MIT (Open Source)
URL: https://storybook.js.org/
GitHub: https://github.com/storybooks/storybook

React Styleguidist

> React Styleguidist is a component development environment with a hot reloaded dev server and a living style guide that can shared with your team.

Styleguidist is similar to Storybook. It also enables us to create a styleguide from our React components which are currently used in an application. However, **Styleguidist** is more implicit than **Storybook** and can be extended with **PropTypes** and **JSDoc** comments. Markdown files in the directory of the components can also be used to further add information on the component.

License: MIT (Open Source)
URL: https://react-styleguidist.js.org/
GitHub: https://github.com/styleguidist/react-styleguidist

Docz

It has never been so easy to document your things!

Docz is a tool that is centered around documentation as the name might suggest. It can also be seen as a styleguide, but it is completely **MDX** based. **MDX** is an extended version of the Markdown format which can also include React components. This way, our components can be described in mdx format and can be imported and used just like regular JavaScript files.

License: MIT (Open Source)
URL: https://docz.site/
GitHub: https://github.com/pedronauck/docz

React Cosmos

Dev tool for creating reusable React components

React Cosmos takes things a little bit further and allows us to include external dependencies, such as React Router or Redux in our component overview, by using the concepts of *fixtures* and *proxies*. This allows us to display and test such components more simply. React Cosmos breaks up the encapsulation of components which we found in the three previously mentioned tools and allows us to move beyond *just* UI components.

License: MIT (Open Source)
GitHub: https://github.com/react-cosmos/react-cosmos

Gatsby

Gatsby is a free and open source framework based on React that helps developers build blazing fast websites and apps

Gatsby is part of the so-called static site generator category, meaning it is a generator for static websites. **Gatsby** allows us to create components using React and GraphQL and then transforms them into static HTML files. **Gatsby** also creates a JavaScript bundle which is loaded as soon as the page loads. Once the bundle has loaded, **Gatsby** makes use of client-side rendering which means that sites are rendered to the user in "blazing fast" fashion as the HTTP overhead is drastically reduced. Gatsby has been started as an Open Source project and still maintains that status today. In May 2018 it received an impressive investment of 3.8 million US dollars.

License: MIT (Open Source)
URL: https://www.gatsbyjs.org/
GitHub: https://github.com/gatsbyjs/gatsby

React Static

React-Static is a fast, lightweight, and powerful progressive static site generator based on React and its ecosystem.

React-Static is an alternative to **Gatsby** and is also a **static site generator**. Gatsby might be the more well-known tool, especially since its last investment. However, **React static** is a serious contender and also boasts with a great and active community.

License: MIT (Open Source)
GitHub: https://github.com/nozzle/react-static

Next.js

Next.js describes itself as "The React Framework" for a number of different use cases, ranging from static to dynamic websites, small to large companies, and mobile to classic websites. Next.js lives up to its claim, as 36,000 stars on GitHub indicate; it is extremely popular within the community. For many, Next.js is a serious alternative to Create React App. As opposed to CRA, Next.js supports server-side rendering out of the box, which is especially important for developers optimizing for SEO.

License: MIT (Open Source)
URL: https://nextjs.org/
GitHub: https://github.com/zeit/next.js

Conclusion

Dear reader, I hope that you have learned about React now and have been able to understand the concepts and topics covered in this book. I have spent almost 1.5 years writing this book. During this time, things have changed constantly and often so drastically that I had to push back the release of this book a few times to avoid having outdated material in it.

Unfortunately, this meant that a few topics could not be explored in the same amount of detail that I would have liked. Some of these topics are not even necessarily part of React and I have thus decided to not push back the release of the book any further. One of these topics is optimizing build setups with Webpack. While I deem this topic very important, I think it would also have exploded the scope of this book. I have searched for similar books on this topic on Amazon and discovered that books with around 500 pages exist for this topic alone.

I have also only mentioned topics such as server-side rendering. Again, while I deem this topic very important, I have also learned that its usage and resulting benefits do not always outweigh the costs.

If you find any issues or mistakes in the book, please let me know and raise an issue[43] on GitHub! Be it spelling mistakes, grammar mistakes or even mistakes in the content — I want this book to be as useful as possible to you. As I have self-published this book, I did not have access to an editor as many big publishing houses do, but I wanted to keep control over all rights and publishing channels which ruled this out. This means, you can still access the German version of this book at https://lernen.react-js.dev/ which would not have been possible with a publisher.

React allowed me to work on a number of very interesting projects over the last few years. Years in which I have learned an immense amount about Frontend and UI development. It has also allowed me to meet a number of great people which share the passion for React. I wanted to share these experiences and learning with the community which is why the German HTML version will be free and remain free for the years to come.

If you want to support my work, you can order a copy of this book on the regular channels or buy the e-book in Kindle, Apple Books or Google Play book format and read it on your favourite device. I also love hearing about new great projects with React in Berlin, so please get in touch if you have a project that might be of interest.

If you are curious, you can learn more about me and my work on https://www.manuelbieh.de. By the way, this website has also been built using Gatsby (a tool I told you about in one of the chapters).

I look forward to hearing your feedback — be it positive or negative! You can reach me at @manuelbieh on Twitter.

Links

- [1] https://github.com/manuelbieh/react-book/issues
- [2] https://www.gitbook.com
- [3] https://github.com/reactjs/rfcs
- [4] https://github.com/reactjs/react-codemod
- [5] https://github.com/facebook/react/issues?
  utf8=%E2%9C%93&q=is%3Aissue%20is%3Aopen%20umbrella
- [6] https://github.com/creationix/nvm
- [7] https://github.com/coreybutler/nvm-windows
- [8] https://atom.io/packages/language-babel
- [9] https://marketplace.visualstudio.com/items?itemName=dzannotti.vscode-babel-
  coloring
- [10] https://github.com/babel/babel-sublime
- [11] https://chrome.google.com/webstore/detail/react-developer-
  tools/fmkadmapgofadopljbjfkapdkoienihi
- [12] https://addons.mozilla.org/de/firefox/addon/react-devtools/
- [13] https://chrome.google.com/webstore/detail/redux-
  devtools/lmhkpmbekcpmknklioeibfkpmmfibljd
- [14] https://addons.mozilla.org/de/firefox/addon/remotedev/?
- [15] https://www.javascriptstuff.com/react-starter-projects/
- [16] https://docs.npmjs.com/files/package.json#name
- [17] https://codesandbox.io/
- [18] https://codesandbox.io/s/new
- [19]
  https://developer.mozilla.org/de/docs/Web/JavaScript/Reference/Global_Objects/Promise
- [20] https://developer.mozilla.org/en-US/docs/Web/API/HTMLLabelElement/htmlFor
- [21] https://www.w3.org/TR/DOM-Level-3-Events/
- [22] https://michelebertoli.github.io/css-in-js/
- [23] https://www.styled-components.com/docs/basics
- [24] https://github.com/emotion-js/emotion
- [25] https://github.com/zeit/styled-jsx
- [26] https://github.com/cssinjs/jss/tree/master/packages/react-jss
- [27] https://github.com/FormidableLabs/radium
- [28] https://github.com/callstack/linaria
- [29] https://github.com/reduxjs/reselect
- [30] https://www.i18next.com/overview/configuration-options
- [31] https://locize.com/

- [32] https://www.lokalise.co
- [33] https://react.statuscode.com/
- [34] https://this-week-in-react.org/
- [35] http://reactjsnewsletter.com/
- [36] http://newsletter.fullstackreact.com
- [37] https://reactdigest.net/
- [38] https://tinyreact.email/
- [39] https://undefined.fm/
- [40] https://reactpodcast.com/
- [41] https://github.com/chantastic
- [42] https://syntax.fm/
- [43] https://github.com/manuelbieh/react-book/issues

www.ingramcontent.com/pod-product-compliance
Lightning Source LLC
LaVergne TN
LVHW081516050326
832903LV00025B/1510